Identifying Talent, Institutionalizing Diversity

JIANNBIN LEE SHIAO

Identifying Talent, Institutionalizing Diversity

Race and Philanthropy in Post–Civil Rights America

DUKE UNIVERSITY PRESS DURHAM AND LONDON 2005

© 2005 Duke University Press. All rights reserved.
Printed in the United States of America on acid-free paper ∞
Designed by Rebecca M. Giménez. Typeset in Adobe Minion
by Keystone Typesetting. Library of Congress Cataloging-in-
Publication Data appear on the last printed page of this book.

To my parents,

Wen-Tsai and Fang-Zu Shiao,

and my sister,

Lihbin Lee Shiao

CONTENTS

TABLES AND FIGURES

Tables

Figures

ACKNOWLEDGMENTS

For giving me the intellectual freedom to undertake an unusual project and the instrumental support to see it through, I am indebted to my dissertation committee members in the Department of Sociology at the University of California at Berkeley: Troy Duster, Neil Fligstein, and Michael Omi. For invaluable commentary before, between, and after faculty office hours, I relied on my writing group—Kamau Birago, Robert Bulman, Rebecca Chiyoko King-O'Riain, and Pamela Perry—in addition to many other graduate student and junior faculty colleagues in sociology and ethnic studies, at Berkeley and beyond. Ann Swidler, Kim Voss, Samuel Lucas, and Michael Burawoy contributed much needed advice on research design and theoretical framings, and I also benefited extensively from responses to my presentations for the American Sociological Association, the Association for Asian American Studies, and the Stanford Center for Organizational Research. Pursuing this research would have been much more difficult without Dissertation Improvement Grant #9711757 from the National Science Foundation, a Humanities Graduate Research Grant from Berkeley, and a Dissertation-Year Fellowship from the University of California. Beyond the ivory tower, I owe immense debts to Sandra Liu, Norbert Hendrikse, and the YANGS, especially Raymond Lin, for helping me keep academia in perspective.

During the years of its maturation into a more widely accessible manuscript, I have benefited from the advice and encouragement of many others. My senior colleagues in the Department of Sociology at the University of Oregon had the foresight to foster a mutually supportive community of junior faculty and to invest us with the time and space to pursue research. For keeping me sane during my transition from graduate student to assistant professor, I am indebted to Mia Tuan, Jocelyn Hollander, and the "new faculty" happy-hour group. I also extend my thanks and appreciation to my research assistants, Hava Gordon, for assembling the scholarly literature on the Ford

Foundation, and Brett Clark, for conducting the first nonspecialist reading of every chapter. I am grateful as well to the University of Oregon for research support and space and especially to our undergraduate students for keeping me "relevant" and regularly reminding me why I have chosen this vocation.

The anonymous reviewers for Duke University Press provided critiques that were really just excellent. From both their agreements and disagreements with each other, I learned important lessons about how to refine the manuscript to bridge its many possible audiences. Although the three reviewers were responsible for inspiring its ambitious goals, I must bear the blame for wherever it fails to reach its potential. Because this book is my first, Raphael Allen is also my first editor, and therefore, as a social scientist, I must admit that I have no basis for comparison. That said, I cannot imagine how I would have completed this project without his empathy, intelligence, integrity, good humor under pressure, and, of course, his enthusiasm for the work of Joss Whedon.

My respect and thanks go to the many foundation trustees, foundation staff, local experts, and directors of nonprofit organizations who spent valuable time sharing their perspectives with me and teaching me about their professional world and life missions. I was awed by their commitment, experience, and insight. The conditions of our interviews preclude my thanking them by name; however, I can thank certain key facilitators for my research. John Kreidler was instrumental in helping me locate and interview former San Francisco Foundation personnel. Similarly, Russell Jeung introduced me to many directors of ethnic organizations in the San Francisco Bay Area. David Hammack invited me to give a seminar at the Mandel Center for Nonprofit Organizations and introduced me to a very welcoming and helpful community of Cleveland scholars. And Lynne Woodman of the Cleveland Foundation raised my expectations immensely for how foundations could assist external research into their own activities, even those relating to the too often taboo subject of race relations.

Last but hardly least, I cannot do enough to express my gratitude to my family for their generous, loving support throughout this project. My parents, Wen-Tsai and Fang-Zu Shiao, have always believed in me, even when my life choices looked strange to their immigrant sensibilities. My sister, Lihbin, has long been both my best critic and my biggest fan. My partner, Nancy Toth, met me in the midst of my struggling, ahem, writing this book; nevertheless, she agreed to stick around and made the final sprint more than worth the effort.

I am eternally grateful to you all.

1

Diversity, Philanthropy, and Race Relations

Bill and Melinda Gates are giving $1 billion to fund scholarships
for minority college students in the hope of producing "a new
generation of leaders."—Seattle Times, 16 September 1999

When the Bill and Melinda Gates Foundation announced its Millennium Scholars Program, it articulated in one moment two of the most intriguing phenomena for Americans: affluence and race. Though some commentators disagreed with the race-consciousness of the Millennium scholarships, none suggested that Bill Gates had stolen from his predominantly White Microsoft employees and customers to give to undeserving youth of color. Though Americans might decry his company's monopolistic practices, they also admire its results and tend to attribute such success more to personal leadership than to the combined activities of the firm. Furthermore, though few Americans would require their rich to act like nobility, the media routinely praise acts of charity and philanthropy as enlightened self-interest, the American "free market" version of noblesse oblige. Still, race relations have been so influential throughout U.S. history that one might have expected the Gates announcement to rile more than a few feathers. This book is about a quiet transformation in U.S. race relations: the institutionalization of diversity policy among elite private organizations in the wake of a conservative backlash against the progress of racialized minorities.

With the scholarship initiative, Bill and Melinda Gates joined the long ranks of White philanthropists who have devoted a portion of their wealth to the education of non-Whites. In distinction from the historic philanthropists, however, the initiative targets not only African Americans but also American Indians, Alaska Natives, Asian Pacific Americans, and Hispanic Americans—a diversity of ethnoracial groups refracted from the ongoing shifts in U.S. demography. Despite the usual individualism trumpeted in news coverage of philanthropy, there were also signs that the Gates initiative was not entirely free to address social changes in whatever manner might please the Gateses. This book thus examines the emergence of diversity policy by focusing on the political and institutional realities behind the generosity of philanthropic institutions seeking to privately intervene in U.S. race relations.

The system of segregation known as Jim Crow would have provided southern Blacks with even worse schools if not for the intervention of northern philanthropists. Their critics, however, charge those philanthropists with cowardice for not confronting southern racists directly, if not also for privately covering up the systemic hypocrisy behind "separate but equal" education. In addition to evaluating the available political opportunities, philanthropy has also had to work through a preexisting institutional landscape, especially since it often has the finances but not the infrastructure to pursue its goals. Consequently, the young Gates Foundation has contracted the administration of these diverse fellowships to the over fifty-year-old United Negro College Fund, to which the Foundation left the task of convening other racialized minority organizations, including a new Asian Pacific American Advisory Committee.[1]

Given the political and institutional worlds in and through which philanthropy makes "private policy," studies of patronage confront unique questions at a tangent to those postulated by classical theorists of "social classes, bureaucracy, ideology, and charisma" (Lagemann 1999, ix). How much freedom does government actually permit organized philanthropy to pursue unpopular causes? How unique are philanthropy's contributions if it relies on the same nongovernmental actors participating in government contracts?

These structural challenges for organized philanthropy raise parallel concerns for diversity policies, which likewise have risen from political origins, thrive in elite private institutions, and yet purport to influence U.S. society in ways beyond the capability of government. How much autonomy does diversity policy actually have from the racial politics from which it arose? Can diversity policy be more than a weak form of affirmative action? Would it survive without affirmative action mandates? How unique is the impact of diversity policy if the targeted intergroup relations are between already politically defined actors? Can diversity policy replace unequal group competition with new relationships? Would it survive if it attempted to veer from federal racial classifications? The answers lie not in a "perfect" policy model for all institutions or a "perfect" situation with visionary leadership from all groups, but rather from an examination of how the imperfect, field-specific policies arose in response to imperfect, locally specific situations. Accordingly, this book answers these questions through the story of how two philanthropic foundations arrived at diversity policy three decades after the civil rights movement.

In the middle of the twentieth century, when Edsel Ford's Foundation sponsored "desegregation experiments," segregationists boycotted Ford Motor Company products and facilitated the congressional investigation headed by Eugene Cox (D-Georgia) charging "that America's largest private philanthropic foundations had been infiltrated by communists who funded subversive activities" (Raynor 1999, 200). By the late twentieth century, however, times had changed. By then, foundations were following other notable institutions that were committing themselves to policies pursuing something called *diversity*. Repudiating a "one size fits all" model of American culture, many institutional fields declared instead that they would value cultural differences as central to their varied missions. Increasingly, this notion of culture has included gendered, sexualized, and other social differences, but even in its most inclusive form, Americans have understood that "diversity" refers primarily to valuing ethnoracial pluralism.

On learning of this topic, many individuals, including race and ethnicity scholars, are no doubt wondering, Why *foundations*? Some will assume that ethnic studies should focus on the marginalized and historically underrepresented rather than privileged groups and their elite institutions. Others will question the need for a narrow focus on foundations in race relations theory, rather than a wider focus on Whites or on the affluent classes, which are predominantly, but not exclusively, White. This chapter provides substantive and theoretical answers to these concerns, but a personal response might interest the reader and better prime her[2] for the sociological explanations to come. It may be surprising that the book grew out of research that began not with foundations but with a youth gang whose pan-Asian character made it an anomaly for the usually middle-class phenomenon of panethnic formation. However, these youth were in regular contact with the middle-class staff of a pan-Asian nonprofit organization, for whose afterschool program I volunteered as a tutor. When the agency later hired me as a strategic planning consultant, I discovered that the design of its new programs often depended on what the staff believed foundations would support. The usual story of the racial and ethnic formations occurring between the gang and the agency would involve the factors of ethnic group identification, shared experiences of racism, emergent collective traditions, and the state racialization of distinct class segments. What these usual understandings miss, though, are the role of foundations in providing rare venture capital for developing new racial projects and, more generally, the role of private organizations in moderating the interplay of racialized minority groups and the larger society. Rather than only dutifully mediating the interests of constituent groups to the government, these organizations also feed back and influence the groups themselves because these institutions are the means by which the groups relate to one another.

It is a mistake to characterize all race relations as equally "political" when significant aspects are quite institutional rather than exclusively subject to group solidarity or intergroup conflict. On the one hand, Americans across the political spectrum do tend to view race relations as a "struggle," whether between Whites and non-Whites, democracy and racism, or the moral majority and the special interests. Within this metaphor, racial political theory has largely adopted the Gramscian distinction between a war of maneuver and a war of position (Omi and Winant 1986, 1994)—in other words, between movements to end racism "in a single stroke" and efforts to end its effects by means of a "long march" through various societal trenches. On the other hand, the theoretical emphasis that scholars give to solidarity and conflict may be excessive if the trenches in question operate by distinct institutional logics or possess particular relationships with each other. In fact, foundations adopted diversity policy not because people of color united to demand it or because the federal government required compliance to it but for institutional reasons, namely, protecting their ongoing project investments from an increasingly hostile context or securing their historic niche within local political regimes. Similarly, racial and ethnic groups can behave institutionally rather than only politically or traditionally. Substituting "race" for "class" in the Marxist distinction between objective class membership and subjective class identity, I suggest a critical role for the emergence of non-White institutional behavior. The development from being a "race in itself" to becoming a "race for itself" may pivot on an important threshold wherein the process of collectivization requires institutionalization or the adoption of organizational forms recognizable to others outside the group. In contrast to a purely political approach to studying race relations, an institutional approach might thus view the risk of co-optation not as exogenous to non-White insurgency but as inherent to its growth and effectiveness.

I rest the arguments in this book on three years of research on the racial/ethnic priorities and debates of the San Francisco Foundation, the

Cleveland Foundation, and the national philanthropic field of which they are members, from the civil rights movement to the advent of philanthropic diversity policy. Studying the period from the 1960s through the early 1990s, I interviewed forty-five foundation trustees, program officers, local political informants, and directors of grant-seeking nonprofit organizations in the two metropolitan regions of the San Francisco Bay Area and the Greater Cleveland Area and also analyzed the oral history transcripts of deceased foundation personnel.[3] In addition, I reviewed decades of each organization's annual reports and studied the trade magazine of the Council on Foundations, currently titled *Foundation News and Commentary.*

The 1965 Hart-Cellar Act established immigration trends that will continue to reshape the racial and ethnic composition of U.S. society into the twenty-first century. Although diversity policies in philanthropy and other private institutions have typically addressed the new immigration, I argue that the new immigration was only one of the forces behind their advent. In fact, these organizational policies have significantly reflected previous institutional experiences with race relations. Notwithstanding the plethora of how-to manuals, workshops, and conferences on managing the new demographics of the United States, how organizations previously "did race" still shapes how they now choose to "do diversity."

Many institutional actors employed the demographic "threat" to rearticulate racial politics anew. In this chapter, I first integrate disparate discussions of diversity policy into a sociological "ideal type" with four dimensions, by which to evaluate philanthropic diversity policies. Second, I argue that the complex nature of diversity policy necessarily emerged from private, nongovernmental institutions rather than U.S. legislation and laws. Third, I explain why studies on diversity in the new millennium should attend to not only the national demographic shifts but also their uneven local impacts and institutional receptions. Last, I outline the remaining chapters that make my argument in this book and suggest an alternative chapter sequence for readers more interested in an organizational analysis than a racial and ethnic account.

The Many Faces of Diversity Policy

By the 1990s, organizational diversity became a symbolically resonant policy with which leaders of private organizations tried to resolve a host of anxieties: about the demands of African Americans, the rise of non-Black people of color, the growing visibility of class differences between and within groups, and the ascendancy of conservative political interests. Consequently, discussions of diversity have been extremely wide-ranging in subject matter, from multiculturalism in higher education to corporate diversity management to the new Asian and Latino immigration to political correctness to globalization to the new Whiteness studies to racial reparations. In outlining this chapter's first task of mapping out a sociological analysis of diversity policy, I argue that discussions of diversity policy have involved combinations of its four major aspects: (1) its path-dependence on its "older sibling" policies of affirmative action and multiculturalism; (2) its greater breadth of race relations concerns in comparison to the civil rights era's emphasis on Blacks and Whites; (3) its recombination of domestic and international intergroup relations; and (4) its return to or reinvigoration of the concern for intergroup coexistence beyond competitive group politics.

Diversity policy began as a movement to put a protective spin on affirmative action and other explicitly racial policies that were under attack by conservatives; however, it developed beyond its utilitarian origins. The effort to shield affirmative action practices from declining federal enforcement and to hide goals of equality and justice under more acceptable goals actually resulted in new organizational policies that rhetorically connected productivity and difference. In higher education especially, these new policies highlighted the importance of difference by broadening the public image of policy beneficiaries beyond African Americans to other ethnoracial groups and illuminating the historic invalidity of the melting pot ideal for immigrants of color. As these strategies succeeded in shifting policy foci from equality/justice to productivity/difference, they also opened the door to challenges articulated within the new framework of demographic justifications. Although continuing racism invalidated the melting pot, rising intermarriage and "mixed-race" identification have begun to undermine the ethnoracial categories that diversity policy inherited from affirmative action. The possibility that sociodemographic heterogeneity could be more productive than homogeneity raised the additional question of whether *some* heterogeneities might be more productive than others. If affirmative action were diversity policy's older sibling, their parents were arguably the civil rights struggle and the changing international context. However, though diversity policy favors its parents more equally than does its sibling, its specific combination of civil rights and immigration concerns remains quite open. Also, the failure of civil rights enforcement to change intergroup relationships ironically became an opportunity to change the historical asymmetry of so-called minority policies into symmetric intergroup relationships. Their complexity suggests that private institutions have been a briar patch for race-specific social policy.

BEYOND AFFIRMATIVE ACTION
AND MULTICULTURAL REVISIONISM

In the 1990s, a mélange of diversity policies emerged in many fields, most notably in education and business management. In higher education especially, popular commentators have alternately noted and mocked the proliferation of programs and debates, such as graduation course requirements for multicultural competence, disputes over affirmative action in admissions, the popularity of ethnic student organizations, and campus responses to hate speech. Noted less by outsiders, but equally important for college insiders, have been the issues of faculty diversity, culturally appropriate student services, preorientation programs for students of color, and various group-specific official programming such as heritage months and awareness weeks (Valverde and Castenell 1998).

Similar programs have emerged in business management, though accompanied by less controversy. As Erin Kelly and Frank Dobbin observed, "Over the space of a quarter of a century, efforts to integrate the workforce were transformed, in management rhetoric, from an onerous requirement of federal law to a valuable means to increasing organizational effectiveness" (1998, 961). However, they also argue that most diversity management techniques are simply renamed components of embattled affirmative action programs. They acknowledge that the old and new programs differ in their stated philosophical missions: whereas the old affirmative action programs aimed for equality by targeting injustice, the new diversity management strives for greater productivity by valuing difference. They nevertheless conclude that diversity management amounts to a weak version of affirmative action, rationalized in terms closer to traditional business goals than to legal compliance, but shorn of its most effective techniques. For years, however, critics of affirmative action have questioned its effectiveness given its common provocation of negative reactions from nonbeneficiaries. The response of diversity policy advocates to this critique of affirmative action has been to aim at altering the organizational culture to minimize such backlashes (Cox 1993). Unfortunately, the culture audit—the technique with the potential to refocus older practices within a diversity framework—can be quite costly; consequently, few organizations actually implement the main technical innovation of the diversity management movement (Kelly and Dobbin 1998).

The management literature's analytic distinctions between the goals of equality and productivity and the tools of justice and difference are helpful in navigating the larger morass of diversity debates prevalent in schooling. In education, liberals often assume the two goals to be synonymous, employing the slogan "Excellence Through Diversity," while conservatives demand that educators not sacrifice excellence for diversity.[4] In the 1980s conservatives argued that multicultural revisionism and student services based on "victimology" were obscuring the core truths in the traditional canon and destroying the integrity of the traditional campus. Meanwhile, liberals countered that reforms in teaching and campus life were uncovering hidden truths behind an arrogant Eurocentric universalism and creating a new community freer of historical prejudices. Diversity advocates of the 1990s rhetorically reconciled the political conflict by linking productivity and difference and subsuming equality and justice as important but distinctly secondary concerns. As in corporate management, educators converged on diversity as a common goal, an event well symbolized by the publication of emeritus culture warrior Nathan Glazer's *We Are All Multiculturalists Now* (1997). In brief, Glazer acknowledges that his earlier optimism for institutional colorblindness as the means for bettering race relations proved to be unwarranted. In a complex argument, he alternately questions the actual productivity of diversity policy, admits his preference for institutional multiculturalism over governmental interventions, defends its bedrock integrationism beneath the "alienating" rhetoric of difference, and asserts its inevitability in the face of continuing racial inequality. Though Glazer has not found the productivity-difference connection entirely convincing, he now argues that recognizing differences may be a necessary first step toward the older goal of colorblindness.

THE UNEVEN PUSH OF DEMOGRAPHY

Significantly, the new race-conscious programs have also differed from earlier civil rights–oriented policies by their consideration of the ongoing dramatic shift in U.S. demography, largely driven by immigration trends initiated by the 1965 Hart-Cellar Immigration Act. The influx of new immigrants fresh from distinct cultural milieus has facilitated a synergy of quantitative and qualitative shifts in how Americans conceive of assimilation and integration. I suggest that the increasing numbers of linguistically and visibly different Asian Americans and Latinos have fueled a central argument of diversity policy: *racially distinct* groups will integrate into the larger society along *culturally different* paths from earlier European immigrants. Rather than melting into a single "Anglo" cultural pot, Americans have instead melted into quintuple pots of Asians, Blacks, Latinos, Native Americans, and Whites—what historian David Hollinger (1995) has termed an ethnoracial pentagon—historically institutionalized in federal racial classifications. If the ethnoracial pentagon were to hold true for future Americanization processes, then the United States is in the midst of a demographic transition from a majority White population to a majority-minorities or majorityless national population. By the year 2050, the U.S. Census estimates that the population will be 52.8 percent White, 24.5 percent Hispanic, 13.6 percent African American, 8.2 percent Asian American, and approximately 1 percent Native American. The centennial year of the Hart-Cellar Act may see the non-White proportion surpass the 50 percent mark. Future Americans may remember Hart-Cellar not only for ending long-standing racism in immigration and naturalization policy (Takaki 1993) but also for finally removing the founding *Herrenvolk* stain of White privilege from U.S. political citizenship (Winant 1994).

These prospects, however, arise from population projections that do not take into account two significant phenomena: the rising frequency of majority-minority intermarriage and the growing social acceptance of the offspring from these unions as mixed-race individuals (King and DaCosta 1996; Rockquemore 1999), rather than simply members of one or the other ethnoracial population.[5] The racialized minorities contributing the greatest increases in intermarriages—Asian Americans and Latinos—are also the groups growing the fastest from immigration. This fact undermines the Census assumption of solely in-group fertility and suggests that the projected demographic transition may not arrive in the twenty-first century, if ever.

Nevertheless, both the raw magnitude of the new immigration and its racial distinctiveness from the "huddled masses" hailing from Europe have provided strong incentives for popular, governmental, and institutional responses. Though the demographic transition may never materialize, I argue that another kind of diversity transition is occurring. This *cultural* transition is suggested by the increasing porosity of the ethnoracial pentagon, pushed by the overstated but still significantly increased demographic presence of Asians and Latinos, and being channeled by the mélange of institutional policies seeking to reconcile productivity, difference, equality, and justice. By the mid-1990s, for example, Americans' kinship networks were already more heterogeneous than the concept of the pentagon might expect. One in 7

Whites, 1 in 3 Blacks, 4 in 5 Asians, and 19 in 20 American Indians were related through their extended families to someone of a different racial group (Goldstein 1999).

Many schools and cities now regularly "celebrate diversity" in their public rituals and daily practices. The 2000 Republican National Convention even sought to recast its image from an exclusive party defending White male privileges and "traditional values" to a party actively inclusive of racial minorities and cultural differences. The state of Iowa may be designing the boldest diversity policy yet. In a *New York Times* article entitled "Short of People, Iowa Seeks to Be Ellis Island of Midwest," Pam Belluck (2000) reported that state officials have made a proposal to make the entire state into an "immigration enterprise zone" by exempting it from federal immigration quotas and establishing "diversity welcome centers," in the hope of offsetting Iowa's declining population base and revitalizing the flagging economy. One proponent has articulated the state's needs in revealing terms: "We need a doctor from Ghana, a schoolteacher from Brussels, a journalist from Calcutta. What we don't need is 5,000 more Mexican meth dealers." That some Iowans perceive certain groups as more "productive" than others falls short of the political message of many diversity proponents but is consistent with its demographic rationale for social policy. Their interpretation of diversity's potential, however, is also a far cry from the earlier criticisms of affirmative action and diversity policy's "middle sibling," multiculturalism.

THE NECESSARY BUT INSUFFICIENT
PULL OF CIVIL RIGHTS

Often forgotten in millennial celebrations of diversity is that up through the early 1990s, public reactions to its antecedent shibboleth, multiculturalism, were as ambivalent or even hostile as present reactions have been pragmatic and embracing. At the time, a host of popular and academic commentators wrote about secondary schools and college campuses as the major battlefields in a culture war for the meaning and future of American life. While traditional conservatives like George Will and Rush Limbaugh derided ethnic studies and feminist studies scholarship as weak-minded victimology, neoconservatives warned of a growing political correctness threatening to impede cultural literacy (Hirsch, Kett, and Trefil 1987) and fragment civic unity (Schlesinger 1992). At heart, they argued that leftist professors and administrators were wasting time "coddling" African American and feminist students to the point of neglecting White male students and thus diminishing the whole campus community. Their criticisms of especially race-conscious programs put liberals on the defensive—until the appearance of the controversy over Asian American admissions to elite institutions.

So long as the multiculturalism debate remained centered on Blacks and Whites, liberal discourses on "difference" and "equality" also remained interlocked, if not practically synonymous. However, when Asian Americans charged that top universities were using quotas to limit their enrollment and when conservatives joined the controversy to blame those quotas on affirmative action "quotas," the mostly liberal and White administrators of these universities finally modified their positions. In the face of criticisms that they were diminishing rather than increasing the diversity of their campuses, they made a *retreat from race* (Takagi 1992) and precipitated a broader shift outside the academy to a new social class basis for affirmative action and other social policies. Indeed, even after the return of a Democratic president to the White House, liberal commentators like Todd Gitlin (1995) expressed disappointment with the political left for an internally and nationally divisive obsession with identity politics. Given this political context, the transformation of the antidiversity and diversity-queasy America of the Reagan, Bush, and first Clinton administrations into the pro-diversity nation of the 2000 Republican National Convention is thus quite surprising.

The roots of the earlier negative reactions to multiculturalism lie in the aftermath of the post–World War II civil rights movement, sometimes called the Second Reconstruction. The collective memory of the movement has become a resonant symbol for varied, even antagonistic groups. For neoconservatives like Nathan Glazer, the Civil Rights Act of 1964 and its multiplied consequences completed the unfinished business left by Reconstruction-era promises made to "colored people" after the Civil War but then broken with the rapprochement of northern and southern Whites (Bloom 1987). Since the promise of equality has now been fulfilled, they regard racially preferential policies such as affirmative action, minority contracting, and even certain aspects of voting rights legislation as simply excessive. Multiculturalism was thus just another such policy verging on or even directly promoting "reverse discrimination" against Whites, especially White males. To liberals, the civil rights movement simply repeated the plot of the earlier Reconstruction, with racial progress stalling yet again after southern "Negroes" left de jure second-class citizenship behind for the de facto second-class citizenship of their northern and western coethnics. The above public policies thus remain necessary, but in the absence of a clear target like state-sanctioned Jim Crow, a unifying rationale is difficult to articulate in simple terms. Multiculturalism similarly had an inherently inchoate character that thus naturally provoked negative reactions. Even its supporters were divided between de-emphasizing race-specific policies for universal policies (Wilson 1978, 1987, 1996) and emphasizing the continuing need for addressing racial problems "head on" (Takagi 1992).

To yet others, the real movement of significance was not the early civil rights focus of the Southern Christian Leadership Conference and its leader, Dr. Martin Luther King Jr., but its role in readying Negroes to demand *Black* Power and thereby inspiring other cultural-political movements: second-wave feminism, Red Power, the Chicano movement, the Asian American movement, and even the group consciousness of multigenerational European ethnics (Evans 1979; Omatsu 1994). Thus, race-targeted public policy barely begins to improve race relations because it fails to address the cultural and community empowerment issues prevalent at the grassroots, far below the debates of academics and politicians. By this bottom-up definition, multiculturalism as a cultural movement was fundamentally different from federally mandated policies seeking to restore rights and redress representational imbalances. Yet somehow, this marginalized culturalist emphasis on profound ethnoracial *difference* became the heart of the more successful diversity policies.

THE CHANGING CONTEXT OF INTERNATIONAL RELATIONS

I suggest that an important explanation lies in the international context for domestic race relations. An often overlooked aspect of the postwar civil rights struggle is its international context and how that facilitated the diversity transitions, both demographic and cultural, that recent diversity policies have tried to exploit and address. The fall of the Berlin Wall and then of the Soviet Union were events of global significance. Unless one lived through the cold war or is otherwise familiar with how it affected U.S. domestic policies, however, one might view its importance as somewhat academic. It is arguable, though, that without the cold war, there might not have been a successful civil rights movement. Although the continent that became Europe was a relative backwater in world civilization before the fourteenth century AD (Abu-Lughod 1989), the consolidation of its peoples into nation-states and the subsequent development of those countries into colonial powers would transform the globe (Blaut 1993). If the twentieth century was the "American century," it was also a beneficiary of the earlier European revolution and its institutionalization of "race" as a global hierarchy. European colonialism, however, exhausted itself in the two World Wars, leaving the United States and the U.S.S.R. as superpowers in a world full of colonized, largely non-White peoples heading for national independence.

The resultant competition for the allegiances of the new Asian, African, and Latin American nations made de jure segregation in the U.S. South not only a glaring domestic embarrassment but also a thorny international liability. In this climate, U.S. laws that reserved the right of naturalization to Whites and excluded immigration from Asia and the Pacific also made a mockery of U.S. claims to be the "leader of the free world." Nevertheless, when the Hart-Cellar Act passed into law, its proponents expected little change in the ethnic composition of immigration streams into the country. President Johnson in fact explained his support of the bill as a "corrective . . . for southern and eastern European immigrants" (Hing 1993, 40), whose numbers had also been reduced though not outright banned, as Asian immigration had been. That Hart-Cellar would further transform racialized minority communities, already in ethnic renewal cycles as a consequence of the Black Power movement (Espiritu 1992; Nagel 1996), was not a concern. That the new populations would precipitate a domestic sense of external demographic "threat" (Borjas 1999), much less a cultural transformation, was completely unanticipated.

The conservative backlash to the new immigration, however, was primarily a reaction to the contemporary international context, rather than the earlier civil rights struggle. White Americans' "sense of group position" (Blumer and Duster 1980) is affected not only by their relations with other Americans but also by their relations with other nations, since their domestic majority status also permits their taken-for-granted identification with the entire nation. In the 1980s, the United States appeared to be in danger of losing its economic preeminence to previously "inferior" nations, either because the latter's products had "invaded" U.S. consumer markets or because their labor markets were too great a "seduction" for U.S. manufacturing plants. For many White Americans, the distinction between civil rights and immigration has remained too subtle to be significant (Rubin 1994). Nevertheless, the two concerns did not become "social problems" simultaneously. As noted above, the initial backlash against multiculturalism was mainly directed against African Americans rather than the new immigrants of color. Later, with Japan's rise as an economic power and Mexico's increasing availability for factory relocation, popular discontent with international competition cast a shadow mainly on Asian Americans and Latinos. More recent international shadows on domestic race relations include the tension between the myth of global economic integration among equals promulgated by multinational corporate marketing and the "war" against terrorism led by the U.S. executive branch.

Perhaps not surprisingly, the direct beneficiaries of civil rights and immigration policies have only inconsistently formed a united political front. Although the 1980s saw the resurgence of "Third World" coalitions of Asian Americans, Blacks, Latinos, and Native Americans, they were often only either temporary alliances or confined to college campus settings. And even these linkages fractured in the wake of the 1992 Los Angeles riot and rebellion. In 1994 California voters passed Proposition 187, curbing the legal claims of undocumented immigrants on state services. On November 9, 1994, the *Los Angeles Times* reported that its exit poll found that African American and Asian American voters were both split in support of and against the proposition (roughly 45 percent favoring and 55 percent against), while Whites supported it 59 percent to 41 percent and Latinos were overwhelmingly against it (78 percent to 22 percent). Two years later, California voters passed Proposition 209, repealing affirmative action in state policies. This time, the *Los Angeles Times* reported on November 7, 1996 that while Whites were again the only group in favor of the proposition (63 percent to 37 percent), the other groups opposed it by different margins, Latinos and African Americans overwhelmingly so (roughly 75 percent to 25 percent) and Asian Americans in equal measure to White support (61 percent opposing to 39 percent favoring). Thus, an inconsistent inclusion of civil rights and immigration issues complicates how any given speaker or institution constructs pro-diversity and diversity-queasy positions. While an antidiversity position opposes any attention to either issue domain, the other two positions might more complexly combine attention to Black civil rights and Asian and Latino immigrants, or even a broader articulation of concerns, for instance, Asian, Latino, and Native American civil rights, Black immigrants, or even Native American sovereignty. In brief, one might be pro-diversity with respect to certain groups and issues and diversity-queasy with regard to others.

WHITES IN DIVERSITY

The above examples might lead one to note the one consistent finding: a majority of White Americans object to diversity, whatever its definition. On the other hand, the conditionality of each opposition can lead one to less strict interpretations, and also explains the absence of a complete repeal of the

1964 Civil Rights Act or a return to the more restrictive immigration codes of the century before Hart-Cellar. After all, opponents of Proposition 187 argued that it forced voters to conflate fiscal concerns about undocumented migrants with racist stereotypes that they might have otherwise opposed. Similarly, opponents of Proposition 209 argued that its phrasing as the repeal of "racial preferences" misled voters otherwise supportive of affirmative action and multiculturalism. Critical commentators have more strictly interpreted these diversity-queasy reactions as indicative of *hegemony*, a political system that rules not through categorical exclusion but through selective inclusions (Winant 1994). Each White reaction—"colorblind" concerns about crime and safety, racially preferential federal policies, and illegal migrants—thus disciplines old and new Americans of color alike by policing the cultural boundaries of their social acceptability. Implicit in this critique, however, is also the policing of White behavior along a racist versus nonracist boundary defined by whether and how Whites weigh the potential consequences of implicitly racial policies for their fellow citizens.

Other commentators have observed instead a real increase in the tolerance of Whites for non-Whites, a trend documented in Clem Brooks's (2000) examination of the effects of civil rights attitudes on voting behavior. Contrary to popular views of the U.S. public as having partisan "mood swings" and to scholarly research on the relative superficiality of White "goodwill" for non-Whites, Brooks found a steady rise in liberal voting patterns, not merely surface attitudes. In fact, he argues that this trend suppressed the margins of Republican presidential victories in the 1980s below what they would have been otherwise and foreshadowed a Republican realignment to embracing diversity in order to remain competitive with Democratic candidates.

At a certain level, whether we should view diversity queasiness as a more subtle or even insidious opposition to racialized minorities or a transition to an acceptance or even embrace of them as fellow Americans is arguably a simple matter of pessimism or optimism. At another level, the issue pivots around the more substantive question of whether diversity policies and their surrounding debates asymmetrically target non-White acceptability while leaving White attitudes and behaviors untouched. At best, this asymmetry conflates diversity concerns with non-Whites and results in efforts to encourage "normal," racially unmarked Americans to either exoticize, patronize, or pity the "other" Americans. At worst, it promotes subtle discrimination by institutionalizing a closer scrutiny of non-Whites for social acceptance and asking them to be more "tolerable" to Whites. Both scenarios would embed in intergroup-related policies an assumed relationship between White judgments and non-White "objects."

Viewing diversity policy instead as symmetrical practices seeking primarily to change intergroup relationships rather than group representations is 180 degrees from Kelly and Dobbin's (1998) view of diversity management as a self-amputated form of affirmative action. As a substitute for affirmative action, diversity policy would indeed be a weak organizational compliance to legal assessments of institutional culpability and liability. I suggest, however, that as an effort to alter relationships, diversity policy attempts to achieve what affirmative action never could: a re-membering of the formerly excluded and a re-creation of community on new terms. While it is this aspect of diversity policy that fueled the earlier conservative denunciations of multiculturalism as political correctness, the same criticisms could easily have applied to conservative calls for a "return to traditional values." For that matter, any cultural change movement runs the risk of being charged with becoming a "thought police" when it is viewed through the lens of legal culpability and punishment, dominant in civil rights law.

BEYOND BACKLASH CONTROL:
NEW RELATIONSHIPS AND COMMUNITIES

As critical legal scholars of race have argued, however, these Western legal principles and their traditional civil rights practices become increasingly incomplete and even irrelevant the further removed a given situation is from the classic model of de jure, intention-laden discriminatory actions and conspiracies. Although Yamamoto's (1999) theory of interracial justice is based on cases of interracial apologies and reparations, I argue that his conclusions have important implications for our understandings of diversity policy. Rather than begin with traditionally Black-White models of racism and antiracism, his analysis models interracial justice on interminority conflicts, wherein each group has a limited measure of power over the other and which occur in "borderlands" where historically oppressive situations have undergone sharp demographic, economic, and political change.

As a process, interracial justice projects may begin with civil rights goals, but they attain enduring resolutions only when interpersonal "rights talk" gives way to intergroup performances of reconciliation and reunification. Civil rights laws and legal cases aim at policing behaviors to alter the "bodily" representation of federally protected categories in a given situation. They seek to find *culpability* for clear crimes, punish perpetrators, and assign to victims awards that are financially commensurate with the harm done to them. By contrast, interracial justice aims at raising collective awareness of the cultural representations informing interpersonal tensions in order to alter intergroup relationships. It defines *complicity* as benefiting from the unequal relationships that structure the immediate interpersonal situation irrespective of intent to harm, assigns a broad responsibility to "right wrongs," and makes reparations that address underlying grievances between groups. Rather than measure diversity policies against the "ideal" of legal compliance, we can assess both diversity policy and affirmative action along the broader conception of interracial justice, which articulates both quantitative and qualitative goals for social change.

Privatism in Diversity Policy and Racial Formation

The complexity of diversity policy's four major aspects[6] contrasts with the relative simplicity of the federal approach to race relations: the protection of victims. The closest that antidiscrimination law comes to approximating the scope of diversity policy is the principle of reasonable accommodation in disability protections. The aforementioned distinction between affirmative action and diversity policy approximates the difference between ignoring the existence of a disability (a version of colorblindness) and accommodating its presence.[7] Even the latter legislative mandate, however, would fall short of the fourth aspect's goal of changing core organizational cultures and intergroup relationships.

Perhaps it should not be surprising, then, that diversity policies emerged first from within private institutional settings and have proliferated most quickly there rather than following from public sector mandates. Private institutions, especially the elite organizations that are financially endowed and professionally oriented, are less vulnerable to changing political climates than government offices. Nevertheless, the private origins and contexts for diversity policy have been lost in the very public debates about its desirability and effectiveness. In the wake of feminist proclamations that "the personal is political" and scholarly paradigm shifts highlighting the vast interpenetration of formal electoral politics and "external" social inequalities, it may seem somewhat antiquated to assert a difference between "private" and "public" spheres. However, the distinction intended here has a conditional character that does not deny the embeddedness of private institutions in public politics. In fact, it is the public sphere that grants the private sphere its measure of freedom to distinguish itself from the activities directly under the jurisdiction of the democratic state. This argument imports into the political sociology of race relations particular insights of neoinstitutional organizational sociology in order to correct for the tendency to characterize all racial phenomena as equally "political," that is, open to contestations, electoral or otherwise. As Fligstein has outlined, "Organizations operate in three contexts of what could be called institutional spheres: the existing strategy and structure of the organization, the set of organizations comprising the organizational field, and the state" (1991, 312). This study of diversity policy thus amends theories of racial formation by calling attention to the second context, the interorganizational culture and relationships that influence organizational policies in directions beyond the political interaction between organized agendas and state responses.

Of the private institutions that have developed diversity policies, organized philanthropy deserves special attention because it is an especially ambitious and autonomous institutional field. Philanthropic diversity, or, to use the field terminology, *philanthropic pluralism*, differs from its higher education and corporate counterparts in its orientation to both internal and external relationships. Higher education evaluates its success by attending primarily to student experiences, campus climate, and the availability of resources throughout its units. Corporate management evaluates its success by attending to customer loyalty, employee commitment, workplace climate, and the maximum use of human resources in work groups. By contrast, grant-making foundations direct their diversity policy not only internally, like other private institutions, but also externally to shaping the level and character of intergroup relationships involving the grantee organizations, their client populations, and other significant alters. In brief, whereas most private institutions focus their diversity policies narrowly to the recruitment of talent into themselves, philanthropy also constructs policies for the broader purpose of *identifying talent for society at large.*

By highlighting philanthropic diversity policy, this book contributes a unique perspective to scholarship on racial formation, which has recognized the strongly political character of race relations but not the deeply private aspects of U.S. politics. By racial formation, I refer principally to Michael Omi and Howard Winant's conception initially set forth in 1986: "We use the term racial formation to refer to the process by which social, economic, and political forces determine the content and importance of racial categories, and by which they [the aforementioned forces] are in turn shaped by racial meanings" (61). In distinction from previous definitions that reduced race to ethnicity, class, or nation, they defined race as a politically structured system of classifications: "There is a continuous temptation to think of race as essence, as something fixed, concrete, and objective . . . And there is an opposite temptation: to see it as a mere illusion, which an ideal social order would eliminate. In our view it is crucial to break with these habits of thought. The effort must be to understand race as an unstable and 'decentered' complex of social meanings constantly being transformed by political struggle" (68).

Omi and Winant advanced a social constructionist definition and anchored its relativism to political process, emphasizing the struggles between national states and social movements, that is, the civil rights movements of the 1960s and the conservative reaction of the 1980s. Thus, they defined race as an enduring element in U.S. political culture, which provides a structural context for racial phenomena examined by other scholars: segregation, differential returns to human capital investments, comparative school performance, antipathy, exceptional events or crises, identity, and group traditions and social capital. In effect, Omi and Winant have insisted that sociologists not abandon the study of U.S. politics to political scientists, who have been less likely to theorize its racial dimensions (Hero 1992).

Pervading the contestations between social movements and the state, foundations represent a *private* policy infrastructure for the nonprofit movement organizations. The racial formation paradigm assumes a traditional analytic split between macro and micro levels in the social world. In this framework, the racial state is of primary importance at the macro level, while at the micro level, collective identities are of primary importance, though families, ethnic communities, and even multiracial coalitions are also significant features. Joining these micro and macro levels of racial life are the social movements and racial projects (Omi and Winant 1994) that shuttle between them, mostly by rearticulating new group identities into demands for state action. In turn, these contestations themselves function as dramatic stages on which the racial state delimits demands to what it deems acceptable racial common sense.

However, social movements are not only bundles of collective will and effervescence. They also have institutional form in an ongoing and not simply reactive nonprofit sector. To discuss diversity only in terms of demographics, public policy, and interest groups is to close our eyes to the reliance of governmental activities on certain kinds of private organizations, known in other countries as nongovernmental organizations or NGOs. The U.S. nonprofit sector handles social responsibilities administered by the public sectors of social democratic nations, which have been the ideal typical states of political sociological theory. Health care is a popular example, but one must also consider the explosion of government contracting for social services since the 1960s (Smith and Lipsky 1993). While social movements may exploit the nonprofit form (Gronbjerg 1993), the nonprofit form also disciplines social movements in ways more nuanced than simple co-optation (Espiritu 1992). Importantly, the nonprofit form pressures movements to transform political demands into mission statements within grant economies and interorganizational cultural fields, within which foundations are influential. However, because nonprofits are generally nonpolitical, hence nonpublic, and yet institutional, hence not reducible to identity, they fall off the map of the racial politics theorized by racial formation scholars.

Among nonprofits, philanthropic foundations have an elite status as organizations whose capital endowments render them less dependent on external sources of revenue than other nonprofits. In fact, they function as private governments for other nonprofits through their disbursement of capital gains that the Internal Revenue Service partially releases from taxation obligations. Furthermore, their relations with each other as a field of mutually oriented organizations (DiMaggio and Powell 1991) provide the basis for policy debates relatively autonomous from public sector debates on race, ethnicity, and other social issues. Their relative *in*dependence from electoral accountability and their relative *inter*dependence on independent discourse provide an autonomous policy infrastructure among elite nonprofits. Foundation policies thus index a privatist culture and infrastructure for nondemocratic forces that influence legitimacy despite their externality to the formal political system.

Putting Diversity in Its Place

Besides providing a political history and elaborating the private base of diversity policies, I also consider the geographically uneven impact of the national diversity transition. If indeed "race is place" (Chideya 1999), examining diversity solely as a national phenomenon squashes the distinct nuances arising between regions as spatially and culturally disparate as the West Coast and the Midwest. Historically, White workers cornered privileged employment in the U.S. labor market, resulting in its nineteenth-century racial dualities: for men, between higher-wage jobs with opportunities for advancement and low-wage, dead-end, marginal jobs; and for women, between motherhood and paid domestic work, including parenting their employers' children in addition to their own. However, these White over non-White dualities varied by region as the non-White group varied from African Americans in the South, Mexicans in the Southwest, and Asians on the West Coast and Hawaii (Glenn 1992). The migrations of southern Blacks during the World Wars to the North and West muted these variations, but not for long. The uneven regionalism of post-1965 immigration has magnified those earlier local differences as the new immigrants initially concentrated on the coasts and the Southwest, and then later spread to the South. As private institutions shifted from the "one size fits all" model of national culture to diversity policy, the regional reality behind "national" culture has also shifted. In earlier times, popular culture assumed that the leading edge of American culture was east of the Mississippi River, where Black-White dynamics dominated race relations. As the twentieth century closed and much of the national economy migrated westward, popular culture also shifted attention to the West Coast, in particular California, where less bipolar intergroup relations have reigned for a much longer time. To use Yamamoto's (1999) terminology, the center of American culture has shifted to the borderlands, where historic oppressions and recent transformations collide and recombine, but by no means have these regions converged on a single model of intergroup diversity.

Accordingly, my research focuses on local philanthropies in the context of the national philanthropic field to pay attention to the significant geographical variations in the institutionalization of diversity policy. For this reason, I selected two far-flung community foundations as the cases to represent locally oriented organized philanthropy. Rather than operate social services or other programs themselves, as do operating foundations, community foundations make grants to others who operate such projects; in other words, they legitimate particular projects from pools of possible projects, exemplifying the external orientation making philanthropy unique among private institutions. Instead of being focused on a particular industry or field of activity (e.g., primary education), community foundations pursue broad missions, delimited primarily by geographic scope; therefore, their contribution to the public good is broad, like the public sector. Whereas individual donors control family foundations (e.g., the Gates Foundation) and annual donors in aggregate control federated funding (e.g., the United Way), public boards instead control the community foundations. In the large and mature community foundations on which I focus, the board members are the appointees of local establishment leaders: the mayor, the president of the Chamber of Commerce, the president of the United Way, the presidents of elite local universities, presidents of the trustee banks, among others, plus a certain number of self-perpetuated (i.e., board-elected) members. Therefore, the public governance of community foundations refers not to electoral accountability but to leadership by a varied group of relatively insulated, private, and local stakeholders.

To weigh the relative impacts of the post-1965 immigration and historic civil rights concerns, I compared the high immigration-receiving region of the San Francisco Bay Area in the state of California with the low immigration-receiving area of the Greater Cleveland Area in the state of Ohio. Out of the eight major community foundations examined by the National Committee for Responsive Philanthropy (1989), I chose the San Francisco Foundation and the Cleveland Foundation because of the contrasting demographic changes experienced in their respective metropolitan areas. Both the Bay Area and the Cleveland Area were roughly 10 percent foreign-born in 1960 (U.S. Bureau of the Census 1964a, 1964b) but divergently experienced the post-1965 rise in immigration, becoming 25 percent and 5 percent foreign-born, respectively, by 1990 (U.S. Bureau of the Census 1973a, 1973b, 1981a, 1981b, 1993a, 1993b). These two foundations were thus faced with either the continuation of race relations dominated by Black-White dynamics or the significant addition of other intergroup dynamics. Additionally, they are comparably sized institutions, both being in the top ten of the largest community foundations. With respect to endowments, the Cleveland Foundation has approximately $1.5 billion in assets, and the San Francisco Foundation has almost $.75 billion (The Foundation Center 2003).

Another reason for my attention to both local and national milieus is more theoretical: to weigh the relative contributions of translocal debates about race, that is, racial discourse, and the local maneuvers for influence, that is, crude political interests. These theoretical factors are significant because of the split in ethnic studies, including the sociology of race and ethnicity, between culturalist and structuralist studies of race relations. For proponents of Marxist theory and its upending of the Hegelian Spirit to favor materialist over idealist interpretations, the popularity of discursive analysis might seem a horrific intellectual counterrevolution. It was one thing for social constructionism to complicate the base-superstructure relationship and burden economic determinism with explaining the new identity-based social movements, but it was a whole other thing for the new cultural studies to argue that the mode of production was itself a discursive effect. Rather than resolve this debate, the more pragmatic goal here is to explain my use of discourse in addition to the more traditional sociological conception of ideology.

An important advantage of conceiving of ideas and beliefs as "discourse" has been to reveal their portability, or, as William Sewell (1992) has noted, their transposability, a characteristic generally lacking from the sociological concepts of ideology. Ideological analysis links the explicit arguments and their hidden assumptions to their *speakers* (e.g., the question of *whose* ideology) and their collective interests. By contrast, the analysis of ideas as discourse severs the subjects constituted in them from their *carriers*, whose collective interests are only contingently related to the ideas put forth. Rather than distinguish between true and false beliefs, discursive analysis makes all consciousnesses "false," that is, historically constructed or imagined (Wetherell and Potter 1992). The appeal of discourse to its carriers is legitimacy rather than personal gain or group honor. Crudely put, we can analyze power relations in terms of complexity rather than simply conspiracy.

This approach allows sociologists to study the interplay of multiple ideas and beliefs, but it risks abstracting these concepts out of the contexts in which people and institutions employ them. We can maintain those contexts, however, by identifying discourses in translocal media and then examining their effects on local practices and transformations in specific local contexts. Because community foundations are primarily oriented to local regions and yet are part of a professional field with national discourses, they are excellent subjects of study for weighing how both extralocal discourse and local interests influence organizational diversity policies.

In sum, a sociological evaluation of diversity policy depends on understanding its political history, private institutional basis, and geographic scope. Ironically, for a policy premised on inclusiveness and envisioning a new nation, diversity is both strongly a creature of nondemocratic, only loosely accountable social forces, and practically a captive of local exigencies and interests. Foundation diversity policies uniquely reveal how private institutions have negotiated the inherent complexities and contradictions of attempting to institutionalize a revolution in race relations.

THIS INTRODUCTORY CHAPTER has reviewed a number of debates on diversity policy and argued that its development in organized philanthropy provides a unique window on its surprising emergence as a widely resonant symbol in the wake of a political backlash against the post–World War II civil rights movement. The review followed a theoretical map for diversity policy, which highlighted (1) its negative development out of earlier racially preferential policies, (2) a broader "post-Black" attention to race relations, (3) the historical context of civil rights and international affairs, and (4) the potential for moving intergroup relations beyond asymmetry and narrow "rights talk." The complexity of these dimensions to diversity policy called attention to its institutional life within private organizations and fields. This privatism was then related to the racial formation paradigm, whose theoretical dominance in ethnic studies has directed scholarly attention to the political construction of racial categories and projects. Finally, I discussed the historical, methodological, and theoretical importance of geographically specific and comparative research on U.S. race relations.

Chapter 2 empirically introduces an institutional approach to understanding diversity policy through an explanation of how and why foundations as a field shifted their focus from the historical support of Black colleges to the "pluralism in philanthropy" of the 1990s. Rather than preceding the social movements of the post–World War II period, the institutional character of philanthropy actually emerged through foundation experiences in race relations.[8] From the civil rights movement onward, foundations modeled their general discussions of minority issues on their experiences with African Americans and Black issues. Almost all discussion of immigration trends, international relations, and deviations from the traditional White/non-White asymmetry in racial discourse enter through Asian-, Latino-, and Native American–specific issues but remain marginal to the general discussions until the 1980s. Thus, I distinguish between diversity as a demographic phenomenon with potential social consequences and diversity as a strategic organizational response to political crises. Throughout these shifts, foundations maintain and reconstruct their unique role of identifying talent as distinct from the federal civil rights goal of protecting victims. The shift in demographics does not provide a substantive rationale for diversity policy; instead, it primarily becomes a rhetorical opportunity for preserving preexisting racially liberal programs.

Chapters 3 and 4 consider the impact of these national institutional shifts on local organizations amid divergent demographics and distinct political environments. These chapters combine the nationally oriented racial formation theory with the insights of urban sociologists on political regimes to provide an account of local-level processes of racial formation. Before continuing to chapters 3 and 4, however, organizational scholars may find it more intuitive to read the remaining chapters out of order. While chapter 2 is an account of national racial politics, it also functions as a "new institutionalist" analysis of field-level racial processes. Instead of immediately exploring whether and how national politics influence local politics (chapters 3 and 4), some readers might wish to stay on the topic of field-level dynamics by first turning to chapters 5 and 6. As they return to chapters 3 and 4 before reading the concluding chapter, organizationally minded readers will discover that the analysis has shifted from neoinstitutionalism's emphasis on communities of like organizations to the emphasis of "old institutionalism" on single organizations impregnated by their local environments (Perrow 1986). In effect, I argue that social scientists should pay attention to both institutional processes in addition to their reliance on each other. By comparison, the readers who read the chapters in order will learn, first, that local racial politics diverge from national politics in significant ways and second, that institutional processes moderate the different levels of racial politics and their interrelationship. In brief, I argue that demographic change has played a relatively passive role in the political and institutional formulation of diversity policy.

Chapter 3 examines the development of foundation policy in the baseline low-immigration region in the Midwest and tells the story of how the regional philanthropy less impacted by immigration ironically had greater institutional opportunities for diversity policy. From the civil rights movement to the 1990s, the Cleveland Foundation was led by two White males and one Black male, whose executive directorships demonstrated the Foundation's connections with local corporate and political elites. With local clout that also attracted national attention, the Cleveland philanthropy built institutional bridges between Blacks, Whites, and other groups within the regional community. Its early pursuit of the goal of "strengthening the role of Blacks in the community" continued its top-down orientation as it chose to reshape its local nonprofit sector within a philanthropic *greenhouse.*

In a parallel fashion, chapter 4 examines the development of foundation policy in the high-immigration region on the West Coast and tells the story of how the regional philanthropy surrounded by greater demographic heterogeneity made more innovative yet also less substantial diversity policies. Up through the mid-1990s, the San Francisco Foundation was led by three White men whose executive directorships evidenced the Foundation's isolation from local politics. Without significant local or national allies, the San Francisco philanthropy responded to the sudden population changes mainly by encouraging its grantee organizations to adopt inclusiveness as a value. Although the organization initiated policies with a post-Black constituency well in advance of the national political crisis, they developed largely along philosophical and ideological paths. The Foundation's otherwise innovative early goal of "making differences helpful rather than harmful" remained a passive accommodation to an unpredictable local political context, as it chose to gingerly handle its local nonprofit sector as a *wild garden*. Like chapter 2, the interregional comparison in chapters 3 and 4 strongly warns against conflating the magnitude of demographic diversity with the substance of diversity policy.

Chapter 5 connects the comparative regional histories with the national field by focusing on the nigh omnipresence of the Ford Foundation in both the local foundations' distinct policy strategies and the national field's diversity turn. With almost $11 billion in assets, the Ford Foundation is the third largest foundation in the United States (The Foundation Center 2003). For decades, Ford magnified the already greater resources of the Cleveland Foundation and entrenched the philanthropy in national policy networks, while the San Francisco Foundation experienced an additional isolation from not only possible local allies but also national networks. In the wake of Reagan's election, however, these long-standing networks lost their legitimacy, and the Ford Foundation's response led to a new relationship with the San Francisco Foundation. Meanwhile, at the national level, the racial projects of the Carnegie, Ford, and Rockefeller philanthropies eclipsed the projects benefiting historically Black colleges. During the Reagan-Bush years, the Ford Foundation used its international development experience as the model for pluralism in philanthropy by way of its earlier impact on Native American–specific issues. Ford's search for new political allies and legitimacy in the 1980s facilitated the broader field's attention to the new demography, especially on the West Coast, and simultaneously captured and updated racial philanthropy with its experiences collaborating with community foundations in the Midwest since the 1960s. In organizational terms, Ford facilitates the philanthropic shift to diversity policy when it lends its clout to reduce the price of innovation (Becker 1995) for local institutions on the West Coast. In racial terms, Ford's historic preference for liberal elite intermediaries effects an ambivalent commitment to social change. The chapter wraps up the book's primary argument about the historical emergence of diversity policy.

Chapter 6 presents a secondary argument about diversity policy: the institutionalism that characterized its design and adoption also pervades its relative validity for foundation actors themselves. While the preceding chapters demonstrate the relative utility of diversity for maintaining institutional distinction and status in the face of a new, politically conservative context, this chapter examines one of the policy's major consequences: the rise of new insiders in the historically White and Eastern institution of philanthropy. Like its older, sibling policies of affirmative action and multiculturalism, diversity policy assumes that group membership influences individuals' life experiences, perspectives, and potential contributions to society. In actual philanthropic relations, however, institutional locations segment these "cultural" differences, nearly invalidating the group-based premise of the policies in question. While racial/ethnic inequalities remain salient outside the foundations, incomplete social change has occurred within them, reproducing the external intergroup tensions *within* the institution itself while simultaneously segmenting them *between* institutional statuses and geographies. In fact, it is the new insiders of color and/or region who advocate the alternatives to elite-directed philanthropy, emphasizing the more symmetrical relations absent from White and midwestern conceptions of philanthropic racial policy. Ironically, these foundation actors, who actually "walk the talk" instead of treating diversity policy primarily as a shield for traditional policy, are peculiarly concentrated in the most powerful organizational positions and the less central geographic region.

Diversity policy is thus institutional in both origins and effects, as I discuss in chapter 7 while revisiting questions of privatism and racial formation. I explore the implications of the development of philanthropic pluralism for understanding the broader diversity transition in U.S. society as evidence for an increasingly visible and critical aspect of race in the post–civil rights era: its extensive *institutional segmentation*, where success or failure in one institutional domain does not necessarily signal success or failure in others. An institutional approach to racial formation theory advances its development from a description of historical contingencies to an exploration of how race remains coherent despite its extensive situational fragmentation. To illustrate, I show how institutional segmentation accounts for the noted proliferation of both "good" and "bad" multiculturalisms and how it complicates certain monolithic predictions of Black exceptionalism from the new American embrace of diversity. Last, I argue that the emergence of institutional segmentation suggests a new methodological approach concerned with the relative coherence of race relations across institutional settings—between politics and the other institutional domains, between the domains, between domains and their geographically embedded members, and between elites and other domain members.

2

Race Talk in the National Magazine
of Foundation Philanthropy

What we do best is identify talent.

A former member of the program staff for the Cleveland Foundation made the above statement to me during our interview appointment. Since his years there, he has remained working in the field of organized philanthropy and now directs a foundation whose assets rival those of his former organization. Performing his leadership in the field, he discusses foundation work in the first person, "What we do," and highlights its unique contribution to society, being the "best" at identifying "talent." Pervading the foundation discourse about race and ethnicity, this metaphor of the talent search diverges from the related U.S. federal and legal terminology of "protected categories" that regulate the government programs. From the view of nonprofits, however, the existence of a coherent foundation logic may seem elusive. Because nonprofits are heavily dependent on government contracts (Smith and Lipsky 1993), they may experience the rationales attached to philanthropic support as excessive to the actual dollar amounts and view foundations as idiosyncratic or simply capricious. Nevertheless, I argue that a consistent, alternative cultural logic distinguishes foundation projects from U.S. racial politics.

Between 1960 and 1990, many private institutions changed the way they thought about race and ethnicity, from an exclusive focus on African Americans to a focus on a diversity of major groups. Emblematic of this shift, the national magazine, currently titled *Foundation News and Commentary*, published in 1990 a special issue on "Pluralism in Philanthropy," which both explained and singled out for praise the charitable traditions of four culturally distinct "groups": Asians, Hispanics (Latinos), Blacks, and Indians

(Native Americans). The cover for the special issue aesthetically communicated the contours of the new focus on diversity (figure 1). Beneath the magazine title sat four equally sized panels arranged in a two-by-two grid, framing illustrations of four faces that possessed distinct features racially identifiable as Asian, Black, Latino, and Native American; were rendered comparable as tribally styled or "native" masks, anthropologically positioned in relation to the "civilized" magazine subscriber; and ultimately framed philanthropic diversity as the sophisticated appreciation of non-White cultural objects by a racially unmarked, implicitly White subject. On the other hand, while this reading of the art suggests an old politics of colonialism behind the symbolic appeal of the new policy, I would also argue that the social factors behind diversity policy cannot be reduced to this political symbolism. Indeed, the articles in the issue were far less colonialist in content.

Noting that the world population was "82% non-White" and that the U.S. population was increasingly non-White, the issue posed the question of how the four groups' traditions might blend with mainstream philanthropy. This focus stands in contrast to the magazine's near exclusive focus in the 1960s on supporting what were then called "Negro colleges," or once-segregated but now "historically Black" institutions of higher education. I argue that why foundations shifted their attention from African Americans to multiple equivalent groups is tied to why the new concern for cultural competence (group-based) displaced the old focus on educational uplift. In brief, an account emphasizing institutional-cultural autonomy provides a significantly fuller explanation than demographic or political accounts can by themselves.

This chapter explores the institutional considerations moderating foundation perspectives on diversity policy by elaborating the philanthropic cultural logic that has characterized foundation responses to demographic trends and political events. It empirically examines the emergence of diversity discourse in the foundation field through an analysis of the major ethnoracial themes published in its national magazine from 1960 to 1990. By focusing on when specific racial themes appear, disappear, and become coherent, I show how the ascendancy of conservative politics was a stronger goad for foundations to reshape their racial and ethnic debates than the actual arrival of immigrant people of color. I discuss how the trope of "identifying talent" distinguished racial discourse in the foundation field from the trope of "protecting victims" in federal policy and trace the development of philanthropic thinking about race after the civil rights movement to its arrival at diversity policy. To the historic Black-White framing of

Pluralism in Philanthropy

race relations, I contrast the broader attention of diversity policy to the four "food groups" of Asians, Blacks, Latinos, and Native Americans and chart its appearance in *Foundation News and Commentary*. I compare the expectations of popular and sociological accounts of the emergence of diversity with the empirical development of philanthropic pluralism in the field's discourse about race and ethnicity.

I assert that an institutional cultural logic explains the relative autonomy of foundation "race talk" from broader social changes by arguing that:

1. The historical inclusion of non-Black non-Whites in foundation rhetoric is more complex than the expectations of demographic and political theories.

2. A pseudo-dialectic cultural logic of shifting *identifications* and *talents* better characterizes the trajectory of philanthropic discourse.

3. The characterizations of Asian Americans, Latinos, and Native Americans pivot, respectively, on their relative putative differences from African Americans.

4. The appearance of philanthropic diversity discourse occurs only after the politically conditioned decline of a long-standing Black centrality in the field rhetoric.

I close with a discussion of how the autonomy of foundation discourse increased, ironically, when the broader society became averse to the advancement of non-Whites.

In the popular imagination, diversity policies are direct responses to either demographic imperatives or political forces. For instance, the shift in national demographics has resulted in the necessary consideration of Latinos and Asians along with Blacks and Whites in civil rights policies and national culture. Alternatively, population shifts may be regarded as less important than the post–World War II process of non-White decolonization, countering the historical oppression of the four major minority groups.[1] From this second perspective, diversity policy is just the private sector's participation in (or even co-optation of) the cause of minority advancement. Yet another popular explanation attributes the policy not to population shifts or historically motivated movements but to entitlement demands premised on victimhood. In this account, diversity policy is simply the private mimicry of ill-conceived public policies which have invited innumerable and inconsistent claims from self-serving political operatives. However, none of these three popular stock stories, or even their more theoretical counterparts in sociology, can account for the complex manner by which foundation field discourse shifted to embrace diversity policy. Table 1 summarizes these distinct accounts, including my alternative explanation.

Except for the story of victimhood, each theory predicts the steady accumulation of ethnoracial categories in organizational policy from only Blacks to the four major groups. After the 1965 Immigration Act, the numbers of foreign-born U.S. residents of Asian and Latino origin have geometrically increased. After the breach made by the Black civil rights movement in the 1950s and 1960s, other non-White groups were inspired to form social movements to challenge the status quo. Racial formation theory (Omi and Winant 1986, 1994) provides a more sociological version of the decolonization story by emphasizing not only minority movement formation but also the effects of both minority and conservative movements on the state. The key factor is the prevailing political culture in response to major social movements. Although the state may not concede to every demand of a movement, the movement still forces the state to rationalize its selection of which demands to legitimate. State response is thus a measure of movement

TABLE 1   Hypotheses for the Emergence of Diversity Policies

	EXPECTATIONS	
	Inclusion of Groups beyond African Americans	Rationale for Inclusions
Social Strain		
National Shift in Demographics	Steady accumulation after 1965 from Blacks to diversity	Increasing intergroup relations beyond Blacks and Whites
Social Movements		
Non-White Decolonization	Steady accumulation after 1964 from Blacks to diversity	Social movements of historically oppressed groups
Political Culture (Racial Formation Theory)	Steady accumulation after 1964 until 1980	Non-White activism after 1964 and White backlash after 1980
Policy Effects		
Entitlement Claims Based in Victimhood	Indiscriminate inclusions	Non-White claims and White guilt in the form of special preferences
Political Legitimacy (State Rules and Their Effects)	Steady accumulation after 1964 until 1980	Political opportunities for social service and protest before 1964, advocacy after 1964, and declining opportunities after 1980
Institutional Autonomy		
Field-specific Cultural Logic	Complex dependence on field logic autonomous of political and demographic forces	Institutionally specific responses to major political events

success, even when activists have failed to provoke their desired response. If diversity policy followed such racial politics, however, then the accumulation of policy targets would have ceased or even receded with the 1980 presidential election of Ronald Reagan, which was the result of political unity among three conservative movements: the far right, the new right, and neoconservatives.

The victimhood thesis differs from the above theories because it regards racial policies, whether public or private, as rooted in contemporary special interests rather than historical forces. It predicts not an orderly accumulation but the indiscriminate aggregation of inconsistent claims about history. Ironically, a sociological version of the victimhood story might expect a process of accumulation similar to the above theories. Debra Minkoff's (1995) study of the proliferation of women's and racial/ethnic national organizations after 1955 highlights the same pivotal years as racial formation theory but emphasizes not the impact of movements on the state but the ecological consequences of state policy for organizations. The key factor is the prevailing political legitimacy or clout of particular constituencies and policies as signaled by the state. In Minkoff's account, the political climate for non-White organizations becomes increasingly positive after 1964 but plummets after 1980. More specifically, the post-1964 period sees advocacy organizations surpass both protest organizations and the historically dominant social service organizations, while the post-1980 period witnesses the increasing demise of even the service organizations. In other words, state rules such as protected categories, civil rights legislation, and court rulings have effects independent of whatever historical forces facilitated their emergence. As with the victimhood theory, history is best considered as backdrop and not ultimate cause of diversity policy.

Although most of the above theories predict a similar pattern in the inclusion of non-Black non-Whites into race policy, they differ in their mechanisms and thus also have different expectations for why private organizations shifted attention from Blacks to the four major groups. If foundations were paying attention to population trends, then their rationale for diversity policy might be a growing recognition of intergroup dynamics beyond Black-White relations. If foundations were paying close attention to non-White movements, then their rationale for diversity policy might be the appearance of an expanding number of minority movements. Alternatively, if they were paying attention to successful social movements, then their rationale might shift in 1980 from non-White activism to White backlash. If foundations were paying close attention to random entitlement claims, then their rationale for diversity policy might be a repeating stimulus-and-response pattern of minority claims and White guilt in the form of special preferences. Alternatively, if they were paying attention to state-prescribed legitimacy, then their rationale might shift in 1980 from magnifying non-White advocacy efforts to perhaps pruning and consolidating social service programs for non-Whites.

In actuality, the shift in foundation discourse from focusing on Blacks to focusing on Asians, Blacks, Latinos, and Native Americans evidences what I term an institutional cultural autonomy. Foundations (in their field rhetoric) did respond to social strain as predicted by the demographic thesis, but the strain concerned political events instead of demographic shifts. Although foundations adopted diversity policy in the name of population shifts, their manner of including non-Black non-Whites suggests an autonomously designed response. The aggregation of non-Black non-White groups into foundation rhetoric about race followed a logic more complex than either steady accumulation or indiscriminate inclusion. In addition, though 1980 proved to be an especially salient year, the foundation response did not merely reflect prevailing political culture or legitimacy but instead drew on the institutional culture of the organizational field.

The evidence for my institutional argument comes from analyzing the foundation field's discourse about race and ethnicity, that is, the field-level rhetoric regularly disseminated in its national magazine, *Foundation News*. The magazine actually originated in 1960 as the newsletter of the Foundation Center, the national organization that maintains branch libraries on philanthropic resources for grantors and grant seekers alike in numerous metropolitan areas, including San Francisco and Cleveland. In 1972, the Center transferred the ownership of the publication to the Council on Foundations (COF), which had become the professional association for U.S. foundations in the wake of the 1969 Tax Reform Act (Frumkin 1999).[2] The Council changed the publication's format to that of a magazine but kept its bimonthly publication schedule. Unlike other publications, namely, the *Chronicle of Philanthropy* and *Philanthropy Monthly*, *Foundation News*, which is currently titled *Foundation News and Commentary*, is the national publication for foundations exclusively and does not include other forms of charitable giving, such as individual donations and annual funds, or other forms of philanthropy broadly defined, such as voluntarism.

Before the 1990 publication of the "Pluralism in Philanthropy" issue, the Foundation Center and the Council published 180 issues which contained a total of forty-five articles with significant focus on racial and ethnic issues (table 2).[3] I conceptualize these articles as a significant part of the foundation field's understandings and debates about these issues. They represent the positions and cultural schema that carry fieldwide sanction and legitimacy. When individual foundations or foundation personnel employ these ideas, other field actors may recognize their activities as imbued with the natural authority of the foundation field. These schema are certainly not the only cultural resources that field members may use, for individual foundations

TABLE 2   Racial and Ethnic Articles Published in *Foundation News and Commentary*, 1960–1989

Article No.	Year	Vol.	No.	Title	Page	Discourse
1	1961	2	1	Looking Backward	6	Black
2	1965	6	2	Foundations and the Negro	21	Black
3	1969	10	2	Foundations, Universities, and Social Change: Year of Decision	51	Minority
4	1969	10	3	Foundations and Negro Higher Education	111	Black
5	1970	11	2	Cummins Engine Foundation	59	Black
6	1970	11	3	What's Past Is Prologue	100	Black
7	1972	13	5	Black Perspective on Foundations: Foundations and Society	27	Black
8	1972	13	5	Black Perspective on Foundations: Blacks in Foundations	27	Black
9	1973	14	2	White Philanthropy and the Red Man	13	Native
10	1974	15	2	Foundation Support of Black Colleges	20	Black
11	1974	15	2	Meanwhile, a Question of Funding Apart from Education	30	Black
12	1974	15	6	Foundation Trustees: The Need for Diversity	11	Minority
13	1976	17	1	Power Structure Explored from an Ethnic Perspective	33	Minority
14	1976	17	2	Will It See the 21st Century? Black-Controlled Foundation Determined to Succeed, But . . .	44	Black
15	1976	17	4	Association of Black Foundation Executives (News)	10	Black
16	1976	17	4	Minorities and Foundations: Why the Distrust Lingers	21	Minority
17	1976	17	5	Foundations and Affirmative Action	14	Minority

TABLE 2   (continued)

Article No.	Year	Vol.	No.	Title	Page	Discourse
18	1976	17	6	After Intensive Care: Is a Relapse Ahead for Minority Medical Education?	11	Minority
19	1977	18	2	Association of Black Foundation Executives (News)	3	Black
20	1977	18	2	Two Faces of Chinatown	18	Asian
21	1978	19	3	New Indian Wars	12	Native
22	1978	19	5	For the Business World, vucg Has a Better Idea	17	Minority
23	1979	20	2	On Being Non-Indian	14	Native
24	1979	20	3	Chicano Education Project Organizing for Equal Opportunity	14	Latino
25	1979	20	3	What Bilingual Education Can Achieve . . .	19	Latino
26	1979	20	4	Minorities and Housing: Are the Doors Really Open?	22	Minority
27	1979	20	5	A Helping Hand for the Boat People	12	Asian
28	1980	21	2	Census 1980	14	Minority
29	1980	21	3	Alumni Challenge Grants to Black Private Colleges	25	Black
30	1980	21	3	Mott's Commitment to Black Colleges	27	Black
31	1980	21	5	Hispanic Theater: Not to Be Upstaged	40	Latino
32	1981	22	1	Grants for Black Colleges	4	Black
33	1981	22	1	Bilingual Education and the Hispanic Challenge	20	Latino
34	1981	22	4	Black Belt Counties Organize	13	Black
35	1981	22	4	Self-Help in the Mississippi Delta	17	Black
36	1981	22	4	Hispanic Giving: Challenge of the 80's	25	Latino
37	1982	23	6	One Worthwhile Coffee Klatch	12	Latino

TABLE 2   (continued)

Article No.	Year	Vol.	No.	Title	Page	Discourse
38	1983	24	4	Affirmative Action: Gains and Costs	55	Minority
39	1984	25	2	To Live on This Earth	18	Native
40	1984	25	5	Serving the Least of These	58	Black
41	1984	25	6	Developing Leadership in Minority Communities	40	Minority
42	1986	27	3	Starting Over: Indochinese Refugees Americanize through Self-Made Support Centers	16	Asian
43	1988	29	1	Native Profit	18	Native
44	1988	29	5	Votes of Confidence	26	Minority
45	1988	29	6	Into the Donor's Seat	62	Minority

typically also participate in other fields such as local politics and related professional arenas. However, although the other fields may be influential, they do not directly bear the authority of foundations as a class of organizations. Even when nonphilanthropic ideas carry the day, others may view the outcome as abnormal, self-serving, or even perverting the purpose of the institution.

Of the forty-five articles, I classified thirty-two as "group-specific" and thirteen as more broadly "minority." Each of the group-specific articles referenced racial and ethnic populations that fell into only one of the four major non-White categories: Asians (3 articles), Blacks (18 articles), Latinos (6 articles), and Native Americans (5 articles). The preponderance of the group-specific articles suggests that the ethnoracial categories employed in diversity policy were not imposed just for the sake of simplifying a previously less restricted discourse but instead built on preexisting and widely accepted group boundaries in field rhetoric. In contrast, the minority articles referenced populations that fell into multiple categories; however, their relative attention to individual categories corresponded with the frequency of the group-specific articles. Every article in this set included Blacks, and their inclusion of the other non-White categories roughly correlated with how often the medium published group-specific articles about the same categories (table 3).

TABLE 3   Frequencies of Group Appearances in
Minority Articles and in Group-Specific Articles

	Inclusions in Minority Articles	Group-Specific Articles
Blacks	13	18
Latinos	9	6
Native Americans	5	5
Asian Americans	3	3
White ethnics	2	0

Last, I classified the content of the forty-five articles into thirteen distinct themes: eleven repeating topics and two topics in unique articles. Only one theme, self-help, crossed group-specific boundaries; the self-help articles were present in the discourse about Asians, Blacks, Latinos, and Native Americans but not in the general minority discourse. I titled the other twelve themes model minority myth (Asians), refugees (Asians), uplift (Blacks), nationalism (Blacks), professionalism (Blacks), bilingualism (Latinos), sovereignty (Native Americans), economic independence (Native Americans), equality (minorities), Black vanguard (minorities), technical attention (minorities), and leadership development (minorities).

My analysis of the inclusion patterns and rationales demonstrates that although the new immigration starts in the 1960s, it is not until the conservative presidency of Ronald Reagan that a post-Black diversity policy begins to cohere. Until the 1980s, foundations use their experiences with African Americans and issues identified with them as models for discussing minority issues—with the notable exception of American Indian issues. Only after the Reagan revolution does foundation discourse about Blacks ebb, and Native American philanthropy implicitly becomes the new model for minority discourse. This form of institutional-cultural autonomy suggests a general process for how diversity policies achieved popularity in other private institutions, such as higher education and corporate management. While these policies ostensibly address a demographic phenomenon and its social consequences, they are actually strategic institutional responses to political crises.

The Complex Inclusion of Non-Black Non-Whites

In the minority articles, the inclusion of non-Blacks veered from the popular expectations and their sociological variants. First, the inclusion of groups did not follow a stable primary logic of demographics, social movements, or policy effects and in fact followed multiple themes, some of which individually corresponded with decolonization and victimhood. Also, the pattern of group aggregation was neither steady accumulation, as most of the theories would expect, nor indiscriminate, as the victimhood thesis predicted. Instead, the magazine produced multiple themes with distinct inclusion tendencies, and yet every article also followed a historically static hierarchical rule for inclusion—in violation of the equal positioning of groups in diversity policy. Although the categories in philanthropic pluralism were not new, their structural equivalence was indeed a historical deviation.

Four distinct themes rather than a single logic constituted the general discourse about minorities: (1) equality, (2) Black vanguard, (3) technical attention, and (4) leadership. Although Black vanguard resembled the decolonization story and technical attention resembled the victimhood story, neither movements nor state effects was the primary rationale for the transition in focus from exclusively Blacks to Asians, Blacks, Latinos, and Native Americans. In fact, a discussion of the distinct themes illustrates the heterogeneity of their assumptions, arguments, and recommended courses of action.

Equality is the topic of the first article in the general discourse about minorities. The 1969 article assumes as background the social movements of its time, especially "the Negro movement for equality," and asserts that foundations need to respond carefully to these concerns. To quote its central argument: "A philosophy of concern is developing rapidly: a concern for individuals as expressed by the young peoples; a social concern as expressed by the Negro movement for equality. These concerns have jogged the conscience of the nation. Our responses to these concerns will determine the quality of life here. All else flows from this" (Kunen 1969, 57). The writer recommends that universities should recognize the societal duties of foundations and conduct social research useful for improving philanthropic interventions, rather than relate to foundations as merely sources of financial support.

Black vanguard is the topic of five articles of the minority discourse published from 1974 to 1983. These articles assume as background the ongoing societal efforts to integrate minorities in mainstream institutions and call for foundations to voluntarily comply with and even be exemplars of broader efforts to deal with racial and ethnic inequality. They directly define minorities as groups underrepresented in positions of power and influence because of historical discrimination and figure Blacks as the *exemplar* minority group. Their writers suggest that foundations should support efforts that go beyond nondiscrimination to affirmative action, especially on their own boards of trustees. In 1976, one author, James Joseph, secretary of the board of the Council on Foundations, makes explicit the taken-for-granted centrality of Blacks: "Minority Americans—whether they be black, Chicano, or native—are rejecting the hierarchical pluralism that has lifted up the cultural standards of one group as normative and regarded everything else as deviant. They have opted instead for an egalitarian pluralism in which sameness and difference are held together in a creative tension . . . No discussion of foundations and minorities can conclude without mention of the new movement to develop an indigenous philanthropic infrastructure in the black community" (23). In this article, Joseph figures Blacks as the leading group among minorities, not because the others intentionally follow what Blacks do but because the phases of consciousness in Black history constitute the basic model for all minorities. As hinted in the other articles, integration is the lever for broad social change.

Technical attention is the theme of four articles published from 1976 to 1980. In brief, whereas Black vanguard conceptualized integration as a tool, technical attention viewed it as an end in itself. The articles focus not on appropriate foundation concerns with minority groups directly but instead on appropriate foundation concern with grantees serving minorities, that is, case studies of good grant making. Consequently, the assumed backgrounds and recommendations are highly specific to each article's topic. However, their basic rationale is identical: where there is *less* for minorities, there should be foundation intervention to promote *more*, whether it is medical practitioners (1976), business consulting (1978), fair housing (1979), or census enumeration (1980). To illustrate from the 1978 article: "New York City's Volunteer Urban Consulting Group [VUCG] is a leader in providing nonprofits and minority businesses with professional expertise . . . the key reasons for VUCG's success . . . financial operations and management are the main areas in which VUCG aids its nonprofit clients; *it steers clear of program-related problems or fundraising aid*" (Abarbanel 1978, 17–19; emphasis mine).

Last but not least of the minority themes, *leadership* is the topic of three articles published between 1984 and 1988. The articles assume as background the need to sustain the creation of minority leadership in the economy, politics, and philanthropy. The writers recommend the systematization of leadership development, seen retrospectively as having been an ad hoc affair

TABLE 4   Group Inclusions in Minority Discourse by Theme and Year

Theme and Year	Groups Included
Equality	
1969	Blacks and Latinos
Black Vanguard	
1974	Blacks plus
1976	Blacks, Latinos, and White ethnics
1976	Blacks, Latinos, and Native Americans
1976	Blacks plus
1983	Blacks plus
Technical Attention	
1976	Blacks, Latinos, and Native Americans
1978	Asians, Blacks, Latinos, and White ethnics
1979	Blacks plus
1980	Asians, Blacks, Latinos, and Native Americans
Leadership	
1984	Blacks, Latinos
1988	Blacks, Latinos, and Native Americans
1988	Asians, Blacks, Latinos, and Native Americans

thus far. Moreover, rather than push a general goal of integration, the actual suggestions are highly specific, targeting community development corporations, voting rights organizations, and community foundation outreach efforts. To illustrate the complexity of this new logic, I quote from a 1984 article: "Well recognized leaders who have emerged from CDCs [community development corporations] include Franklin A. Thomas, president of the Ford Foundation and former president of the Bedford Stuyvesant Restoration Corporation . . . Mayor Henry Cisneros of San Antonio, who formerly worked for the Mexican American Unity Council . . . now there is a new generation of CDC leadership, expanding the body of minority leadership throughout the nation" (Martinez and Carlson 1984, 41). In sum, experience shows that community development corporations are good training grounds for minority leaders; for that reason, foundations should support their continuance.

Together, the four themes do not guide a steady accumulation from a minimum to a maximum number of major groups. Instead, each minority theme has a distinct tendency for including groups (table 4).

TABLE 5   Frequency of Inclusion Patterns in Minority Articles

	Articles
Blacks plus	4
Blacks, Latinos, and Native Americans	3
Blacks, Latinos	2
Blacks, Latinos, Native Americans, and Asians	2
Blacks, Latinos, White ethnics, and Asians	1
Blacks, Latinos, White ethnics	1

The equality theme comes from only one article, but it is notable that Blacks are not the only group mentioned in the first general minority article. Although the 1969 article focuses on Black social movements, it mentions both Negroes and Mexican Americans. Similarly, most of the Black vanguard articles discuss only Blacks in detail while referring to other non-Whites simply as "other minorities," that is, a general aggregation. Some articles, though, mention Latinos and one other group, either White ethnics (e.g., Jewish Americans) or Native Americans. In contrast, the technical attention articles have a somewhat broader core of groups, although Blacks remain central in their contents. These articles usually mention Latinos and sometimes one or even two other specific groups. The leadership theme possesses multiple core groups. Significantly, the articles in this theme always mention both Blacks and Latinos, and their discussion of even Native Americans is more substantial than discussions of non-Black groups in any of the other three themes. As might be expected, leadership is the minority theme that directly precedes the special issue on philanthropic diversity published in 1990.

Although the minority articles do not include non-Blacks through a steady process of accumulation, their inclusions are not indiscriminate. Besides the thematic structuring of the shift to a diversity of groups, the minority discourse also rests on a stable hierarchical rule for group inclusion (table 5).

First, the field rhetoric always includes Blacks. Second, if any other groups are specifically mentioned, the rhetoric always includes Latinos. Only if Latinos are included does the field discourse also mention Native Americans or White ethnics. And the discourse mentions Asians only if it has already mentioned populations in the three other categories. In other words, a static hierarchy guided the inclusion of groups, notwithstanding the multiple themes that bridged the shift in foundation attention from Blacks to a diversity of groups. From 1960 to 1990, no minority articles violate this hierarchy; there are no Asian-Black articles, no Jewish-Native articles, and no Latino-Asian articles. In sum, the structured complexity of the shift from Black to diversity in racial philanthropy reveals limits to popular and sociological accounts that simply privilege demographic imperatives or political forces. I suggest that, instead, an institutional cultural logic motivates and moderates how foundations respond to those external factors.

An Alternative Explanation: Institutional Cultural Autonomy

Instead of reflecting demographic and political conditions, the inclusion of non-Black non-Whites into the minority articles depended on the changing conception among foundations of the purpose of their involvement in race relations. As their institutional mission shifted, so did their discourses about both specific groups and minorities in general. An internal philanthropic logic informs how foundation rhetoric responds to the external context. This logic is better characterized by the metaphor of a talent search than the metaphor of protected categories, whether for redressing historical wrongs or creating special entitlements. Indeed, in the United States, philanthropy has traditionally distinguished itself as an alternative to government programs under the ideology of privatism, the belief that the private sector is superior to the public sector in the design if not also the provision of social goods (Hall 1987). Whereas government programs protect anonymous individuals from disadvantage, foundation interventions identify and single out for recognition the talented efforts that demonstrate the capacity of private action unfettered by public regulation. In foundation rhetoric about race and ethnicity, the adoption of diversity policy or philanthropic pluralism occurs with the shift to a strategic conception of philanthropy modeled on discourse about Native Americans.

A pseudo-dialectic between two elements constitutes the talent search in race-relations philanthropy; these elements are the identification of talent for consideration and the judging of talent in competition, in other words, defining the pool of candidates and selecting the grantees. I identified three types of talent identification of philanthropic candidates: *good causes*, first appearing in 1961; *good works*, first appearing in 1973; and *good strategies*, first appearing in 1970. In the minority articles, the three modes of identification make their first appearances, respectively, in 1969, 1976, and 1984. I also identified four types of ideal talent or model grantees: *higher education*,

TABLE 6 First Appearance of Three Types of Philanthropic Identification

Looking for ...	Primary Components	Attention Directed to ...	Year in Minority Articles	Year and Category in Group-Specific Articles
Good Causes	Rationales for foundation involvement	Community or class of persons	1969	1961 (Black)
Good Works	Targets for foundation support	Grantee organization	1976	1976 (Black)
Good Strategies	Rationales for particular targets	Planned outcomes	1984	1973 (Native American)

first appearing in 1961; *radical perspective*, first appearing in 1970; *effective tactics*, first appearing in 1976; and *inclusive expertise*, first appearing in 1984. In the minority articles, the four definitions of talent make their first appearances, respectively, in 1969, 1974, 1976, and 1984. Each article combined one identification with one or two talents, and, with only one exception, each theme's articles combined the same identification and same talent(s).

Over the decades, the shifts between identifications occurred with shifts between talents. When new identifications appeared, new talents also appeared, either immediately or soon after, and vice versa. In a given year, the discourse included current elements and old elements, but over time, new elements replaced the current ones, which in turn became the new old-elements while the old old-elements joined the historical repository of older elements.

The dialectic between identifications and talents, however, was somewhat asymmetrical; while articles sometimes combined a current identification with an older talent (preceding the current talent), they never combined a current talent with an older identification (preceding the current identification). In brief, older identifications were largely abandoned or remained viable only with older talents, but older talents remained in the toolbox for combination with newer identifications. This asymmetry suggests that the ability to change how foundations identify candidates is more powerful than the ability to alter how foundations select grantees. Nevertheless, the second element is not reducible to the first element; thus, I elaborate them separately below. Tables 6 and 7 summarize my definitions of these cultural elements.

TABLE 7   First Appearance of Four Types of Talent or Model Grantees

Recognition of . . .	Examples	Year in Minority Articles	Year and Category in Group-Specific Articles
Higher Education	Black colleges	1969	1961 (Black)
Radical Perspective	Transformative Black perspective	1974	1970 (Black)
Effective Tactics	Fellowships for minority students	1976	1976 (Black)
Inclusive Expertise	Combination of technological and economic acumen with Native resolve	1984	1984 (Native American)

From 1961 to 1983, the articles identifying good causes emphasized the rationales for foundation involvement with particular groups or classes of persons. The exact nature of involvement was secondary to the need to get involved. Of the four themes of the minority articles, equality and Black vanguard were the instances of good-cause philanthropy. The equality article promoted the need for foundations to respond to the social concerns of Blacks for equality, and the Black vanguard articles argued that foundations could leverage deep social change through voluntarily integrating their own personnel. In the group-specific articles about Blacks, the articles composing the theme of nationalism further argued that the integration of Blacks into philanthropy would transform the basic assumptions and practices by which foundations operated. These articles implied that foundations should identify talent by looking for racial and ethnic groups that made for good causes.

From 1976 to 1981, the articles identifying good works emphasized the targets of foundation support, that is, particular grantee organizations for non-White concerns. The rationales in these articles were reduced to responding to disparities of any sort with technically specific solutions. Of the minority themes, technical attention was the instance of good-works philanthropy. The article quoted above (Abarbanel 1978) promoted a business consulting effort that refused to debate organizational mission or build constituency or resources and instead focused on strengthening the managerial capacities of its organization-clients. In the group-specific discourse about Blacks, an article in the theme of professionalism (Coombs 1976) argued that Black-controlled philanthropies were idealistic efforts doomed to failure because excluding Whites from trustee boards also reduced the needed flow of White capital into endowments. By contrast, Black integration into mainstream philanthropy was a more effective and enduring tactic for improving philanthropic attentions to Black communities. These articles implied that foundations should identify talent by looking for grantee organizations that did good work.

From 1973 to 1988, each of the articles identifying good strategies made a case for specific targets with particular rationales, that is, well-planned outcomes for non-White communities. This type of identification thus synthesized the preceding types of foundation intervention. Among the minority themes, leadership was the instance of good-strategy or strategic philanthropy. The article quoted above (Martinez and Carlson 1984) recognized community development corporations as the proven training grounds for minority leadership. The writers argued that foundations had a responsibility for improving the quality of non-White community leadership because of the limits imposed by either the nature of "soft sector" training or the prevalence of discrimination in corporate careers. Community development corporations provided minorities with the experience in economic development that careers in the social services could not provide and the level of responsibility that corporate glass ceilings barred from minority executives. Among the group-specific articles about Native Americans, strategic philanthropy was uniquely prevalent as the preferred type of identification. The very first article in the discourse argued that foundations had the responsibility to support the twin goals of Red Power—political-legal sovereignty and economic independence—because in the past, foundations had erred promoting a coercive assimilationism with disastrous consequences. These articles implied that foundations should identify talent by looking for new plans that employed proven strategies.

In review, the four types of ideal talent or model grantees were higher education, radical perspective, effective tactics, and inclusive expertise. In the minority discourse, the equality article highlighted the importance of higher education in providing knowledge and solutions for broad social challenges, that is, the Black and youth social movements. In the group-specific discourse about Blacks, articles in the theme of uplift singled out historically Black colleges as the ideal recipient of philanthropy for racial and ethnic issues. The uplift articles uniquely divided between early articles published from 1961 to 1974 identifying Negro colleges as good causes and later articles published in 1980 and 1981 identifying the support of Black colleges as a good strategy. In sum, these articles asserted the general benefits of promoting higher education, whether in society at large or among African Americans.

By contrast, from 1970 to 1983, the articles highlighting a radical perspective asserted the revolutionary potential of non-White activism and concerns. In the minority discourse, the Black vanguard articles proposed that Blacks were at the vanguard of minority empowerment movements; by supporting African American activism, foundations could radically improve how they did philanthropy. In the group-specific articles about Blacks, the articles in the theme of nationalism argued that Black perspectives would be transformative when integrated into foundation thinking. In the group-specific discourse about Latinos, articles similarly featured the group as a new vanguard; in brief, specific Latino activism had the potential of shifting U.S. society beyond an internationally embarrassing tendency for monolingualism.

The 1976–1986 articles highlighting effective tactics were oriented to grant recipients rather than ethnoracial groups. In the minority discourse, the technical attention articles singled out as important philanthropic targets the integration of medical practitioners, the provision of business consulting for minority organizations, the continued support of fair housing organizations, and the enumeration of non-White populations in the U.S. Census. The above theme of bilingualism actually combined the talent of a radical perspective with a tactical focus on specific "Hispanic" organizations that agitated for bilingual programs in education and employment. The theme of professionalism in Black discourse was even more oriented to the organizations receiving foundation support rather than the group benefiting from the intervention. One article quotes a foundation professional who evaluates Black-controlled foundations on pragmatic rather than normative grounds: "The reality of America should tell the people at [a Black foundation] that white people who give away money want to be stroked with appreciation. They want to sit on your board not really to keep tabs on you, but to assure themselves that without their presence, your foundation just could not work. And the damn sad thing about it is that they are nearly always right" (Coombs 1976, 47). In direct repudiation of good-cause philanthropy, the unnamed source, a "Black who is a former staff member of the Ford Foundation" (47), advances good-works philanthropy because good intentions were not enough; worse, they could interfere with selecting the most effective solution.

After 1980, the group-specific articles highlighting effective tactics shift from making a broad set of recommendations toward a single tactic: supporting self-help or mutual aid organizations. In every group-specific discourse, Asian, Black, Latino, and Native, articles consistent with this theme advance the tactic as the best strategy. The only exception is the discourse about Blacks, which also includes articles in the theme of uplift, albeit distinctly from the earlier articles that exclusively highlight the intrinsic value of higher education. Similarly with the shift to self-help, however, these later articles characterize supporting Black colleges not as synonymous with group advancement but as a strategic choice. Strategic philanthropy thus arrives in implicit form with a tactical target, suggesting that responding to racial disparities is an insufficient rationale. Instead, the appropriate identification must target organizations that leverage broader effects for non-White populations.

From 1984 to 1988, the leadership articles of the minority discourse elaborate strategic philanthropy by introducing inclusive expertise as the new ideal-talent. The shift to strategic intervention becomes explicit in the preference for philanthropy that not only has the potential for broad effects but also develops enduring and reliable leadership for non-White communities. In brief, the best talent becomes the capacity for leadership with "feet in both worlds": both proven success in the White mainstream and recognition in a non-White community. As noted above, community development corporations become the target for the rationale of developing leaders with the capacity to encourage minority economic development. The other minority articles similarly articulate the value of inclusive expertise for community foundations and electoral politics. In the group-specific discourse about Native Americans, the articles tellingly begin to repudiate political-legal confrontation as a solution for social problems. One article recognizes the talent of a leader who was "a pragmatist of the eighties . . . [who] began her career as a grassroots organizer in the rhetorical seventies" (Margolis 1988, 23). Her current agenda and the implicit recommendation to foundations was to combine technological and economic acumen with Native resolve. In a sense, inclusive expertise is simultaneously a validation of activist experience and a negation of its direct value: the talented are those who have learned, to borrow a book title, that "protest is not enough" (Browning, Marshall, and Tabb 1984).

In sum, the pseudo-dialectic between shifting definitions of identification and talent accounts for the nondemographic and nonpolitical character of the field rhetoric in the thirty years before the emergence of foundation diversity policy. Furthermore, this theoretical characterization reveals the relative recency of the cultural elements constituting philanthropic pluralism: strategic philanthropy and inclusive expertise. If there were a steady accumulation of non-Black non-Whites in the minority discourse, then it begins not in the 1960s but in the 1980s, during which time theories of political culture and political legitimacy expect a reversal of accumulation patterns. Similarly, the appearances of most of the talent search elements in the group-specific articles about Blacks before their appearance in the minority discourse (tables 6 and 7) suggest the belated nature of the structural equivalence among Asians, Blacks, Latinos, and Native Americans found in diversity policy. Until the 1980s, foundations learned how to identify racial talent primarily through their experiences with African Americans. I suggest that foundations learned an alternative way of identifying talent from the group that, ironically, most "resisted" their earlier Black-White modeling of race relations, that is, Native Americans.

Non-Black Non-Whites: From Margin to Resource

In 1990, philanthropic pluralism features Asians, Latinos, and Native Americans as groups that are parallel and equal to African Americans. For decades before, however, foundation rhetoric about non-Black non-Whites largely reflected the centrality of Blacks in the field discourse that differentiated Asians, Latinos, and Native Americans as illegitimate non-Blacks, legitimate new Blacks, and sovereign non-Blacks, respectively. The three non-Black non-White groups actually share one important characteristic: a relatively incomplete level of racialization in contrast with both Whites and Blacks. Ethnic, national, and tribal divisions have internally differentiated their respective "racial" experiences more so than they have the histories of European and African Americans. However, the articles of the field rhetoric discussed this commonalty in inconsistent ways to characterize non-Black non-Whites in comparison with African Americans. These Procrustean comparisons render the discourses about Asians and Latinos into satellites of the Black and minority discourses while freeing the Native discourse to pursue its own planetary orbit. The special characteristics of the latter group-specific articles permitted Native Americans a unique autonomy from Black centrality, a situation that in turn facilitated the production of the cultural elements that ironically would assemble as philanthropic diversity policy.

"Asian Americans" and "Latinos" are social categories that, under certain conditions, become panethnic identities (Lopez and Espiritu 1990); likewise,

"American Indian" and "Native American" are categories that sometimes become socially salient as supratribal identities (Nagel 1996). By contrast, African slaves were forced into a hypervisible "Black" ethnicity, while European immigrants have voluntarily assimilated into an invisible "White" ethnicity, often mislabeled as "American" culture. Historically, the racialization of Pakistanis, Hmong, Vietnamese, Filipinos, Japanese, Chinese, and other groups coheres around the stereotype of them all as perpetual or "forever" foreigners; however, each group experienced that same process in different periods and with shifting intensities. Likewise, the racialization of Mexican Americans, Puerto Ricans, Cubans, and other groups occurred across different periods and with shifting intensities. As for Native Americans, armed conflict, treaties, and political-legal agreements between specific tribes and the U.S. government extensively segmented their historical relations with White Americans. In addition, the majority of the Asians and Latinos in the contemporary period have arrived since the "Great Transformation" of the 1960s (Omi and Winant 1986, 1994). Most of their family histories in the United States do not include the centuries when the social tracking of diverse ethnic memberships into racial statuses occurred with overt state support.

Despite their common distinction from Whites and Blacks, foundation discourse about Asian Americans, Latinos, and Native Americans pivots instead on certain putative differences from African Americans. While the internal diversity of Asians is magnified to define the category as purely descriptive and nonsensical, the internal diversity of Latinos is minimized to render the category identical to "Black." And for Native Americans, internal diversity is observed for the purpose of accurately naming specific tribes, but the group-specific discourse persists in recommending common interventions for all "Indians."

Between 1977 and 1986, the field magazine published three articles on Asian Americans. The first article engages popular views of the group as both successful and unfamiliar by discussing its distinct historical experiences with discrimination and the internal complexity of the panethnic category. It argues that despite Asians' demographic growth, foundations have shown an ignorance of Asians comparable to that of the average American. Instead of addressing long-standing social problems, foundations tend to substitute the model minority myth of Asian success for a deeper understanding of history, needs, and complexity.

Ignoring these claims, the two subsequent Asian articles emphasize only Vietnamese refugees from Southeast Asia, and one minority article notes Asian internal diversity without any mention of discrimination. The former articles make no explicit connection between themselves and the earlier article on Asian Americans, and the latter connects them only categorically: "Chinese traditions vary widely from those of Japanese, Koreans, Laotians, Samoans and dozens of other Asian ethnic groups" (Curtis 1988, 63). Silent on historical discrimination, the field discourse includes Asians in the Black-centered discourse only selectively: as disadvantaged refugees and as a mantra-like litany of diverse ethnics, but not as a "real" (i.e., historical) racial minority.

In comparison to the sparse and paced publication of Asian discourse, group-specific discourse about Latinos flares, with twice as many articles but within a shorter period, from 1979 to 1982. Against the backdrop of demographic growth and the passage of bilingual education legislation in Colorado, Latino articles argue that because conquest brought Latinos into the United States and subsequent (historical) racism segregated them, foundations have the responsibility to support their primary means for integration and civil rights, that is, bilingualism. However, as one writer cautions, "Government cannot be for Hispanics in the '80s what it was for blacks in the '60s. America's Third Sector is confronted with the opportunity to fill, at least partially, the vacuum created by a new set of economic realities" (Garcia 1980, 25). The articles also elaborate two complications for foundation intervention: whether bilingualism is a compensatory program or a political movement, and whether it is a Latino or group-specific social need or a national good. One article synthesizes these two tensions by advising that although the United States needs all of its citizens to be bilingual, advocates of bilingualism should work for that day covertly, demanding only compensatory programs in the present. Significantly, the Latino articles substitute (Latino) language rights for (Black) civil rights, compare Latinos in the 1980s to Blacks in the 1960s, and figure Latinos as the new vanguard whose advancement also will promote the advancement of the mainstream.

Latinos were therefore subsumed in the Black-centered discourse as "new Blacks," while only select Asians were included as disadvantaged newcomers, not as subjects of historical discrimination. Whereas the simple invocation of Asian diversity became a basis for selective exclusion, the discourse about Latinos both compared the histories of subgroups and cast those distinctions as ultimately minor. Although "Asians" existed only as a social category, an author of an article about Latinos argued that "what [they] share in common . . . far outweighs the differences among them, and this is a broad sense of ethnic identity based on allegiance to a shared mother language and culture" (Pifer 1981, 23). This differentiation suggests that the two groups were being judged for their relative capacity to join or replace Blacks as the vanguard minority group whose needs and agendas transcended the interests of other groups.

By contrast, even though Native Americans were often subsumed as just another group in the minority articles, the articles about Native Americans constituted the most autonomous of the group-specific discourses. From the outset, Native discourse constructed their experiences as distinct from both the mainstream, that is, White Americans, and other non-Whites. These articles directly posed major ethical questions: Should historical considerations be considered in present intergroup relations? What stance should foundations take toward the autonomy of minority groups? What are the new solutions for a better future? In sum, extraordinary historical discrimination was the primary subject of the Native discourse.

Special conditions permitted Native discourse to be uniquely autonomous. From 1973 to 1988, the majority of the Native articles had a single author, Richard Margolis, who began as a freelance contributor and became a member of the magazine's editorial staff. Access to Native discourse thus was mostly restricted to one specialist rather than multiple authors. This singular authorship insulated Native discourse from the Black centrality within the field discourse. In contrast to the rhetoric framing Asian Americans and Latinos, the discourse about Native Americans did not measure them (unfavorably) against a Black vanguard. As a result, articles discussing their experiences with historical discrimination did not interpolate Black history and in fact distanced Natives from such comparisons. Asserting the uniqueness of Native history, one article asserted: "All too readily, those in organized philanthropy will acknowledge that Indians are another oppressed minority, suffering difficulties because of racism and seeking full equality under the law. That may be true, but if we stop there and insist on looking upon Indians only as individual citizens then we commit the greatest violence of all. We begin the denial of the right of Indian peoples to exist as political entities" (Folk-Williams 1979, 18).

From the start, themes in Native articles responded primarily to each other, not to themes in Black or even minority discourse. In particular, an intense dialogue emerged between the themes of political-legal sovereignty and economic independence, distinct from developments in discourse about other groups.

The initial article, "White Philanthropy and the Red Man" (Margolis 1973), explicated the resurgence of foundation interest in American Indians as the direct product of Indian "tribalism," actually supratribal militancy rather than tribally confined nationalism. It outlined three strategies for foundation intervention: continuing efforts at assimilation, political-legal sovereignty, and economic independence. Because philanthropy had a shameful past role in coercive assimilation, the article asserted that White attempts at philanthropy for Native Americans had to recognize the necessity of preserving the integrity of Native cultures and abandon the first strategy. The theme of sovereignty was an argument for foundation support of legal justice and political autonomy for Native peoples targeting either specific court battles in 1978 or specific legal rights organizations such as the Native American Rights Fund in 1984.

The theme of economic independence responded to the group conditions, as did sovereignty and also the strategy of sovereignty itself. The initial article presented both themes as more valid alternatives to assimilationism, especially in the face of growing Native militancy. In fact, the two appeared as complements: while sovereignty protected tribal borders and conducted foreign relations, economic independence shifted reservation livelihoods from dependence on U.S. government assistance programs to reliance on profits from tribally owned businesses. Later articles in 1984 and 1988 presented economic independence as the more necessary and more practical strategy, citing the failure of sovereignty to alleviate reservation poverty. Where economic independence was also viewed pessimistically, the pessimism lay not with the choice of strategy but with attempts at implementation: "As throughout the Third World, the lesson here is all too familiar: instant development will not work" (Margolis 1984, 27). The last article highlighted the success of one grantee, First Nations Financial Project, and directly opposed its mission to that suggested by political-legal sovereignty. It quoted the organization's founder: "Development is the tedious job that remains after the rhetoric of revolution and independence has been spent" (Margolis 1988, 23). Angry "young" rhetoric characterized the goal of sovereignty, opposing it to a more mature goal of economic independence, characterized as the hard work of uniting Indian culture with mainstream economics.

From the start, Native discourse selected and emphasized good strategies, originating the identification of strategic philanthropy in the field rhetoric well before its full appearance in minority discourse. Native discourse also provided the conception of talent highlighted later in the minority articles about leadership: inclusive expertise or the command of both mainstream and minority cultural competencies. The latter theme defined "true" minority leaders as those who could muster minority constituencies for mainstream politics, who learned mainstream economics from managing minority corporations, and who adhered to minority traditions of benevolence that could be recruited into mainstream philanthropic institutions. The articles on philanthropic pluralism subsequently drew on this definition of talent to cast affluent, successful, and charitable non-White individuals as the carriers of traditions that did not impede their mainstream participation. Both minority themes were extensions of the trajectory of "maturing" beyond confrontational demands to developing an "indigenous" self-sufficiency that combined "technological and economic" acumen (i.e., success in White society) with "Native resolve" (i.e., non-White culture).

In sum, the cohesion and independence of Native discourse produced alternatives to the Black-centered racial philanthropy that had dominated foundation discourse for at least three decades. And it was those alternative cultural elements that were employed to construct philanthropic diversity policy in the late 1980s and early 1990s. At the start of this chapter, I characterized the foundation adoption of diversity policy as a shift in the meaning of race from the historic Black-White frame to the four food groups. I employ this metaphor from the old U.S. Department of Agriculture nutritional guidelines to describe how philanthropic pluralism constructed the four groups as equally necessary targets for foundation involvement in U.S. race relations. I also suggest that the metaphor contrasts with how field discourse previously characterized non-Whites as distinct "dishes" and constructed minority articles as "meals" guided by how well particular non-Blacks "tasted" when combined with each other but especially with Blacks. Therefore, I can restate and elaborate the hierarchical rules for the inclusion of non-White groups into the minority articles in the following way:

1. Blacks are the *central entrée.*
2. Latinos are the best complement for Blacks as the *second entrée.*
3. Either Native Americans or White ethnics can be added after Latinos, but never have both Natives and White ethnics in the "same meal," like *soup and salad.*
4. Asian Americans can be included only after three other dishes, like *dessert.*
5. Never have all five dishes in one meal, or else risk creating a *buffet* that demonstrates little capacity for judgment.

In the next section, I argue that the metaphor of food groups replaced that of taste combinations only when the latter lost significant political legitimacy in the 1980s.

The Origins of Diversity Policy in the
Political Crisis of Black Centrality

Thus far I have described the institutional logic structuring foundation rhetoric about race and ethnicity and distinguished the specific elements that directly preceded the appearance of diversity policy. However, although the philanthropic adoption of diversity policy did not simply reflect demographic imperatives or political forces, the shift to philanthropic pluralism was not an entirely internal affair. On the one hand, while demographic change may have provided a passive basis for expanding philanthropic discourse beyond Whites and Blacks, it does not appear to have provoked the significant shifts in how foundations identified racial talent. On the other hand, political conditions, events, and crises do appear to have triggered the major reconsiderations of institutional mission. Over the course of three decades, political events punctuate the shift of field rhetoric from Negro educational uplift to philanthropic pluralism.

Of the three major shifts in foundation field discourse, the last shift—the move toward diversity policy—is in fact the one most opposed to the prevailing political conditions. Echoing the decolonization narrative, the first shift from an early White paternalism to a "radical" Black perspective follows the collapse of the civil rights coalition and the rise of nationalist movements. The second shift from transformative identity to the goal of interracial parity possesses multiple and thus ambiguous connections to political events and also witnesses the rise of Asian and Latino group-specific articles. Third, the foundations shift toward diversity policy in reaction to the new Republican presidential administration of Ronald Reagan. In brief, although earlier non-White movements prompted the philanthropic construction of a Black-centered rhetoric about race, the foundations craft a "post-Black" discourse to limit the effects of conservative political forces.

FROM WHITE PATERNALISM TO BLACK VANGUARD

Between 1961 and 1983, Black authors rearticulated good-cause philanthropy by challenging the historic talent of higher education with the new talent of a radical perspective (figure 2). They introduced the new conception of talent into group-specific articles about Blacks before recasting the general discourse about minorities in a similar mold. Until 1969, foundation rhetoric about race and ethnicity mentioned only "Negroes." The first articles about "Blacks" were paternalist in nature and concerned with their *uplift* for the purpose of ensuring the presence of a college-educated class. The post–

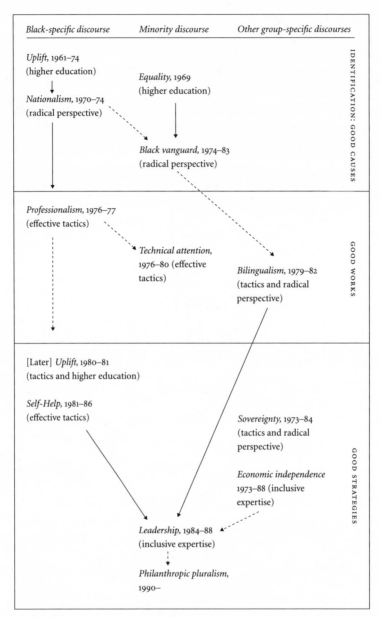

FIGURE 2 The trajectory of discourse about race and ethnicity in *Foundation News and Commentary*, 1960–1989. Theme is set in italic; talent highlighted in parentheses. Solid line indicates replacement of talent; dotted line indicates diffusion or addition of talent.

World War II civil rights movement culminating in the Civil Rights Act of 1964 had no effect on this theme, despite the heavy involvement of students from Black colleges starting in 1960 with the sit-in in Greensboro, North Carolina (Bloom 1987). In fact, published in eight articles from 1961 to 1981, uplift remained the most enduring theme in the field discourse. After 1969, however, new themes temporarily eclipsed uplift in the field rhetoric.

By the mid-1960s, the Black-led civil rights movement had fragmented into entrist (i.e., moderate) and radical factions (Omi and Winant 1986) that split over the utility of nonviolent direct action as a strategy. Not until after the Reverend Martin Luther King Jr.'s assassination in 1968, though, did foundation rhetoric shift. In a new kind of article, Black foundation staff argued for philanthropic responsibilities beyond fostering an educated Black elite who could assimilate into White society. "We are the Blacks who cannot forget," proclaimed one author, arguing that foundations should support integration in not only education but also philanthropy itself (Joseph 1972, 32). These authors asserted the importance of a "Black perspective on foundations" that would change how foundations operated, that is, *nationalism*.

Subsequently, in 1974, minority articles begin proliferating, and their annual number comes to rival that of the group-specific articles about Blacks. Ignoring the White withdrawal from racial politics, foundations produce a discourse about minorities, similar to the new theme in Black articles. In the theme of Black vanguard, these new minority articles become increasingly inclusive of non-Blacks, though they remain dominated in content by Black issues. In addition, they follow a terminological shift from "Negroes" to "Blacks" already noticeable in the Black discourse as well as either a shift in the race of the authors from White to Black or the emergence of racial self-identification as a source of legitimacy. Although most of the articles do not mention specific non-Blacks, some articles do mention Latinos, Native Americans, and White ethnics. Tellingly, one of these articles argues that Latino and Native movements will follow the same path as Black advancement and advances an overarching theory of minority politics of which Black nationalism is the leading edge. Not surprisingly, later articles about Asians and Latinos recognize the centrality of Blacks in foundation discourse, whereas Native articles explicitly distance themselves from it. Ironically, however, in the same year, 1974, in which the talent of radical perspectives diffuses from Black discourse to minority articles, it vanishes from its source.

Between 1976 and 1982, radical aspirations for social change receded, and simultaneously, the more "superficial" rhetoric expanded to include non-Blacks (see figure 2). In the talent search logic, the talent of effective tactics and the identification of good works emerge to challenge, respectively, the talent of radical perspectives and the identification of good causes. As before, these twin challenges begin in the Black articles before diffusing to the minority discourse; however, in this second shift of field rhetoric, the diffusion occurs within a few months of its emergence rather than taking years. In addition, although invocations of radical perspective disappear from Black discourse, the new Asian American and Latino articles invoke the old talent in combination with the new talent of effective tactics. Unfortunately, the presence of multiple changes also makes this second shift difficult to parsimoniously explain. Instead, population shift, politics, and institutional process each provide partially plausible accounts.

In 1976, the articles about Blacks suddenly repudiate the theme of nationalism for the theme of professionalism. The pivotal article cites "Black foundation executives" at historically White institutions who argue that the founder of a nationalist enterprise "made a big mistake when he insisted on having an all Black board of directors" (Coombs 1976, 47). The articles suggest that Blacks should pragmatically pursue social advancement through professional channels within White-controlled institutions. In a sense, the theme exchanges an attempted pluralism of philanthropic missions and practices for a pluralism simply of representation as a more effective tactic than radical aspirations. Good-works philanthropy also arrives as the same articles begin directing philanthropic attention to organizations such as the Association of Black Foundation Executives instead of simply ethnoracial groups or classes of individuals.

When group-based historical discrimination wanes in the rationales for philanthropic attention, a more inclusive minority discourse also appears. Subsequent minority articles further expand group inclusion to Asian Americans, the last of the four major groups, as they showcase specific grantee organizations that have been successful with improving the lot of minorities. Rather than elaborating foundation responsibilities, these technical-attention articles merely highlight the disparities between Whites and non-Whites that grantees seek to close. Rather than support the groups whose movement perspectives might transform philanthropic relations and U.S. society, foundation rhetoric reorients its attention to organizations with good tactics, solid track records, and efficient operations. Telling of the declining clout of radical perspectives, the authors of minority articles cease sharing their own racial/ethnic group identity. The assumed "problem" is no longer that philanthropy was White in character and hence culturally inappropriate for certain populations, but that certain nonprofit grantees were not sufficiently efficient or otherwise effective.

Despite the ascension of good-works philanthropy, however, the talent of radical perspective retains a measure of institutional legitimacy. After the disappearance of the good-works philanthropy from minority articles in 1980, the trade magazine published an additional Black vanguard article in 1983. Stronger evidence for the survival of the old talent, however, is its use in the first article in the Asian discourse and, most significant, the emergence of the discourse about Latinos in 1979. Although the Latino articles mainly highlight case studies of exemplary grantee organizations and their proven effective tactics, they also suggest the potential of Latinos as "new Blacks" whose cause of bilingualism promises to transform U.S. society.

Many factors—demographic change, political legitimacy, racial conflict within the foundation world, and field institutionalization—contribute to this second shift in field rhetoric. First, changing demographics may have provided an opening for the arrival of good-works philanthropy. Increasing numbers of non-White immigrants may have made a Black-focused discourse vulnerable to the advancement of a more inclusive though more superficial talent, one that coincidentally increased the legitimacy of non-Black, specifically White, authorship. During the 1970s, the 1965 Immigration Reform and Control Act was finally implemented in full; its passage completed a withdrawal from long-standing race-based immigration policies and established large immigration quotas by hemisphere. However, not until the late 1970s did the foundation rhetoric pay group-specific attention to Asian Americans and Latinos. Therefore, just as population shift alone cannot account for their increasing inclusion in the minority discourse, so too is it insufficient for explaining their inclusion in the wider racial and ethnic rhetoric.

With respect to political events, the 1972 Equal Opportunity Act belatedly provided enforcement mechanisms for earlier civil rights advances and changed the political climate for legitimate organizational action (Minkoff 1995). These provisions may also have encouraged foundations to abandon the heady but less predictable path of societal transformation for the simpler and more predictable goal of interracial parity. In fact, the process of identifying good works that address social inequalities and choosing the most effective organizations is arguably a philanthropic version of the advocacy turn predicted by the political legitimacy thesis.

Alternatively, the foundation discourse suggests the internal repudiation of radical perspectives because of White donor reluctance to support projects motivated by Black power. Only one article in good-works philanthropy invokes racial self-identification for legitimacy and does so to assert the negative views of Black foundation staff toward Black-controlled foundations. Rather than acquiescing to the political legitimacy of advocacy work, foundations might instead have resolved an internal conflict over the relationship between Black power and White wealth. Specifically, Blacks in philanthropy may have chosen to distance themselves from "radical" positions to maintain good relationships with their predominantly White donors.

Another dynamic internal to the foundation field may be responsible for the shift to good-works philanthropy: the 1970s professionalization of the foundation world (Frumkin 1999). After the congressional inquiries that culminated in the 1969 Tax Reform Act, foundation staff and trustees learned to view their tax-exempt status as politically vulnerable. Through a series of meetings, certain individuals agreed to professionalize foundation work by standardizing their organizational practices, formalizing their relationships with grantees, systematizing their communications with the non-foundation world, and (critically important) achieving widespread conformity to these preceding goals. In brief, they sought social closure over their activities to insulate themselves from external, especially political, interference. Although Frumkin characterizes this process as "professionalization," what these select philanthropic actors actually achieved was not status as a profession like medicine or law. After all, the Council on Foundations does not strictly train, credential, or license foundation staff, much less trustees. Instead, the Council and its backers more narrowly achieved a defensive (re)institutionalization of foundations as a field of (more tightly) mutually oriented organizations. Professionalism, technical attention, and the good-works framing of philanthropy for Latinos may have been part of an elite bid to distinguish the field from the political causes pursued by grantees while shifting philanthropic rationales from political to technical justifications. Whatever the combination of demographic, political, and institutional influences on the second shift, however, it would take the 1980s to effect the decline of Black centrality in the field rhetoric.

In 1980 Ronald Reagan took office as president of the United States, prompting the emergence of an implicit strategic philanthropy in the group-specific discourses, all converging on self-help as their common theme. As a combination of rationales and solutions, the new articles reversed the tendency of good-works philanthropy to de-emphasize historical rationales for foundation involvement in racial and ethnic affairs. Addressing any interracial disparity was no longer a sufficient solution in the new political climate; foundations had to choose between following the prevailing political conservatism or adopting a new direction for philanthropic priorities on race. When Americans elected Reagan for a second term, foundations chose to elaborate their strategic philanthropy and promoted the new racial talent of inclusive expertise or the combination of minority "culture" and mainstream "skills." The philanthropic pluralism of the 1990s was thus an extraordinary effort on the part of organized philanthropy to channel an ongoing "political selection" of non-White civic and political participation (see figure 2).

Initially, the aforementioned Latino articles and a surge of Black articles (i.e., group-specific discourses) eclipse the minority articles. In Black discourse, the later uplift and self-help grantees become the most reasonable to fund under the new presidential regime. Overnight, addressing parity was no longer the most efficient or necessary goal; instead, good tactics required a deeper rationale, even if that would only be the selection of efforts on implicit criteria. Unlike previous shifts in the discourse about Blacks, the repudiation of the past themes does not accompany the rise of self-help and the reappearance of uplift. Instead, professionalism simply disappeared, suggesting the complete incompatibility of technically premised philanthropy with a nationally triumphant conservativism.

Subsequently, the group-specific discourses about Blacks and Latinos disappear, and more inclusive minority articles resurface. Significantly, not until 1990 does the magazine publish another Black-specific article. In place of the Black discourse that had long heralded changes in the minority discourse, the new minority articles draw on elements from Native discourse, asserting that foundations could strategically support grantees with clear and mature tactics for advancing minority interests. While self-help continued to frame the decade's last Asian American and Native American articles, leadership became the last theme in the minority discourse. These articles consolidate the field rhetoric about race and ethnicity into a strategic

	Blacks	Blacks and other minorities	Blacks and Latinos	Blacks, Latinos, and White-ethnics	Blacks, Latinos, and Natives	Blacks, Latinos, White-ethnics, and Asians	Blacks, Latinos, Natives, and Asians	Asians	Latinos	Natives
1960										
1961	1U									
1962										
1963										
1964										
1965	2U									
1966										
1967										
1968										
1969	4U		3E							
1970	5N 6U									
1971										
1972	7+8N									
1973										9S+EI
1974	10U 11N	12BV								
1975										
1976	14+15P	17BV		13BV	16BV+18TA					
1977	19P							20MMM		21S
1978						22TA				
1979		26TA						27R	24+25B	23S
1980	29+30LU						28TA		31B	
1981	32LU, 34+35SH								33B 36SH	
1982									37B	
1983		38BV								
1984	40SH		41L							39S+EI
1985										
1986								42R+SH		
1987										
1988					44L		45L			43SH+EI
1989										
Total	18	4	2	1	3	1	2	3	6	5

Notes: The numbers represent codes for particular articles. The dotted lines mark the years in which the tenth, twentieth, thirtieth, and fortieth articles were published.

Theme Abbreviations:

U = Uplift	BV = Black vanguard	MMM = Model minority myth
E = Equality	TA = Technical attention	B = Bilingualism
N = Nationalism	L = Leadership	EI = Economic independence
P = Professionalism	R = Refugees	LU = Later uplift
S = Sovereignty	SH = Self-help	

FIGURE 3 The annual pace and group foci of articles published in *Foundation News and Commentary*, 1960–1989

emphasis on organization types that can survive and perhaps challenge the new political climate: community development corporations, voting rights organizations, and community foundations' outreach efforts to non-Whites.

Not only does attention to Blacks and Latinos shift entirely from group-specific discourses to minority articles, but the frequency of all race- and ethnicity-related articles ebbs for the first time since 1970 (figure 3). While the first ten articles of the total discourse appears over a fourteen-year period (1961–1974), the twentieth, thirtieth, and fortieth articles about race and ethnicity appear much more quickly, in 1977, 1980, and 1984, respectively. By 1989, however, the magazine has published only five additional articles: two focusing, respectively, on Asian Americans and Native Americans—groups that had been marginal to the rhetoric for decades—one minority article that includes Blacks and Latinos, a second minority article that adds Native Americans, and a third that further includes Asian Americans. The issue dedicated to philanthropic pluralism arrives a year later, completing an institutional divergence from prevailing political conditions.

Conclusion

Like other U.S. institutions, foundations adopted diversity policy in the 1990s. The specific experience of organized philanthropy reveals the in-completeness of demographic and political stories for the prioritization of diversity in the private sector. Foundations created their version of diversity policy by both consolidating and expanding their preexisting rhetoric about race and ethnicity in response to a new political climate that de-legitimized their historic philanthropic interventions. I suggest that private policies about race and ethnicity exhibit an institutional cultural autonomy wherein private actors have the option to employ a field-specific logic to construct their responses to political events. Significantly, diversity policy is not simply a post-Black scope that updates racial policy to new demographic condi-tions. Like the new immigration, non-Black inclusion had begun decades before the 1990s; however, it was sporadic and governed by rules for appro-priate taste combinations of Blacks with specific non-Blacks. Only during the 1980s did foundation rhetoric shift to regularly including non-Blacks as food groups equal to Blacks. Significantly, the election of Reagan triggered more changes in racial discourse than only a post-Black scope. Also integral to the mode of philanthropic pluralism were its new strategic interventions and emphasis on inclusive expertise. In brief, political opportunity and institutional culture mediates the connection (if any) between demography and organizational racial policy.

In the foundation field, the shift to diversity was actually the third in a series of shifts in its rhetoric about race and ethnicity. The logic guiding these shifts was a talent search composed of an asymmetric dialectic between changing conceptions of how foundations identified candidates for funding and of the criteria by which foundations recognized the most talented among the candidates. The dialectic between identifications and talents was asymmetric in that the field rhetoric regularly recycled old talents for combination with new identifications but never resuscitated old identifications for combination with new talents. Furthermore, the foundation rhetoric contained both a core set of discourses about Blacks and minorities in general and marginal discourses about Asian Americans, Latinos, and Native Americans. Ironically, diversity policy emerged late, only after the political de-legitimization of the historically central Black discourse, and from a reconstruction of the minority discourse using elements innovated in Native discourse, the most independent of the marginal discourses.

While the Reagan revolution set off the adoption of diversity policy, the latter's embeddedness in an older cultural dynamic demonstrates the relative autonomy of the organized philanthropy from national politics. Nevertheless, the evidence also suggests that politics were never far from the institutional decisions that prompted the earlier shifts. In fact, the autonomy of foundations was politically selective and moderated heavily by non-White insiders to the institutional field. Despite growing White ambivalence to non-White activism, especially as the latter moved out of the South, the field magazine published articles written by Black foundation insiders who encouraged foundations to value radical perspectives and aspirations for broad social change. During the politically and institutionally chaotic years surrounding the second shift, it was again Black insiders who wrote the critical articles calling for pragmatic instead of nationalistic policies and decisions. Even the professionalization of the field was a response to a major political event, the 1969 Tax Reform Act and its regulation of charitable institutions. Indeed, the greatest show of foundation independence is the field rhetoric's creation of philanthropic pluralism in divergence from the conservative political climate of the 1980s. Ironically, then, the relative autonomy of foundations from the public sector depends somewhat on the national defeat of the racially liberal political party. Whether the rhetoric of food groups diversity has permanently replaced the historic Black centrality in taste combinations may thus depend on how foundations interpret the new Republican initiatives to embrace diversity and rearticulate how Americans value it.

Still unknown are the effects of the field discourse on individual foundations, their grantees, and broader social environments. Instead, this chapter has identified the ideas imbued with fieldwide legitimacy and diffused to the subscribers of *Foundation News and Commentary*. At the level of the field rhetoric, the types of identification demarcate distinct historical periods, while the types of talent are historically sequential in their appearance but remain legitimate when new talents emerge. As combinations of identifications and talents, the themes are somewhat recyclable, like talents. However, whether the field members experience these discursive shifts in the same way cannot be determined from the rhetoric alone.

Beyond operating as an all-powerful national hand setting policy for all philanthropies and nonprofits, the foundation field rhetoric may instead function as a "toolbox" (Swidler 1986) of legitimate priorities, or even less significantly as a museum of past successes useful for legitimizing new priorities but without yielding present legitimacy. At the level of field members, individual organizations are not mandated like government agencies to follow the decisions of higher jurisdictions. In addition, the grantee organizations of individual foundations may have resource dependencies broader than foundation grants. And both individual philanthropies and their grantees also exist in real local geographies and not simply national political or institutional discourses. The scope and character of the legitimacy imparted by the cultural logic and its themes thus may vary widely, depending on the competing pressures faced by the individual organizations in their external contexts.

AS SUGGESTED IN the introduction, one might envision a different sequence of chapters, which would next present the remaining field-level processes (chapter 5), segue toward organizations (chapter 6), and close with the organization-level processes (chapters 3 and 4). Instead, I have chosen the existing plan of chapters to continue redressing the demographic determinism that pervades many popular and academic perspectives on diversity policy and secondarily to model the interconnectedness of the two institutional processes. Accordingly, in the next two chapters, I explore how the Cleveland Foundation and the San Francisco Foundation experienced, within their respective metropolitan regions, the trajectory of their national field rhetoric. I reveal their respective ethnoracial priorities through examinations of their executive directorships from the 1960s through the 1990s. In both the Greater Cleveland Area and the San Francisco Bay Area, local histories channeled foundation practices in ways only partially consistent with the field discourse. Although foundation directors employed the national discourses, they did so in ways that diverged from both each other and their common institutional field. This organizational divergence had as much, if not more, to do with their local political and institutional embeddedness as with their demographic trajectories.

3

Business Philanthropy in
the Greater Cleveland Area

Diversity in this town means that you can find
forty polka bands playing on Friday night.

A staff member at the Cleveland Foundation made the above statement, suggesting that references to diversity in Cleveland often refer to European-origin ethnicities. In interviews, many Cleveland staff and trustees emphasized that the association of the term "ethnicity" with Asians and Latinos was a relatively new idea for their metropolitan area, if not their entire region. In recent years, they have welcomed non-Black non-Whites into their conception of race-relations philanthropy and have been amenable to recasting that older priority as "diversity policy" as long as it excluded White ethnics. The persistence of the Black-White focus, however, contrasts with the Cleveland Foundation's early involvement in strategic philanthropy, defined as the articulation of specific purposes with specific solutions or, as termed in chapter 2, the identification of good strategies. In fact, the Foundation's first use of strategic philanthropy predates by two decades its appearance in the national magazine, where writers would advance this form of talent identification as the singular vehicle for philanthropic diversity policy. Furthermore, the Foundation has long sought to intervene in minority communities by familiarizing minority leaders with the White mainstream. By introducing high-profile Black and later other non-White leaders to White CEOs, the Foundation sought to develop a form of inclusive expertise, again years before its advent in field discourse about race and ethnicity. In a sense, philanthropic pluralism arrived in Cleveland well in advance of even the 1965 liberalization of racist immigration laws.

The Cleveland adoption of strategic philanthropy in the early 1960s was associated with the infusion of national philanthropic and federal dollars into the redesign of the Cleveland Foundation, from an amateur charity supporting good works into a leading institution nurturing good strategies. Three of its subsequent and major race-relations projects suggest the evolving organizational culture that became the basis for the Foundation's diversity policy. Each project figures strongly in the racial objectives of distinct and successive executive directorships. In the three directorships spanning 1960 to 1990, these race-related programs consisted of two citywide governance committees and one citywide consciousness-raising project.

Over this period, race policy generally meant initiatives that, in the words of a former staff member, "strengthened the role of Blacks in the community." Under Executive Director James "Dolph" Norton, it convened the Businessmen's Interracial Committee on Civic Affairs (BICCA), which became the major meeting place for Black community and White corporate leadership to formulate policy recommendations to manage the social movements of the 1960s. The next director, Homer Wadsworth, created the Greater Cleveland Project as the informational clearinghouse and outreach effort to prepare Cleveland for school desegregation in the 1970s and curb outbreaks of racist violence against Blacks. Wadsworth also initiated the Greater Cleveland Roundtable, which functioned as the conduit for minority affairs into Cleveland Tomorrow, the organization that adopted the task of "rebuilding Cleveland" in the 1980s. When Steve Minter succeeded Wadsworth in 1984, he continued the Foundation's involvement with the Roundtable and Cleveland Tomorrow—as its first African American executive director and the only person of color among the six men to head either the Cleveland Foundation or the San Francisco Foundation since the post–World War II civil rights movement. Specifically, the Foundation's success with racial projects that combined business leadership, professional knowledge, and grassroots input reveals how much the Cleveland Foundation has been a cornerstone in its local political system (Tittle 1992).

This chapter examines the development of foundation policy in a low-immigration metropolitan region in the Midwest and tells the story of how the Cleveland Foundation chose to reshape its local nonprofit sector within a philanthropic greenhouse. With local clout that also attracted national attention, the organization was able to build institutional bridges between Blacks, Whites, and other groups within the regional community. I discuss the Foundation's evolving culture, racial/ethnic priorities, relations with grant-seeking nonprofits, and *integration with* local politics by comparing the administrations of its fifth, sixth, and seventh executive directors: James Norton, Homer Wadsworth, and Steve Minter, two White males and one Black male. This chapter relies on my in-depth interviews with trustees, staff, and grantees in the Greater Cleveland Area; transcripts of oral history interviews with (Families 1982–85) Norton, Wadsworth, and their trustees, archived at the Western Reserve Historical Society of Case Western Reserve University; and thirty years of the Foundation's annual reports. I am also indebted to Diana Tittle's (1992) extensive social history of the Cleveland Foundation.

First, I introduce the Cleveland metropolitan area by outlining its historically recent demographic characteristics, economic fortunes, and patterns of neighborhood segregation. Second, I introduce the Cleveland Foundation by noting its pioneering origins and the changing ethnoracial composition of its staff and trustees. In brief, the composition of the Foundation staff shifted from exclusively White males to include a few African Americans and a female majority, while the trustees shifted from almost exclusively White males to include African Americans and a White male majority. Third, I discuss in turn the three directorships, highlighting, on the one hand, their respective managerial styles and racial priorities and, on the other hand, their relations with external actors and the local events that informed their decisions and dispositions. I argue that local circumstances both facilitated the early infusion of external support into the Foundation and enabled the implementation of its subsequent racial priorities. For three decades, Cleveland's corporate-dominated urban regime has remained an effective partner in philanthropic initiatives that have addressed local socioeconomic strains, political insurgency, and neighborhood segregation. I close with a discussion of how local political exclusivity has actually permitted the foundation that is less impacted by immigration to attract greater opportunities for developing diversity policy from extralocal institutions such as the federal government and national foundations.

The Greater Cleveland Metropolitan Area

Depending on who one asks, Cleveland is either "the mistake by the lake," an "All America City [*sic*]," or an important nexus of the major trends in U.S. urbanism, for better or worse (Perry 1995). A major industrial center since the turn of the century, its economy lost thousands of manufacturing jobs in the national, post–World War II shift to a service-based economy. The simultaneous resurgence of westward population movements drained the midwestern metropolis, while within the area, the twin phenomena of sub-urbanization and White flight dramatically shifted the population balance between city dwellers and suburbanites. Starting in the 1980s, however, city boosters began calling attention to the city as a national example of post-industrial urban revival. As in other major cities, intergroup relations have also pervaded Cleveland history. Rather responsibly, its major community foundation has coordinated large-scale racial initiatives for decades.

On the one hand, the awesome scope of the economic downturn might have prompted Clevelanders of all races and ethnicities to pull together. World War II had been a boon for the city, reviving a local economy hit hard by the Depression of the 1930s. Subsequently, however, the city lost both population and economic activity in its major sector of heavy industry. "By the early 1970s, [a net] 20,000 people were leaving the city each year" (Miller and Wheeler 1995, 44). In addition, while gains in suburban jobs kept pace with losses in city jobs, those gains have largely been in service jobs that pay less than the traditional blue-collar work that the new jobs replaced. As late as 1991, however, "more than one in four jobs in Greater Cleveland [re-mained] a manufacturing job [whereas] in the nation as a whole it was one in five" (Hill 1995, 67). The uneven effects of both deindustrialization and recent "recovery" have resulted in a Cuyahoga County unemployment rate that reached 12 percent in 1983 before falling to half that by 1988 and a county poverty rate that reached 16 percent in 1983 and continued rising to 19 per-cent by 1988.[1] Although employment has risen, so has economic insecurity.

Despite these dire straits, the persistent prevalence of residential segrega-tion suggests the limits of a "mass unity" explanation for the region's recur-ring efforts to address race relations. As in most nonwestern U.S. cities, residential segregation in Cleveland follows the traditional "chocolate cities, vanilla suburbs" pattern, wherein most Blacks live within city limits and most Whites live outside and commute into the city solely for work and recreation. In addition, the Cuyahoga River splits the city into segregated west and east sides. The west side is organized along squares and includes much of the historic European-ethnic neighborhoods. The near west side, just across the river, has become the home of a small Latino population, once mostly Puerto Rican but now with greater Latino heterogeneity. Anec-dotal evidence suggests that when the Latino population began growing, officials of the city, county, and parish coordinated actions to encourage the formation of this "ethnic place." On the near east side or downtown, a small Chinatown exists; however, these few blocks are not predominantly Chinese or even Asian, residentially or commercially. The east side is arranged along hills and includes the vast majority of the Black population in the Greater Cleveland Area. The suburbs are both mostly White and distinguished collo-quially into first, second, and even third rings that denote a social and physical distance from the central city. According to some of my interview subjects, the first step for European ethnics out of the westside neighbor-hoods is to the panethnic, White ethnic neighborhood of Parma, just south of Cuyahoga County and west of the Cuyahoga River.

In fact, because of the rather systematic ways by which most Clevelanders appear to avoid each other along a Black-White polarity, the scope of the Cleveland Foundation's race-relations philanthropy is all the more impres-sive. In addition, the similarity of the Foundation's historic initiatives to the diversity policies advanced in national philanthropic rhetoric is rather sur-prising given the relative absence of post-1965 immigrants in the metro-politan area. The main post–World War II demographic shift arguably oc-curred before the 1960s, with the influx of African Americans and their confinement and isolation during the 1950s into "Black" neighborhoods. By contrast, the percentage of foreign-born residents actually fell between 1960 and 1990 from 9.7 percent to 5 percent; in comparison, the San Francisco–Oakland area experienced a concurrent increase from 10.8 percent to 21.1 percent (U.S. Bureau of the Census 1964a, 1964b, 1973a, 1973b, 1981a, 1981b, 1993a, 1993b). Table 8 details the shifts in nativity and ethnoracial composi-tion for the Cleveland metropolitan area and city from 1960 to 2000.

Indeed, the primary target of and motivation for the "new" diversity policy remains the historic Black-White divide. Even more recently, over three-quarters of Whites and Blacks in Greater Cleveland would have to move to another neighborhood to achieve an equal distribution with each other throughout the region.[2] In addition, both Whites and Blacks are very isolated among themselves; the average White person lives in a neighbor-hood that is 88 percent White, and the average Black person lives in a neighborhood that is 71 percent Black. By comparison, although 58 percent of Latinos would have to change neighborhoods to achieve an equal dis-tribution with Whites, the average Latino individual lives in a neighborhood that is only 27 percent Latino. Likewise, while 38 percent of Asians would have to change neighborhoods to achieve an equal distribution with Whites, the average Asian individual lives in a neighborhood that is only 5 percent Asian (Lewis Mumford Center 2002a).[3]

Instead of interpreting the Cleveland Foundation's strategic policies as naturally responding to greater needs, I advance an institutional account for the surprising depth of its diversity policy. Rather than emerging from

GREATER CLEVELAND AREA					
	1960	1970	1980	1990	2000
Total population	1,796,595	2,064,194	1,898,825	1,831,122	2,250,871
Percent foreign-born	**9.7**	**6.9**	**6.2**	**5.0**	**5.1**
Percent White[1]	**85.5**	**83.4**	**79.5**	**77.6**	**75.4**
White	1,535,829	1,721,612	1,509,708	1,420,327	1,698,011
Black[2]	257,273	332,614	343,199	353,505	409,343
Native American[3]	479	1,750	2,014	3,232	3,236
Asian American and Pacific Islander[4]	2,449	4,901	13,171	20,027	31,697
Other[5]	563	3,317	4,813	1,266	33,936
Hispanic[6]	n/a	n/a	25,920	32,765	74,648

CLEVELAND CITY					
	1960	1970	1980	1990	2000
Total population	876,050	750,903	573,822	505,616	478,393
Percent foreign-born	**11.0**	**7.5**	**5.8**	**4.1**	**4.5**
Percent White[1]	**71.1**	**61.0**	**52.3**	**48.0**	**39.0**
White	622,942	458,084	299,970	242,723	186,368
Black[2]	250,818	287,841	249,504	233,860	240,362
Native American[3]	391	1,183	1,094	1,447	1,128
Asian American and Pacific Islander[4]	1,474	1,852	3,384	4,806	6,868
Other[5]	425	1,943	2,098	450	9,113
Hispanic[6]	n/a	n/a	17,772	22,330	34,554

1. Whites are "non-Hispanic Whites" only for 1980, 1990, and 2000.

2. Blacks were reported as "Negro" in the 1960 and 1970 censuses.

3. Native Americans were reported as "Indians" in 1960 and 1970, as "American Indian" separately from Eskimo and Aleut in 1990, and as "American Indian" in aggregate with Alaskan Natives in 1990 and 2000. Alaskan Natives were reported as "Eskimo" and "Aleut" separately in 1980 and in aggregate with American Indians in 1990 and 2000.

4. Asian Americans were reported separately as Japanese, Chinese, or Filipino in 1960 and 1970; as those three categories plus separate categories for Filipino, Korean, Asian Indian, and Vietnamese in 1980; in aggregate with Pacific Islanders in 1990; and in aggregate but separately from Pacific Islanders in 2000. Pacific Islanders were reported separately as Hawaiian, Guamanian, and Samoan in 1980; in aggregate with Asian Americans in 1990; and in aggregate but separately from Asian Americans in 2000.

5. Multiracials are aggregated with "Other" because they were enumerated separately only in 2000.

TABLE 8 (continued)

6. Hispanics were not enumerated separately in the 1960 and 1970 censuses and were reported as "Spanish Origin" in the 1980 census. As a result, the 1960 and 1970 statistics for the "Other" category may include significant proportions of Hispanics.

Sources: U.S. Bureau of the Census 1964a, 1964b, 1964c, 1964e, 1973a, 1973b, 1973c, 1973d, 1981a, 1981b, 1981c, 1981d, 1993a, 1993b, 2000a, 2000b, 2000c. For metropolitan area data, I employed the Cleveland Standard Metropolitan Statistical Area for 1960, 1970, and 1980; the Cleveland Primary Metropolitan Statistical Area (PMSA) for 1990; and the Cleveland-Lorain-Elyria PMSA of the Cleveland-Akron Consolidated Metropolitan Statistical Area for 2000. For city data, I employed the Cleveland Urban Place for 1960, 1970, and 1980 and the Cleveland city component of the above PMSAs for 1990 and 2000.

spontaneous episodes of interracial reconciliation or new immigration (which is minor), it arises from the city's historical capacity for civic action. Cleveland is a much older city than San Francisco and its Bay Area companions. Second, the private sector has long had a role in Cleveland civic leadership, and many local nonprofit institutions celebrated their seventy-fifth or later anniversaries during the 1990s. Relatedly, the midwestern city's history includes a Black middle class with roots well before World War II, unlike western Black communities, which relied overwhelmingly in the 1960s on leadership from the ranks of southern migrants. Third, amid its historic segregation can be found islands of racial integration. These eastside neighborhoods are anchored in part by infrastructural investments in Case Western Reserve University but also by intentional policies. In at least one neighborhood, the community employed property tax relief for homebuyers whose racial group happened to be underrepresented during the year of purchase. Unlike western cities, Cleveland has had the time and fortune to produce many institutional legacies. Indeed, the Cleveland Foundation itself is one of these long-standing legacies that provide the Greater Cleveland Area with local precedents and tools for social investment.

The Cleveland Foundation: From an Almost All-White-Male to a Mostly White-Male Institution (1914 to the Present)

In important ways, conservatives like Frederick Lynch (1997) could point to the Cleveland Foundation's commitment to race-relations philanthropy as a clear refutation of the diversity-management goal of a diverse workforce. Instead, the composition of the Foundation might suggest that a more efficient diversity-management goal is simply regular engagement with and knowledge about the local non-White population. After all, White males have dominated the leadership of the Foundation since its very beginnings, and its origins were steeped in the progressive mission of addressing urban social problems. Although its staff became majority White female by the 1970s and an African American man became its director in the 1980s, the trustees have remained largely enmeshed in an "old boys' network" of White businessmen.

The Cleveland Foundation is the pioneer community foundation and was the creation of Frederick H. Goff, president of the Cleveland Trust Company. Having been an attorney for John D. Rockefeller, he devised a local version of the national foundation, albeit with a then unique form of leadership. From its start in 1914, the community foundation would be an unusual philanthropy controlled not by individual dynastic families but by "leading citizens" or the heads of local elite institutions. When Goff was determining the form of his "community trust," the standard leadership for a private corporation was a self-perpetuating board. He broke with tradition only after his wife convinced him that a publicly representative board was not an example of "nut radicalism" (Tittle 1992, 31). Instead, he secured public, non-self-perpetuating leadership for the Cleveland Foundation through a unique arrangement. The board that would become known as the Distribution Committee "would consist of five people, two selected by the Cleveland Trust Company, and one each chosen by the mayor of Cleveland, the senior judge of the United States District Court, and the senior probate judge of Cuyahoga County" (Hammack 1989, 27), in which Cleveland is located.

These arrangements would be consequential for the group of San Francisco elites when they met to discuss forming the San Francisco Foundation in the 1940s. The role of the pioneer community foundation as a model would continue further into the twentieth century. In the 1960s, the Foundation remade itself, at the initiative of Cleveland philanthropic leaders, into an even closer approximation of the national foundations. And the San Francisco Foundation would later adopt the new form as the growth of its endowments became an opportunity to alter its founding organizational structure.

The Cleveland Foundation began without a director and established in its first decade a survey committee to conduct a number of studies on social problems in Cleveland. "The most enduring contribution of the survey years was to establish a precedent for local philanthropy to act as a civic agenda-setter and problem-solver" (Tittle 1992, 47). Consonant with the operation of an old boys' network or a dense network of White male elites, personal involvement with the Foundation seemed to lead to related positions of authority. In 1919 the Committee hired as its director of surveys Raymond Moley, an assistant professor of political science at Western Reserve University. Even after he left the Foundation in 1922 to become an associate professor of government at Barnard College, the trustees asked him to supervise a final survey, one on higher education conducted by George Zook, then chief of the division of higher education of the U.S. Bureau of Education. After Goff's death in 1923, the first Committee and its subsequent incarnations refocused their efforts to "doling out money to worthy and qualified charities" (65). Meanwhile, Moley went on to become Franklin Delano Roosevelt's campaign advisor.

1954 TO 1973: THE FIRST WHITE WOMEN, THE FIRST BLACK MEN

Despite its relatively passive mode before the 1960s, the Cleveland Foundation would attract more and more contributions to its endowment. By 1960, its total endowment was over $30 million, a level the San Francisco Foundation would not reach until the 1970s. Even at that level, the only professional staff for the Cleveland Foundation was Executive Director J. Kimball Johnson, who, prior to the start of his directorship in 1954, had had a long civil service record in various federal social service agencies.

In the early 1960s, local and national philanthropic leaders came together to initiate a project within the Cleveland Foundation in the hope of modernizing the almost fifty-year-old philanthropic institution. A former member of the Distribution Committee in prior decades, Harold Clark became in the late 1950s the discretionary authority for a trust fund of over $40 million left to his charge by the late Leonard C. Hanna Jr. whose private foundation often collaborated with the Cleveland Foundation. Inspired by efforts at urban renewal in Pittsburgh, Clark established as part of broader strategies a Special Purpose Fund within the Cleveland Foundation. Soon thereafter, he met with Paul N. Ylvisaker, director of the Public Affairs Program at the Ford Foundation, who was looking for ways to replicate a large successful grant to Kansas City in a new urban region. The eventual result was a seed grant to begin the Greater Cleveland Associated Foundation within the Cleveland Foundation. For the directorship of the Associated Foundation, Ylvisaker suggested his former Harvard roommate, James Adolphus ("Dolph") Norton. The Distribution Committee "*was persuaded* that Norton should be retained to undertake a study of the city's philanthropic resources in preparation for making a formal request to the Ford Foundation" (Tittle 1992, 107, emphasis mine). It was the Hanna Special Purpose Fund that would supply Norton's retainer.

The result of the study was a grant proposal to the Ford Foundation "to encourage research on and solutions of community social welfare problems of Cleveland, Ohio and its vicinity; to establish priorities for community action thereon; to make grants for research, pilot, experimental, and other projects toward the solution of such problems; and to encourage wise use of private philanthropic funds" (Tittle 1992, 109). The language was taken nearly verbatim from a speech made by Ford president Henry T. Heald on the kind of community foundation that Ford was interested in fostering (Tittle 1992). That the proposal had wide local support is evident in the identity of its many supporters: all five members of the Distribution Committee, the three trustees of the Hanna Fund, personnel from the Prentiss Foundation, the Beaumont Foundation, the Kulas Foundation, the Mater Fund, the governor of Ohio, the mayor of Cleveland, the president of the Cleveland Chamber of Commerce, the president of Case Institute of Technology, and others (Tittle 1992).

In 1962, the Associated Foundation's first annual report listed Norton as its sole staff. Over the next four years Norton hired a program secretary, an assistant secretary, an associate, and an intern—a total staff of five, including himself. The assistant secretary, Barbara Rawson, was the first woman program officer in the Associated Foundation. In 1967, when Johnson retired, Norton assumed directorship of the combined Cleveland Foundation and Associated Foundation. In his new role, he hired as assistant directors two of his four Associated staff, making Rawson the first woman program officer in the Cleveland Foundation. In addition, Norton hired two staff associates, one of whom was Roland Johnson, the Foundation's first African American staff. By the time Norton retired in 1973, he had a total staff of thirteen: eight in program positions, including three women, and four in support services, including two women.

During Johnson's directorship in the 1960s, the Distribution Committee was an all-White five-member board of four men and one woman, Mrs. Royal Firman Jr. The Associated Foundation's board was even less diverse; all eleven of these appointees of the most high-powered philanthropies in the Greater Cleveland Area were White and male. Even if its official resources were a fraction of the Cleveland Foundation's, its intended clout was unmistakable.

In 1967, when Norton became director of the combined foundations, the two boards were combined into a fourteen-member body. Kent H. Smith, the chair of the Associated Foundation board, was already a member of the five-member Committee and also became the chair for the combined board. The year before, Dr. Kenneth Clement had joined the five-member board as its first African American trustee. In 1970, agreeing to Norton's request, Mayor Carl Stokes appointed Gwill York (listed in the annual reports as Mrs. Scott R. York) to replace Firman as the sole woman. While no other changes in the representation of women and minorities would occur during Norton's directorship, in this same year, the board's membership dropped to eleven with the retirement of three of its former Associated Foundation members, all, of course, being White men.

1974–1983: STAFF DEVELOPMENT
AND (WHITE) FEMINIZATION

While the Committee made a national search for the Foundation's sixth director, it promoted Barbara Rawson to the position of interim director. As such, she became the first woman in the nation to direct a community foundation. In 1974, the Distribution Committee hired Homer Wadsworth, former president of the Kansas City Association of Trusts and Foundations, which had recently been the recipient of the grant that Ford had sought to replicate with its Associated Foundation grants in the 1960s. Within a year, Wadsworth expanded on Norton's administrative structure to hire three "top-notch program officers to handle cultural affairs, health and education, and social services, respectively" (Tittle 1992, 214), two with whom Wadsworth had worked elsewhere and one, Steve Minter, whose ten years in the Cuyahoga County Welfare Department, from case worker to director, made him the organization's expert on the local nonprofit sector. Until Minter's promotion to executive director in 1984, this African American man was the only person of color on the Foundation's program staff and would remain the only man of color on its grant-making staff until 1987.

Wadsworth expanded his staff in both size and scope of functions. Under his annual report editor, Patricia Doyle, the publications staff doubled from three persons in 1974 to six in 1981. By 1976, Wadsworth had a program staff of six men and two women in addition to a support staff of five men and two women, fifteen total. In 1979, Wadsworth promoted Minter to associate director and hired his fourth female program officer in a program staff of seven; therefore, the program staff included a majority of White women just before 1980. In 1981, Wadsworth expanded his nonprogram staff geometrically, from seven persons in the previous year to twenty-four, of whom only two were men. Most of the increase came from hiring female support staff, but Wadsworth also hired two White men who became the start of a managerial staff apart from the program staff. When he retired in 1983, Wadsworth had a total staff of forty-two, including a program staff of ten (including himself): six White women, three White men, and one Black man.

When Wadsworth started his directorship in 1974, the first African American woman, Frances King, would take her place on the Distribution Committee. Interestingly, she is also the first woman whom the annual report identifies by her first name rather than her husband's first name.[4] In the next year, Frederick Coleman would fill in for Kenneth Clement after the latter's passing, as the sole African American male trustee. After Coleman completed Clement's term, David Hill replaced him in 1977, having successfully lobbied the senior judge of the Court of Appeals (8th Appelate District) to appoint him as the Foundation's third-ever African American male trustee. Then, in 1978, Wendy Griswold replaced Gwill York as the sole White woman trustee. In Wadsworth's last years, Black and women representation increased again. In 1982, Mrs. Vincent G. Marotta replaced her husband, who resigned that year; in the next year, the annual report identifies her as Ann Laughlin Marotta as she completed the term of office originally given her husband. She is the first White woman to be listed by her first name, nine years after the first African American woman. In the same year, Wadsworth's last as director, Andrea Coaxum joined the Committee as its second-ever African American female trustee; however, she simply replaced Frances King as the only African American woman on the eleven-member board. In addition, Lindsay J. Morgenthaler joined the Committee and increased the representation of White women to two trustees out of eleven. When Wadsworth resigned in 1983, the composition of his board was seven White men, two White women, one Black woman, and one Black man, relatively similar to his starting board of eight White men, one White woman, one Black man, and one Black woman.

1984 TO THE PRESENT: THE RISE OF BLACK WOMEN AND
THE PERSISTENT MALENESS OF WHITE TRUSTEESHIP
From 1984 through 1990, Minter's program staff grew to fourteen personnel, including one Black man (Minter himself), nine White women, two White men, and two Black women. Only one other Black man, Victor Young, joined the staff in those years and only for two of the seven years; White women thus gained the most representation on program staff in that time. In addition, Minter increased the special managerial staff who did not per-

form grant review, annual report, or support functions to seven personnel (up from Wadsworth's start with two personnel): publications specialist, director of donor relations, information systems specialist, director of philanthropic services, director of communications, chief financial and administrative officer, and executive director of the Grantmakers Forum. Though these staff did not review grant proposals, their function was defined by 1990 as program staff, distinct from the five staff in financial services, nineteen staff in administrative support, the general counsel, and the eleven staff working on the annual report, a total staff of fifty-two.

On the Distribution Committee, diversity shifted slightly by 1990. By then, the Committee was composed of seven White men, two White women, one Black woman, and one Black man. In 1986, the Reverend Elmo Bean replaced David G. Hill as the sole African American man. In 1987, Adrienne Jones, a professor of Black studies at Oberlin College, replaced Andrea Coaxum Taylor as the sole African American woman on the Committee. In 1989, Annie L. Garda joined the Committee, raising the representation of White women to two. By 1994, the Committee was composed of six White men, one White woman, three Black women, and one Black man.

Over the history of the Cleveland Foundation, the representation of White males has steadily declined. For decades until the 1960s, the Committee comprised four White men and one White woman. After the merger of the Foundation with the Greater Cleveland Associated Foundation, the Committee comprised twelve White men, one White woman, and one African American man. The twelve became nine when the total board membership dropped to eleven positions. The nine White men became eight when an African American woman was appointed, and then seven when another White woman was appointed. As in San Francisco, Whites remained in the significant majority on the board. However, unlike in San Francisco, White *male* members also remain in a significant majority. Ironically, the local old boys' network and its important ties to similar networks in other locales and even nationally arguably served to magnify the racial initiatives of the Foundation's executive directors.

The Norton Years (1962–1973): Creating the Model for Elite-driven Strategic Philanthropy

[As a faculty member, I got] a very small [grant of] about $5,000 or so, funded by the Cleveland Foundation for a group of men who wanted to inquire as to whether philanthropy really could provide leadership in a community. Could it be used for leadership? In the course of our making that study, some of the people who were principals behind it were convinced, and I was convinced, that it could be a leadership base.—James Adolphus Norton, Families 1982–83

When Harold Clark began looking for an executive for the project that would become the Greater Cleveland Associated Foundation, he sought a man already knowledgeable about social issues. At the suggestion of Paul Ylvisaker of the Ford Foundation, the Cleveland Foundation gave to a local professor of government, Dolph Norton, a grant to explore whether philanthropy could exercise leadership in Cleveland. Soon after, the new Associated Foundation board hired Norton to be its executive director. The grant facilitated an intensive self-training process for Norton on philanthropy and Cleveland, during which his academic knowledge about social issues could be appropriately converted. Nevertheless, while his trustees hoped he would grow into his position, they selected him to be, not a custodian of existing assets, but a strategist for the application of philanthropic wealth.

MANAGEMENT STYLE

In comparison to the passive years of grant making, Norton's directorships at the Greater Cleveland Associated Foundation and the Cleveland Foundation were programmatic, proactive, and simply effective, in no small part due to his board and even donor environments. As an individual, Norton began his directorship with prior experience in racial issues from his higher education career and leadership in an earlier, albeit failed, campaign for metropolitan government in Greater Cleveland. His board trusted him to act in their stead on such matters because, among other things, he had professional experience with hiring and working with African American professionals.

When the business elite whom his board represented decided that an interracial group was needed in Cleveland, they entrusted Norton with the task of identifying the "appropriate" African Americans to invite to the inaugural meeting. When Black community leaders heard that the corporate elites had instructed Norton to exclude anyone from the Congress of Racial Equality (CORE), they told him that the intended association would have no credibility without CORE's presence. Norton's solution was to sneak the head of CORE into the meeting, and years later he still remembered the "sour looks" the White businessmen gave him for doing so. After an intense and emotional meeting in which every Black invitee spoke about discrimination and only three Whites spoke at all, the meeting's leader closed the event with the words, "Dolph will get back in touch with all of you and we'll see where we go from there." Even after Norton's disobedience, the Associated Foundation director remained the linchpin between White and Black leaders.

BICCA emerged from that meeting as the civic space in which Cleveland's White and Black leaders met to attempt to deal with the racial turmoil of the 1960s. Its avowed mission was as conservative as its actual goals were substantial: "They decided that rather than meeting as a single unit they would meet as committees because the object was not to solve the world's problems; it was to solve the inter-racial problems that businessmen had an impact on" (Norton, Families 1982–85).

Norton also showed a personal willingness to be "very close" to both the board and grantees. He described the ideal director-board relationship as one where the director understood the board so well that he could predict how they would vote on proposals and thus be able to advise grantees effectively. Whereas others might have viewed his presence on potential grantee boards as a conflict of interest, Norton credited his presence with providing him with important intelligence. For instance, when an individual threatened to sue the United Appeal for funding the Urban League's integrationist activism, Norton could confide that as a board member of the Urban League, he knew that the United Appeal had never given the organization enough financial support to be called remotely responsible for subverting community values.

His experience and inclinations informed the nature of the programmatic policies he implemented at the Associated Foundation and the Cleveland Foundation. The Associated Foundation was invented to provide a demonstration of how philanthropy might provide leadership for a community: "It was a working principle that no money would be distributed [from the Associated Foundation's official funds] if we could find somebody else to do what was needed to be done . . . We found we didn't have to give away money even if we could because we could get other people who were interested in spending their money for projects . . . Time after time the Associated Foundation would choose the direction in which it wanted to move, set up an advisory committee of public types who would define the direction more clearly and then people would pick up on the projects" (Norton, Families 1982–85).

With this proactive approach, the Associated Foundation became "the civic leadership group in the city up until the time it combined its board with the Cleveland Foundation and began to operate as a joint group" (Norton, Families 1982–85). The initiative-style grant making that Norton oversaw was exemplified in its education project, Plan of Action for Citizens in Education. The Associated Foundation first looked for a leader from a major corporation to chair the project; when that failed, they brought in an attorney from the Boston branch of a prominent Cleveland law firm who had also been active in an earlier civic campaign in Cleveland. After roughly half a year, the advisory committee made thirty-two recommendations, hired a Harvard Ph.D. to staff the effort, and began a transformation of local education, employing various grants, that culminated in the hiring of a new superintendent for the Cleveland public schools.

Another tactic was exemplified in the summer youth program that the Associated Foundation assembled from federal and corporate monies. "What we did was to identify projects that ought to go on, and to put them together so they were a program, rather than just bits and pieces . . . There was something for everybody [for each donor to pick and choose to support]. That left the money the foundation put in, which was a relatively small amount of money, to go to the less attractive but still important parts of a program" (Norton, Families 1982–85). Rather than treat foundation money as the community bank for a selection of incoming proposals, Norton used Associated Foundation funds as a last resort and as "gap filler" funding in larger projects, which his advisory committees supervised and for which he had already convened an even broader range of donations than the community foundation's grants.

Over a short period of time, the Associated Foundation changed the mission of the pioneer community foundation. When the new combined foundations board made Norton the director for both institutions, he brought his adherence to a Ford Foundation philosophy of philanthropy as social jujitsu: "You try just to set the direction of tremendous forces that society has" (Norton, Families 1982–85). He pointed to how the actual costs of social problems were always far greater than anything the Foundation could deliver in grants as the rationale for short-term Foundation funding. "It's not what you're doing that matters, it's what society is doing in the field that matters . . . if the project hasn't begun to pick up support from other places you realize that maybe we were wrong" (Norton, Families 1982–85). Speaking of the Foundation overall, he asserted its character as "a marvelous institution. It was born in conservatism, yet under some of the most forward thinking leadership that you can imagine . . . it has been conservative in a very creative way in the sense that it really has tried to tackle radical problems" (Norton, Families 1982–85).

Under Norton's directorship, the Associated Foundation and the Cleveland Foundation developed a host of priorities, most of which were related to the increasingly Black central city. Despite the scale and effect of the projects employed to tackle these social problems, Norton hardly ever dipped into the Cleveland Foundation's endowment to make grants. Their relative capacity to make external alliances made such capital invasions unnecessary and even unthinkable.

Limited Successes. Ultimately, however, the Associated Foundation's efforts with education and housing were only qualified successes. In the area of education, the Associated Foundation had initiated the Plan of Action for Citizens in Education (PACE). Working on desegregation and other issues, the PACE committee worked toward the hiring of a superintendent, Paul Briggs, whose first five years Norton described as the most exciting time in Cleveland's educational system in decades. "As a result, Cleveland had more black principals by 1970 than all of the five largest school districts in the nation combined. Paul could recruit Black principals and he did that. One committee of [BICCA] dealt with education, and when Paul would go to them and ask them for support for something, blacks and whites would support him" (Norton, Families 1982–85). Unfortunately, Briggs's talent for political maneuvering would also prevent him from taking as strong a stand on desegregation as the Foundation wanted. Likewise, the Cleveland Foundation was not able to apply other kinds of pressure on Briggs: "We never were able to really have the impact on the internal operations of the Cleveland schools that would have helped Cleveland over the bumps. We were able to have a big impact on getting Paul Briggs in as superintendent and through his building years . . . I think we were on as good a track as any major city in the United States. Paul was too good a politician and he knew how to manipulate the school system. He was not innovative in program and was such a dominant personality that he did not develop school teachers and give them their head" (Norton, Families 1982–85). Therefore, although the Cleveland Foundation under Norton was able to identify a community agenda, empower it with elite and nonelite support, and even persuade others to seriously consider, if not hire, their preferred administrator, they could not influence Briggs to implement their desired agendas.

In Foundation efforts at housing development, Norton also admitted quite limited success. As with PACE, the Associated Foundation established the Plan of Action for Tomorrow's Housing (PATH) and employed "the person who later became the housing director for the Cleveland Metropolitan Housing Authority, who then opened up some of the housing for the elderly in sections of the city that had never been opened up before" (Norton, Families 1982–85). However, aside from small-scale victories, Norton was never able to get leverage on the larger forces necessary to be changed to redevelop housing in decaying neighborhoods.

The Expansive Role of Cleveland Trustees. Norton's board and donor environment contributed significantly to the extensiveness of the Foundation's involvement in its community. The Associated Foundation board members were more than sources of advice and information. Rather than seeking to represent distinct community segments, the Associated Foundation started with a board of men who were believed to be able to leverage other sources of philanthropic dollars; by contrast, the Cleveland Foundation's original board always included a token woman, who, anecdotal evidence suggests, was traditionally appointed by the mayor. Only after the Cleveland Foundation absorbed the Associated Foundation did women trustees come to participate in Norton's proactive directorship.

Describing the chair of his board, Norton noted how far the businessmen's commitment could take the Foundation, even without any political or social empathy: "Kent Smith had never really known any blacks. I'm using the term blacks, but in those days we called blacks Negroes. Kent didn't; he called them blacks because that came out of his experiences in World War I . . . he was an absolute realist. He couldn't empathize, that was not it, but he could work with you and he could understand the rationale behind a feeling. Kent knew that something had to be done" (Norton, Families 1982–85).

The rest of the board was as determined as Smith to execute their mission of civic leadership and showed it in their individual willingness to make stands on principle. During the Associated Foundation's support of the Urban League's desegregation efforts, the Urban League brought a lawsuit against a homeowner whose neighbors convinced him to back out of selling to a Black dentist. He countersued the Urban League and threatened to mount a campaign against the United Appeal for its funding of the Urban League. "I talked it over with some of the persons who were leaders on the Associated Foundation board and we decided that we would get together with the people who were heading the United Appeal this year . . . We invited the person threatening action to come in and sit down at the conference room of the Associated Foundation . . . and to explain to them what he was going to do" (Norton, Families 1982–85). Under the guise of giving the man an audience to air his grievances, Norton set the stage for board members to decide how far the Associated Foundation was willing to support desegregation. After two hours of discussion, the man backed down. Norton made a telling analysis of the situation: "These persons [his board and the United Appeal leadership] had the courage of their convictions to say we might lose this time but it's what needs to be done. I think he was intimidated because these were the names he read in the papers all the time" (Norton, Families 1982–85).

Norton and his board were able to build a consensus on what the Associated Foundation needed to do by approaching social issues as problems to be solved. However, Norton did not have such skills before his directorship. In fact, after the first year of his directorship, it was only Kent Smith's intervention and threatened resignation from chairship that prevented the board from firing Norton. Thereafter, Smith started "counseling Norton on how he might communicate more effectively with the board. With men of a practical mind and bent, Norton learned, it was a mistake to begin a discussion of any problem by making an emotional appeal to conscience or proposing a high-sounding solution. Rather, Smith suggested, start with a dissection of the problem and let the answers follow naturally from that—an approach with which businessmen such as he and his fellow board-members were more comfortable" (Tittle 1992, 116). Years later he would claim that the Urban League's residential integration programs were "funded by a group that many people thought was the most conservative group on earth because they were the economic and social notables of Cleveland. If you could give them a problem and they could see the problem and begin to work on what might be done, then they would come to about the same conclusion that anybody else would. They came to the conclusion that that had to be done" (Norton, Families 1982–85).

Establishing a new relationship with his board, Norton remained director and was permitted to make strategic use not only of funding and alliance building but also of his board members themselves. Regarding a juvenile delinquency initiative, he stated that the Associated Foundation had been responsible for locating the principals on its board. "We enlisted Tom Burke from our own board and I served as Tom's second. This was one of the beauties of working in an agency like [the Associated Foundation]. When a leader stepped forward, we could guarantee him that he would have enough backing so that he wouldn't be embarrassed and he would be able to do things" (Norton, Families 1982–85). This loan of board and staff resources meant that the Foundation could actually apply the personal legitimacy of its trustees directly rather than only through the presence of their names in annual reports or other literature. In another instance, Norton reports that the Associated Foundation was able to persuade the chief of police to accept institutional reforms intended to curb police mistreatment of Black Cleve-landers only because of the chief's respect for a board member who actively lobbied on Norton's behalf. Otherwise, the chief would not have moved on the suggestions, out of worry "that he would be criticized for sending his people somewhere else [for police school] where they could get training rather than here where everything was [of course] perfect" (Norton, Fami-lies 1982–85).

Despite his improved relationship with his trustees, though, Norton be-came aware of the limits set by their personal experiences and class interests. Sometimes he succeeded in overcoming these limitations. For instance, he was able to persuade his board to fund a child day-care program, which some members saw as "inefficient." As men who had not taken part in the actual care of their children, they balked at funding a program whose per child cost approached the cost of a prep school education. Norton had to prove that good childcare required paying for more than the "storage" of children while their parents were working. At other times, he was unable to influence them to change their minds. Once he brought his trustees a grant proposal for a program to identify retired miners who had worked in the Appalachians, examine them for black lung disease, and educate them of their rights to federal benefits under black lung disease legislation. The board turned down the proposal because "that was asking too much. This is a coal town and the feeling that we would be identifying people whose lives had been put into jeopardy by actions of the coal companies seemed just too much to take" (Norton, Families 1982–85). Seeming to criticize the Founda-tion's corporate sponsors was out of the question.

However, the aversion to upsetting its donors seemed to be rewarded. Like many donors, Cleveland donors possessed an antigovernment bias that made private efforts more palatable targets of largesse. "Many of the people who are wealthy enough to worry about [bequest money] are biased against giving it to the government to spend" (Norton, Families 1982–85). Cleveland donors tended to leave their trusts unrestricted, demonstrating their faith in the Foundation as a civic institution. In fact, Norton and his staff took advantage of the otherwise threatening 1969 Tax Reform Act to publicize to bank officials the utility of the community foundation in comparison to the increasingly regulated private foundations. Even so, Norton remained con-cerned about the fit between the ethics of a donor's motives and their institution. "You have to be careful how you do it [raising the endowment]. One of the things you do not want to do is to encourage the baser motives of a person who's going to give money. It can be tied up in the wrong ways. That gets to be a problem" (Norton, Families 1982–85).

While his caution may have curbed the growth of the endowment, it also made donating to the Foundation a positive choice rather than simply a last resort. When asked whether Cleveland's problems in the 1960s influenced the donors, he answered that he had earned "the enmity of one of the most powerful men in the city" but "also won the support of some others, including one who has died and left millions to the Cleveland Foundation. He told me that one of the things that really sold him on the Cleveland Foundation was the way we were working on the real tough problems of the day" (Norton, Families 1982–85).

RACIAL PRIORITIES

Norton led the Cleveland Foundation to pursue racial priorities through a definition of race relations philanthropy as "the grants that strengthened the role of blacks in the community" (Norton, Families 1982–85). This priority was a programmatic one, which the Associated Foundation and the Cleveland Foundation pursued not at their convenience but through warding off feelings of great ambivalence. His board addressed these "touchy problems" without a solid mandate from the surrounding Cleveland community and without complete confidence in their grantees. "When you're working on the problems of race and poverty and you're dealing with groups that develop their race consciousness to a high level, it doesn't make you comfortable. Things can go wrong just as well as they can go right" (Norton, Families 1982–85). In other words, Norton and his board hardly felt isolated from the racial currents flowing around them. However, their nervousness was in fact the result of their ongoing engagement with the social flux. How they managed racial inclusion on their own board illustrated their generally conservative approach.

Regarding the rationale by which the Associated Foundation convinced the Cleveland Foundation to adopt the former's structure when the organizations merged, Norton noted, "The Cleveland Foundation, initially, was set up with just five people to serve on its distribution committee. It literally was shaky for a variety of reasons and it did not have the opportunity to add certain significant groups. There was no way in the world they could have a black on that committee or at least not up until that time" (Norton, Families 1982–85). Inclusion through expansion rather than reallocation became the Foundation's policy for implementing its goal of strengthening the role of Blacks in Cleveland.

This policy led to the Cleveland Foundation's active hand in the recognition and incorporation of middle-class Blacks into the Cleveland mainstream and the pacification of lower-class Blacks through calming their relations with police and providing youth with summer alternatives to rioting in the streets. Norton achieved the first effect with a textbook case of comprehensive racial policy. He supported efforts that addressed major problems in racial minority experience: residential segregation (the relative freedom to cross ethnic lines), underemployment (the relative coincidence of economic status and group membership), and lack of civic participation (the relative salience of historical factors on group participation in contemporary society). All of these efforts, however, left the basic structure of economic opportunities untouched.

The Associated Foundation worked with the Urban League to "put together a program in which we would locate blacks who had enough money to move into all-White neighborhoods and then find a way to let them move into those neighborhoods" (Norton, Families 1982–85). An important stake of this support was whether Blacks could provide their children with schooling that was commensurate with their parents' income. The integration of the Shaker Heights neighborhood and hence its public schools was an important component of these efforts. In the realm of addressing employment inequality, Norton's foundations produced programs that had impact beyond even the local scene. For example, BICCA included an employment committee that started "what was called AIM JOBS, which was a special alliance between business and industry and government to identify blacks who were unemployed, give them the training they needed, and help them find jobs, work through 'til payday, and so on. It was to do exactly what the theoreticians are now asserting needs to be done under the Jobs Training Partnership Act. It was done step by step and it was a huge program" (Norton, Families 1982–85). Rather than wait for a federal program, the Associated Foundation produced a local program that would anticipate national efforts. Finally, in the formation of BICCA itself, Norton united the desegregation and economic efforts within a biracial framework for policy discussion and determination. Through BICCA, Blacks' access to power was not limited to political offices; they had access to the powerful private actors whose interests would endure past political administrations.

With such a focus on inclusion into existing social and economic systems, however, Norton's efforts did comparatively less for those who were unskilled or young. The latter would not have a seat in BICCA, could not afford the homes in good school districts, and would have to develop skills before becoming eligible for employment programs. To be fair to Norton, he would have needed the leverage that he felt he lacked in housing and education. Where he was most successful, instead, was in the administration of justice and in summer youth programs. "One of the most interesting sets of problems in those days was the question of law enforcement and racism. All of the police were white and most of the blacks felt that the police were racist and mistreating them . . . We tried to see what we could do that would help government govern better and the police to learn not to be so racist as they were in many of their activities" (Norton, Families 1982–85). With the assistance of a key trustee, Norton managed to support a police cadets program that brought young Black men into the force. Likewise, he took pride in assembling summer youth programs to ward off potential riots. While he recognized that this kind of strategic grant making did not solve the roots of the problems producing riots, he saw it as better than laissez-faire racial governance that saw riots as unpredictable events to which responses could never be planned.

RELATIONSHIPS WITH EXTERNAL ACTORS

With a conservative respect for structural limits, Norton's foundations were able to intervene in substantial urban efforts. In addition to simply attracting federal support for its programs, the Foundation convened or brought together money and actors in important coalitions: national with local philanthropic monies, federal funding with corporate contributions, state agencies with Black nonprofit organizations, all to fund initiatives for youth, jobs, and the very Associated Foundation itself. Under Norton's directorship, the Foundation accomplished these programs through a general policy process whereby their input on federal legislation produced resources, both cultural and financial, which they applied to forward their local agendas. An important ingredient was the virtual match between the Cleveland Foundation and the beliefs of field elites about what the business of philanthropy was. The result was the extensive and intimate involvement of private philanthropy with local government.

Rather than regard the involvement of national actors as a threat to local control, Norton saw the Cleveland Foundation as taking advantage of federal legislation, in one instance, new monies for the prevention of juvenile delinquency. Often, the Associated Foundation became the administration for such resources even without matching funds from the Foundation itself:

"Those [programs] were often times run under the administrative aegis of the Greater Cleveland Associated Foundation even if it didn't have any money in it. We ran a lot of federal money through the programs and it turned into a holding company" (Norton, Families 1982–85). In the area of youth programs, Norton combined federal money with corporate gifts in a comprehensive package that allowed donors to fund particular concerns, leaving the Foundation to support the less popular but necessary components (Families 1982–85).

Local corporate leadership provided direction and legitimacy for federally financed projects, all as part of the Foundation's policy of convening national resources and local power. In the area of employment programs, the AIM JOBS program "was done with business leadership. They got the former head of Philco Ford to come back in and serve as head of that. They brought in some outstanding people. It was a huge organization with mostly federal funds but with a tremendous outlay of effort on the part of business here in the community" (Norton, Families 1982–85). The Associated Foundation itself was financially the collaboration of the Ford Foundation, the Cleveland Foundation, and another local philanthropic giant, the Hanna Fund, whose principals populated the board with an even broader range of philanthropic leaders. And, as mentioned above, the proposal made for Ford's support in starting the Associated Foundation was also signed by local government officials.

The Foundation's involvement with the Tax Reform Act of 1969 and the War on Poverty money that constructed Cleveland's Equal Opportunity Program reveals the process by which the Foundation under Norton was able to attract national resources. During the congressional hearings that would result in increased regulation of foundations, the Cleveland Foundation assumed a position of leadership in the foundation field, especially in the community foundation movement within the field:

> The Cleveland Foundation was the fourteenth biggest foundation in the nation then and still holds about that same rank among foundations. It was perfectly legitimate that I was there. Everyone there was worried about the tax reform act . . . because it was a direct attack on foundations. I had read the bill and recognized that through a quirk in the bill, "public charities" were different from private foundations . . . Before that meeting was over I told the group assembled, "You know, we're going to work with you on this thing all the way down the line but I want you to understand that on some things we may have conflicting interests and

when we do we'll stand apart from you. If it's necessary, we'll fight you on anything that might drag us into some of the fights you are in by yourself." I left that meeting and called up our attorney in Cleveland and told him that we wanted to take on the project nationally. We sent out one hundred letters to the one hundred largest community foundations and were able to establish a common base that community foundations presented to Congress through that whole year. I testified once and submitted testimony a few times. (Norton, Families 1982–85)

The result was that the Tax Reform Act indeed exempted community foundations from the heaviest of the regulations imposed on private foundations, including the initial 6 percent and later 5 percent payout requirement. On his return, Norton and his board took advantage of the new federal standard for philanthropy to discipline the local bank trust officials, who, in Norton's opinion, used excessively conservative investment strategies. "They resisted [less safe investments], but then the tax reform act came along and set a standard . . . and we told them that if private foundations ought to do five percent then surely we ought to do better than that" (Families 1982–85).

Likewise, with respect to War on Poverty funding, the Cleveland Foundation assumed a unique level of leadership among philanthropies and reaped the results of their input. Norton described the Foundation's access to Don Carmichael, a member of a Washington, D.C., task force working on War on Poverty legislation: "He would come back here [Cleveland] to do some work and touch base again. We would have a breakfast meeting at Stouffers-on-the-Square one day a week, and then he'd run back to Washington for the rest of the week . . . Out of that came the Cleveland economic opportunity program which was one of the first large ones funded in the country" (Families 1982–85). For their efforts, not only did Cleveland become the site for one of the first programs, but they were able to persuade the hiring of Ralph Findley, a Black community leader friendly with the Foundation and Norton in particular, as its director in the 1960s.

The result of these efforts was a particularly intensive involvement with local government. So intense and regular was this involvement that Norton developed his own philosophy for understanding it: "One of the problems you have with a foundation is that you're dealing with 'free' money in the sense that if nobody can really question what you do . . . you're likely to get to thinking that you are blessed by knowing what public policy 'ought' to be . . . Yet, at the same time that you have to be careful not to go too far, you have to be careful not to assume that everything government does is right or the most farsighted . . . If it had not been for the Foundation the poverty program would have been another year coming in here and the Community Action for Youth never would have been here. The same thing is true for several programs in the field of administration of justice. We kept the pressure on the city to do things" (Families 1982–85).

Rather than ignore city hall or simply follow their lead, the Foundation tried to work with the city to leverage its substantial resources in directions that Norton and his board felt were wise. Not only did they collaborate with departments, they worked with the chief administrators: the mayors. "We had a lot of projects that were greatly dependent on City Hall and Tony Celebrezze, Ralph Locher, Carl Stokes, and Ralph Perk . . . All those were quite cooperative on some projects" (Norton, Families 1982–85). In fact, there is even evidence of Foundation involvement in selecting both the Republican and Democratic candidates for mayor in the 1967 mayoral campaign, which resulted in the election of Carl Stokes, the first African American mayor of a major U.S. city. "Whatever the new mayor needed in the way of supplemental personnel, discretionary funds, advice or connections to heal the social and economic wounds of the city, [the heads of the newly combined Cleveland and Associated Foundations] stood ready to provide" (Tittle 1992, 160). Beyond supporting the mayor, however, the Foundation under Norton took pains to develop Stokes professionally, to the point of the Foundation's hiring a consultant to assist the new mayor. As Norton reported, "When Carl Stokes came in he didn't have a machine or a group that could move in (strong cabinet members) and help City Hall go . . . I was out of the city and got a telephone call with the word that the mayor was really in trouble and he now wants some help. Could we do something? . . . We set aside a chunk of money and we paid the consultant to go in and work with the mayor" (Families 1982–85).

By the end of the 1960s, the Foundation was a central institution in a web of influence spanning national and local actors.

THE URBAN CONTEXT

These relationships with external actors were impressive in their scope and reliability; however, they could not have existed in the absence of an urban context with stable major players. On the one hand, the Cleveland City Council possesses a district structure with small wards and thus creates a multitude of council representatives. In comparison to San Francisco's eleven districts for .75 million residents, Cleveland possesses twenty-one wards for its fewer than .5 million residents. Such political systems have long been criticized for encouraging provincialism and patronage to the point of producing corruption and ultimately discouraging citywide unity. On the other hand, weighing against potential political divisiveness, Cleveland also possesses a cohesive business elite, an established and sizable Black middle class, and a racial polarization that ironically simplifies the dispersion of neighborhood interests.

The extreme centralization of financial assets in Cleveland exacerbates the usual dependence of local U.S. policymakers on economic elites. Among the Western liberal democracies, local governments in the United States are uniquely dependent on private wealth, in part because the federal government does not make loans directly available to local jurisdictions, which also tend not to cooperatively pool their resources (Swanstrom 1995). These U.S. political traditions deepen the structural need for local politicians to pay attention to potentially mobile wealth. In addition, the relative degree of capitalist cohesion increases the capacity of economic elites to instrumentally influence local politics. During Norton's directorship, federal congressional studies of local bank stock ownership highlighted FDIC statistics showing that "the five largest banks in the Cleveland metropolitan area held 91.7 percent of all the commercial bank deposits in the area, one of the highest concentrations in the [n]ation" (108). While such findings routinely provoke alarm over wealth concentrations, they also reveal a certain stability in Cleveland, a predictability about whom the Foundation could contact if it sought to mobilize resources and allies beyond its own leadership.

Cleveland also has an established, sizable, and integration-oriented Black middle class from which the Foundation could identify community leaders for interracial projects such as the various BICCA committees. This group constitutes an eth-class (M. Gordon 1964) with the capacity to represent its particular social class interests as synonymous with the interests of the entire racial/ethnic group. Its centrality arises from its leadership of the Black church, its organizational leadership of Black coalitions, the demise of radical organizations serving less affluent African Americans, and its representation in a statewide Black political caucus. The Black church is an especially central community institution dating back to its role in the civil rights movement of the 1950s and 1960s. In the early and mid-twentieth century, large urban congregations consolidated the Black migrations from rural areas in the South to urban areas throughout the nation and provided an organizational basis for new identities and cultures of solidarity (McAdam 1982). Along with the historically Black colleges, the churches provided the organic infrastructure that supported the more formal social movement organizations, and although the Black insurgency of the period waned, the churches survived.

In Cleveland, the primary coalition of Black movement organizations seems to have been the United Freedom Movement (UFM), which was led by the local chapters of the National Association for the Advancement of Colored People (NAACP) and the Urban League. Historically dominated by the Black middle class, these organizations led UFM primarily to seek the desegregation of Cleveland schools and neighborhoods. Revealingly, although the NAACP and the Urban League survived the dissolution of UFM and the 1960s more generally, their less middle-class–oriented allies largely did not. The Poor Peoples Partnership (PPP), the Welfare Rights Organization (WRO), Afro Set, the Muslims, and the National Committee to Combat Facism (the Cleveland chapter of the Black Panther Party) either dissolved or survived through becoming social service agencies (Chatterjee 1975). In the political arena, in 1967 Carl Stokes became the first Black mayor of Cleveland, indeed of any major metropolitan area. As noted above, Black Clevelanders elected him to the mayor's office for two terms with substantial White corporate support. Meanwhile, at the statewide level, his brother, Congressman Louis Stokes, built the 21st District Caucus as an independent, largely Black political caucus as an alternative to the Ohio Democratic Party regulars, institutionalizing a pathway for Black political training and ambitions. Like the middle-class NAACP and Urban League, Black political power in Cleveland (and Ohio) survived the 1960s, providing a stable resource for the initiatives of the Cleveland Foundation.

Unfortunately, the paradox of broad ethnic diversity, numerous neighborhood-oriented council representatives, and yet overall institutional cohesion had one last and very important contributing factor: racial segregation. The extreme quality of segregation ensured that the potential dispersion of provincial interests neatly simplified into a political tripod of White ethnics, corporate leadership, and African Americans.[5] Racial polarization discouraged alternative lines of conflict, for instance, a three-way tension between (1) pre–World War II Blacks, Italians, and Hungarians, against (2) corporate leaders, post–World War II Black arrivals, and Poles, against (3) Jews, Puerto Ricans, and Albanians. Therefore, whenever Norton stepped outside the Cleveland Foundation, he found a relatively predictable political landscape, regardless of how fractious the tensions appeared from time to time.

The Wadsworth Years (1974–1983):
Maintaining Elite Discretion in Civic Affairs

When the Cleveland Foundation board hired Homer Wadsworth, the twenty-five-year veteran director of the community foundation in Kansas City, he inherited an organizational legacy that was unique in its concentration of resources. In fact, Wadsworth proudly noted the institution's possession of an immense percentage (approximately 80 percent) of its endowment in unrestricted funds, in contrast to the New York Trust, which was larger and yet had an endowment predominantly restricted to established purposes. Also, because his Kansas City foundation had been the initial grant recipient of the Ford Foundation program that created Norton's Associated Foundation, Wadsworth strongly agreed with the new mission of the combined foundations. He saw the merger of the Associated Foundation and the Cleveland Foundation in the late 1960s as the legitimate starting date for the kind of philanthropy he promoted as its director. Although some viewed Wadsworth as less activist than Norton, the new director shared his predecessor's aversion to the Foundation's earlier role as virtually an "appendage of the Welfare Federation," which he viewed as a poor use of community risk capital. Leadership for Wadsworth meant using and improving the Foundation's unique clout to address the enduring problems pressing at the nervous system of a city that regarded itself as representative of most major U.S. metropolitan areas.

MANAGEMENT STYLE

During Wadsworth's directorship, he did not advance a radically different mission for grant making, but instead developed its tools. Foundation policies under Wadsworth were oriented toward projects of great scale. It was under his directorship that the Cleveland Foundation began making substantial use of its capital, in projects that are now commonly called program-related investments (PRIS). In one characterization of Wadsworth, he was quoted as often asking grant applicants, "Think about where you would like to spend a million dollars" (Doll 1989, 252). In addition, Wadsworth explicitly asserted that something like a third of the grants made by the Cleveland Foundation had been initiated by the Foundation directly or after it had provided technical assistance to the recipient. Bill Doll claims that the Foundation was not "some Olympian force single-handedly rearranging the civic landscape" but was "more like a small-town country store where people come to get advice, give advice, and the storekeeper knows where they can find what they need to solve their problems" (253). Nevertheless, even though the Cleveland Foundation depended on its local allies to achieve its ambitious goals, the country store analogy fails to do justice to its capacities in comparison with other philanthropic organizations.

Wadsworth's most notable initiative of scale was perhaps the Playhouse Square project, which relocated three of the city's major art institutions to downtown Cleveland. The Foundation convened leadership in the local arts field, proposed and received a major NEA grant, and solicited matching funds from corporate donors, raising $13 million in three years. In subsequent years, businesses added over $11 million, the federal and county governments each $3.5 million, and the State of Ohio another $3.75 million. Throughout the project, the Cleveland Foundation provided a stable staff and space for the campaign, headed by Pat Doyle, the arts and culture program officer whom Wadsworth had brought with him from Kansas City. It should be noted that the impetus that pushed the Foundation into the project was its former board member, Gwill York, in her capacity as a representative of the Junior League. In addition to the Playhouse project, the Cleveland Foundation funded other large projects, including a hunger task force in collaboration with the Catholic Church; a housing committee at the United Way; another PRI for housing development in the Hough, the heart of Black Cleveland, a project directed by future director Steve Minter; and the attempted desegregation of Cleveland's public school system in the 1970s.

Its most significant involvement of this time was the Foundation's participation in Cleveland Tomorrow, the organization often credited with the economic revitalization of Cleveland in the early 1980s. Cleveland Tomorrow was an association of corporate CEOs, formed soon after Mayor George Voinovich succeeded his antibusiness predecessor, Dennis Kucinich. With a new mayor in office, a handful of top corporate executives facilitated the Gund Foundation's financing of a management consulting study (by Mc-Kinsey and Company) of Cleveland's economy. The study competed for attention with the Cleveland Foundation–financed RAND study, which made distinct recommendations, including the creation of a local research institute. The community foundation agreed and started the Regional Economic Issues (REI) Program with a $407,000 grant. Although the RAND research findings were initially unpopular with business leaders, Cleveland Tomorrow eventually adopted REI as its research institute rather than develop one internally. The shift in perception is exemplified in Tittle's account of how "Cleveland Tomorrow director Richard Shatten, who had initially dismissed the RAND study as 'data not connected to strategy,' would in time come to regard REI as his association's 'brains' " (1992, 269). REI's director, Michael Fogarty, described the reasons Cleveland Tomorrow chose to work with REI: "Cleveland Tomorrow had raw political power, but that was not the strategy they took. They decided that they needed to be smart about this. Many people would prefer to hire a consulting company to do a three- or four-month study that gives them what they want. That was not the strategy that Cleveland Tomorrow took" (quoted in Austin and Strimling 1996, 11). Regardless of whether Cleveland business leaders actually "decided to be smart" or were somehow coerced by the Foundation, the latter was once again central to the local process for policy determination.

Not surprisingly, Wadsworth worked with a board characterized by a strong faith in the philanthropic institution. Earlier, in Norton's final years, one prominent trustee, John Sherwin, established a large and rather unique endowment, a fund completely restricted to financing the Cleveland Foundation's administrative overhead expenses. Its establishment effectively separated the expenditures for staff and grants and also suggests an adamant belief in a long-term role for the Foundation. Far from criticizing how philanthropy might innately undermine its social objectives by perpetuating the concentration of wealth, Wadsworth's Foundation pragmatically accepted the existing state of affairs. Wadsworth's own evaluation of his board was similarly pragmatic. On the one hand, he was critical of the process for appointing trustees to the board, questioning whether successful businessmen and lawyers necessarily knew the best candidates for a community foundation board. On the other hand, he praised his trustees, whom he saw as following a long tradition of active involvement. In sum, the board embodied the same conservative yet proactive leadership under Wadsworth as it had under Norton. Without exception, his trustees were all Republicans, whereas Wadsworth, like Norton, were lifelong Democrats.

Wadsworth also contributed to staff development. Steve Minter recalled Wadsworth's arrival in 1974 as the most dramatic point in the long-term professionalization of Cleveland Foundation staff. Unlike Norton, for whom program officers were "promising young charges," as one former staff put it, Wadsworth invested more institutionally in their development. "Each of our people have a day and a half a month to pursue their own interests as long as they relate professionally to what they are concerned with. This has two advantages: (1) it gives us a knowledge about operations in other parts of the country . . . and (2) it opens up the possibility of other things they might do in the course of their career" (Homer Wadsworth, Families 1982–85).

Under Wadsworth's leadership, the Cleveland Foundation pursued less expansive racial projects than under Norton's directorship. But even where Wadsworth did not articulate explicit racial and ethnic priorities, he remained involved in related initiatives. After the five-year honeymoon with the school district superintendent whose rise the Associated Foundation and the Cleveland Foundation had facilitated, the Foundations found him to be recalcitrant to desegregating the schools. In fact, during the 1970s, the Cleveland Foundation's most well-known racial involvement was probably its support of the NAACP suit against the district. "Probably the most noteworthy [controversial activity of the Cleveland Foundation] in which we spent well over $1 million was in monitoring every proceeding before the court in the desegregation of schools and providing authentic information to every conceivable organization here in a position to assure that their constituents understood what the basic facts were" (Wadsworth, Families 1982–85). In sum, Wadsworth regarded local school leadership as irresponsibly leading parents astray and being "impossible" in trying to resist court orders as if they had not begun with *Brown v. Board of Education* in 1954.

The Foundation effort included the creation of the Greater Cleveland Project, "a formal coalition of community agencies that would seek to promote public understanding of the issue of school desegregation by locating and training grass-roots speakers, who in turn would educate their neighbors" (Tittle 1992, 222–223). Although the school officials would attack the Project as the Foundation's main subversion of their authority, the Foundation had already begun meeting with Bishop James Hickey of the Catholic Church. Through those connections, the Cleveland Foundation supported the bishop's subsequent policies against White flight to Catholic schools and Sister Brigid Griffen's Committee on School Desegregation.[6] "Bishop Hickey publicly announced that he would not permit the Catholic schools to become a haven for those fleeing court-ordered desegregation, declaring that children were to be admitted to parochial schools only at normal entry points such as kindergarten and the first year of secondary school" (225). Meanwhile, the Griffen Committee achieved as one of its successes the at-home counseling of nearly every Catholic family in Cleveland the week before the incipience of court-ordered busing. "The Cleveland Foundation continued to support the operation of the Greater Cleveland Project as an information clearinghouse until 1981, long after it had become clear to foundation staff and associates that the school district had neither the financial and intellectual resources nor the political will to fully comply with the court's orders" (227). As the Project's director would reflect in resignation, "At least no one got killed" (227).

Another significant racial priority was the demise of BICCA and its replacement almost a decade later with the Greater Cleveland Roundtable. Wadsworth presided over its disbanding, "not because the idea wasn't sound but it had run its course, and it was not delivering, and its leadership was third rate" (Wadsworth, Families 1982–85). In contrast to its eventual situation, he asserted that its original leadership had been first-rate, notably, top leadership from a national law firm. The Roundtable was founded after the election of Voinovich to mayor, after a coalition of civic leaders including the new mayor, Council president George Forbes, Wadsworth, and future Cleveland Foundation director Steve Minter researched other models for interracial leadership. Thereafter, Cleveland's revitalization in the 1980s would include an important civic group that was interracial. The president of the area's Chamber of Commerce would assert the necessity of the Roundtable by reference to the generally bad record of including Blacks in the revitalization successes of other cities (Austin and Strimling 1996).

RELATIONSHIPS WITH EXTERNAL ACTORS
Under Wadsworth's directorship, the Foundation maintained good relationships with the federal government, national foundations, other major foundations, local philanthropies, and local political actors. By the time of his directorship, the Foundation's reputation as a "good operation" had spread widely in federal circles, to the point where the Internal Revenue Service sent officials to observe the Cleveland Foundation and use it as a model of the quality of bookkeeping that the IRS could expect from large foundations. Not only did federal legislation continue to enable new Foundation projects, but the Foundation continued to participate actively in policy formation. As assistant director, Minter recalled how, during Wadsworth's directorship, the Cleveland Foundation participated in a number of federal studies that resulted in programs that included Cleveland in their first rounds of grants. However, when Reagan began his presidency, the federal government withdrew from much of existing public-private policy processes, leaving their former private partners to find new associates.

At the local level, the Cleveland Foundation worked with the Gund Foundation, which had become the largest private foundation in Cleveland, on supporting or convening the major leadership projects of Cleveland Tomorrow and the Greater Cleveland Roundtable. Wadsworth recognized that the size of the Cleveland Foundation was creating pressures for higher-quality grant making: "When you're getting up to the kind of money they're spending now at the Foundation, you can't count on the stuff coming over the transom being up to it" (Wadsworth, Families 1982–85). Consequently, he felt that his staff spent an extraordinary amount of effort on technical assistance simply to improve project quality. With respect to local politicians, he felt that, save for Mayor Voinovich, their quality was resoundingly low, especially, in fact, the minority leadership in Cleveland. In sum, Wadsworth regarded his region as largely poor in quality but fortunate to have such an asset in its community foundation.

THE URBAN CONTEXT

During the directorship of Homer Wadsworth, the Cleveland Foundation initiated many projects of significant scale. However, although the racial projects remained substantial, they possessed a far less ambitious scope and character than those during Norton's years as director. I suggest that the somewhat smaller scale of the racial initiatives primarily reflected the relative availability of the Foundation's traditional corporate allies.

On the one hand, Black leaders continued to consolidate behind integrationist aims that were also supported by Whites living in the wealthier neighborhoods, which were economically inaccessible to most African Americans. That less affluent Whites were more likely to view Black advancement as threatening was, of course, a national pattern. Throughout this period, Black churches remained important sites of political debate and sources of community leadership. In addition to the continuance of a statewide Black political infrastructure, a local politician, George Forbes, would come to fill the void left by the end of Carl Stokes's mayoralty. From 1973, the year before the start of Wadsworth's directorship, to 1989, when Forbes himself would run for mayor, his prominence as City Council president was legendary. "Forbes built his power during a period when federal funds, particularly through community development block grants (CDBG), flowed to the city . . . Forbes, as wily a politician as ever held office, carefully distributed funds to maintain power among his council members. During [a] ten-year [period], for example, more than $34 million was spent on sidewalks and curbings. Other CDBG funds went to various social service agencies, often controlled by Forbes' loyal council members" (Bartimole 1995, 171). During those ten years, Forbes and his all-Democratic council shared power with Republican Mayor George Voinovich, who had the backing of the local corporate leadership.

On the other hand, a strong neighborhood-based populist movement did challenge the corporatist regime, arguably distracting the corporate leaders from acting as stronger partners in Foundation projects. In many U.S. cities of the 1970s, neighborhood movements emerged against the emphasis on downtown development in earlier decades; in fact, both Cleveland and San Francisco elected mayors backed by those revolts. Cleveland saw the rise and fall of Dennis Kucinich, an avowedly antibusiness, progressive mayor who promised to refocus local policy to benefit common people in the inner city. Not enamored of his stance, bank leaders refused to roll over city debt and forced Kucinich to choose between selling off the public utility to its private competitor and bankrupting the city on December 15, 1978. The corporate community represented by the bank interests effectively curtailed the new mayor's political legitimacy, and after his defeated reelection bid, the subsequent mayor, George Voinovich, developed a closer relationship with downtown business elites. With Kucinich's fall, conventional wisdom coalesced, albeit not without detractors, around the idea that business would have to rebuild the city's downtown in order to revitalize the city's economy.

During the years that San Francisco politics saw the rise of the "slow growth" coalition organization San Francisco Tomorrow, Cleveland politics saw the emergence of the organization Cleveland Tomorrow, an association of the CEOs of the area's fifty largest corporations. Forming in the aftermath of Voinovich's election, Cleveland Tomorrow focused its efforts on downtown renewal, to the neglect, charged its critics, of city neighborhoods. Tellingly, the "new BICCA" of the Wadsworth years emerged only after the defeat of neighborhood insurgency and the resurgence of corporate political power. Indeed, the Greater Cleveland Roundtable served as an important institutional bridge between Cleveland Tomorrow and the African American community.

The Minter Years (1984 to the Present): Icon of Unity and Irony

During Steve Minter's directorship, the Foundation maintained a substantial continuity with its past projects; his being African American did not signal a radical transformation of its priorities, but instead seemed to raise local awareness of their racial implications. The "Cleveland Foundation under his direction would perpetuate Wadsworth's interest in institution-building, while quietly but firmly insisting on minority access to and participation in the city's institutional life" (Tittle 1992, 16). Minter was successful at pressing for a renewal of the Foundation's involvement in minority affairs, arguably because he was intimately familiar with its traditions, having helped develop its institutional precedents as a program officer. As a result, he gained a reputation not for deviating from traditions but for being, as one of his former staff lauded, a "great systemizer" of them.

Minter's vision of the appropriate mission of the Foundation was not a radical shift. Like his predecessor, he saw the major change in the organization's history as having been the merger with Norton's Greater Cleveland Associated Foundation, and he identified the grant-making process as fundamentally the same as in the late 1960s and early 1970s. For Minter as for Wadsworth, social problems had not tremendously changed in Cleveland; there were many "recurring issues" and "not a lot of new ideas." Nevertheless, his becoming the Foundation's first African American director inevitably placed a different nuance on the projects he shared with Wadsworth. His race, his professional experience as staff under Wadsworth, and his publicly known personal life as a Black man in an interracial marriage all seemed to raise Wadsworth's approach of fitting racial policies within the broader cross-racial priority of "rebuilding Cleveland" from an implicit necessity to an explicit strategy.

MANAGEMENT STYLE

As the staff member with the longest tenure at the Foundation and in Cleveland, Minter brought to his directorship a strong sense of institutional history. In the 1960s, the Foundation had started concentrating its priorities on equality of opportunity, health and social services, and criminal justice reforms. Over time, it added involvement in housing and economic development, the arts, health, and, of course, the PRIs. By Minter's directorship, the Foundation had cemented its role as a major civic leader and not simply the largest local foundation. Minter also further developed the staff professionalization and expansion that had been two of Wadsworth's main priorities. Tellingly, he reinforced certain organizational myths, such as the lesson Kent Smith taught Dolph Norton in the 1960s: "Don't write those issue papers . . . instead marshal information on what the problem is . . . the 'liberal' vs. 'conservative' slant of the answer will not be realized until later" (Norton, Families, 1982–85) and would be secondary to the achievement of a consensus to act.

He already had long-standing relationships with local business and political leadership at both city and state levels, all of which reinforced the involvement of the Foundation in major policy issues. Described as an innate mediator, he assuaged his board's fears about being asked to rubber-stamp projects by involving them directly in a strategic planning process wherein he confirmed their commitment to the continuing use of the PRIS. Rather than add new priorities, he systematized existing ones and extended them so that the Foundation board and staff all knew that the organization had clear major initiatives: education, neighborhood development, and lakefront development. He could confidently state that of the Cleveland Tomorrow projects identified by the Harvard Business School as significant for the organization's revitalization of Cleveland, the Cleveland Foundation was involved in every effort.

RACIAL PRIORITIES

As with his general management style, Minter's contributions to the racial priorities of the Foundation were personal yet consequential. He embodied the philanthropic talent of inclusive expertise, someone who had feet in both worlds (see chapter 2). On the one hand, he simply continued the Foundation's earlier involvement in schools, public housing, fair housing, and interracial leadership. He completed a cochairship with the director of the Gund Foundation on a committee that recommended that the State of Ohio take over the Cleveland public school system, a culmination of Foundation struggles with the district since the Associated Foundation's initiation of PACE and its subsequent support of the NAACP's desegregation suit. The Cleveland and Gund foundations' support of the Greater Cleveland Roundtable programs to advance fair housing had roots in the Associated Foundation's support of the first efforts to desegregate the Shaker Heights neighborhood. In the area of public housing, Norton's directorship had been the fiscal agent for BICCA in the 1960s; three decades later, federal legislation for public housing monies used language directly out of Cleveland Foundation–financed studies and subsequently funded such programs in Cleveland. Wadsworth had put BICCA to rest, and later Minter and Wadsworth assembled the Roundtable as its substitute.

On the other hand, Minter was the first African American director of not only the Cleveland Foundation but any large community foundation. His presence was as noted by his staff "consequential though not intentional," a distinction that they felt was often lost on local Black leadership. Like other Black leaders, he had risen through social service and government careers and not through the corporate sector. However, he achieved his success through building alliances and networks that significantly crossed racial lines. In Minter, the Foundation gained a director who was not only pragmatically concerned about race but also actively interested in its role in society.

Because of his style, however, it is difficult to classify his effect on the Foundation's racial priorities as either a change in emphasis or an introduction of new understandings. The distinction between intention and consequence is as fine in the motives for his promotion as in the role of race in his organizational policies themselves. His directorship of the Foundation guaranteed his invitation to membership in the Union Club, the premiere social club of Cleveland's social and economic elite, but his race also made him its first African American member ever. Not only had his life been a sequence of firsts as a Black man, but as a partner in an interracial marriage with a White woman he represented for Cleveland something of an icon who actually bridged an otherwise persistently segregated community. Nor was the fact that one of his son-in-laws was a Chinese professor at an Ivy League university lost on the leadership of the local Chinese community. Rather than view the growing Asian, Latino, and Arab communities as "others," he observed their growth—at least, their organizational growth—as quite similar to Black organizational growth in previous years. While the Foundation had historically been involved in Black-White issues, Minter claimed that the lid had been "blown off" the solely Black-White way of looking at race and ethnicity.

RELATIONSHIPS WITH EXTERNAL ACTORS

Under Minter, the Cleveland Foundation had clear continuing relationships with the federal government, other community foundations such as the San Francisco Foundation, local private foundations such as the Gund Foundation, local government, and especially national foundations. From the Foundation's role in the 1969 Tax Reform Act to its alliance in the 1970s with the Urban Institute and the local Chamber of Commerce to plan federal studies, the Foundation has remained intimately involved in the formulation of federal policy. As mentioned above, the Foundation's own local studies provided language for federal poverty legislation, out of which Cleveland became the first city to receive a Hope VI public housing grant. Minter claimed a similar relationship with the national foundations; if they were to select two or three demonstration sites, Cleveland would probably be one of them. And the monies that Cleveland received would be channeled into local government and private sector partnerships with substantial Cleveland Foundation participation.

Having witnessed many of these recurring partnerships, Minter felt little if any anxiety over whether authority was located locally or nationally. For him, the fact that national foundations shaped the rest of the foundation field was not troubling. Though the leadership was premised on top-down hierarchical relations, he asserted that the actual projects themselves were often innovated by the Cleveland Foundation or other peer organizations "from below." He noted that national foundations simply had the resources to seed these innovations across the nation; they could not actually dictate local philanthropic use of them. In fact, he saw different peer organizations as playing different roles in the foundation world and in policy formation. In contrast with places such as San Francisco, which he recognized as better at innovation, he saw Cleveland as better at improvement and especially implementation.

THE URBAN CONTEXT

The directorship of Steve Minter as the Foundation's first African American director embodies the political paradox surrounding the Cleveland Foundation's continuing race-relations philanthropy in the wake of the Reagan revolution of the 1980s. While the popular acceptance of corporate involvement in Cleveland civic leadership helps explain the seeming contradiction, another factor, persistent racial segregation, ironically may account for the surprising persistence of local bipartisanship behind racial policy in philanthropy. As in previous decades, African American leaders remained in important political positions, and again, the persistence of a local Black political infrastructure was evident. In 1989, Council president George Forbes lost his mayoral bid not to any of several White candidates but to another Black politician, Michael White, whom many regarded as Forbes's protégé. "White, who had been promised Forbes's support before Forbes decided to run himself, refused to move over for his mentor" (Bartimole 1995, 173). Despite a frequently heard complaint that Black leaders base their authority excessively on personal charisma, African Americans in Cleveland appear to have developed a persistent organizational basis for leadership development. And like their fellow Clevelanders, local Blacks accept the necessity of corporate economic development for reviving their local economy and ameliorating poverty.

To a rather high degree, residents of the Greater Cleveland Area are accustomed to corporate leadership or at least corporate involvement in the determination of their common civic affairs. Corporate power is viewed as a necessary community resource, which only the unreasonable would seek to exclude from the political and civic process. While some urban politicians ponder how to minimize the inherently negative effects of economic development, Clevelanders view economic development as so basic that its negative effects are seen as the result of either ignorance of its ultimate necessity or improper economic development. Nevertheless, while most residents appear to praise the civic partnerships with business, such as the many coordinated by the Cleveland Foundation, a minority of local residents also wonder whether downtown renewal will actually trickle down to the neighborhoods. In response, while the Foundation invested millions in the redevelopment of Playhouse Square to revitalize both the arts and downtown usage, it also developed similar capital investments or PRIS to address concerns about education and the neighborhoods.

A major critic of the corporate elite in Cleveland and not infrequently of the Cleveland Foundation itself is columnist Roldo Bartimole, a self-appointed critic of private power in the city since the 1960s. Tellingly, one member of the Foundation staff described him as, above all, a brilliant, sharp man who (she is glad) has a voice in Cleveland because he reminds the city of issues that should be on the table. Clevelanders take him seriously, yet many would probably also agree with her second characterization of him as someone "with a screw loose somewhere." Regardless of whether Bartimole is actually unreasonably abrasive with his opinions, it might be a measure of Cleveland politics that one has to be crazy to challenge the legitimacy of corporate influence.

Time will tell whether Cleveland has actually made a comeback. My interviewees frequently provided anecdotal evidence for a reversal of an earlier trend, when their own children had to leave for other areas such as New York City to find work. Instead, the interviewees believed that college graduates especially were returning home to Cleveland because of new job opportunities and also a climate of declining employment discrimination. On the other hand, they also cited continuing and even deepening poverty in their metropolitan area, suggesting the often noted observation that even "successful" shifts to the postindustrial economy produce a polarization of the socioeconomic inequalities. Given the Cleveland Foundation's history of racial policy, it may soon address the question of whether different races and other groups have shared equally in the benefits and costs of the "new" economy.

The survival of this historical focus on race-relations philanthropy amid the national rightward shift in U.S. politics may be assisted, ironically, by Cleveland's persistent racial polarization. Because of local residential segregation, identity-based and place-based political constituencies are one and the same and thus do not come into conflict. For foundations, neighborhood policies seem to be a symbolic code for philanthropy that is unambiguously for the "masses" who would not be found on the foundation's board or even its program staff. In actuality, place-based social policies have occupied a more ambiguous space in U.S. politics. For such policies to target the disadvantaged, public and private institutions must select particular places for attention. Moreover, the residents of these places are often associated with group identities salient for and sometimes even detrimental to the feasibility and design of policies. Taking the twentieth century as a whole, the Democratic Party's support of identity-based politics during the civil rights movement was a deviation from the norm. By the Second World War, Democrats had used urban policy to build a national, White ethnic electorate. Extending this strategy, they absorbed African Americans from the Republican Party by supporting the southern civil rights movement and introducing new federal urban programs under the banners of the War on Poverty and the Great Society (Mollenkopf 1983). In recent decades, Democrats lost ground as their opponents successfully associated them with ethnoracial minority or "liberal" special interests, that is, identity-based constituents. In response, they have sought to recapture their earlier association with universal rather than identity-based policies. At stake in this national partisan struggle is the legitimacy to speak for the newest place-based electoral majority: suburban voters who are predominantly White and middle class, albeit increasingly ethnoracially diverse, but persistently non-Black. This electorate has become almost as politically important as rural oligarchies were before the 1970s (Anyon 1997). Despite what has been called the "information revolution," I suggest that U.S. political culture still favors geographically based "communities of interest" over communities primarily defined by group identities such as those that form around the federally protected categories.

At the local level, however, racial segregation ameliorates the opposition between the "prize" of place and the "necessary evil" of identity. Because of Black-White segregation in Cleveland, neighborhood policy is not a competing alternative to racial policy. Instead, where identity largely dictates place of residence, philanthropic support for place-based policies directly addresses many identity-based concerns and facilitates bipartisan coalitions. In fact, when Latino and Asian grantees express complaints about political exclusion and policy marginalization, it is in part because their client and constituent communities are less residentially segregated from Whites than are Blacks.

Conclusion

From a certain popular perspective, the West Coast has become the moving edge of U.S. culture and society, while other regions, like the Midwest, are either mired in the past or following western trends as best as they can. Commentary about diversity often assumes this view and cedes to the West, especially California, a demographic if not also cultural power to remake the nation. In this chapter, however, a close examination of one "backwater" area suggests a more complex account for the use of diversity policies. In Cleveland, where immigration has not remade the population or culture into an approximation of Californian metropolitan areas, the race-relations projects of its community foundation have been surprisingly advanced. Although a predominant Black-White demography limits the ethnoracial breadth of foundation policy, the Cleveland Foundation's long-standing strategic interventions appear to be the substantive precursor for the philanthropic pluralism advanced more recently in its field's national discourse. How did the model for diversity policy arise from the foundation with the more limited ethnoracial demography?

If we view the Cleveland Foundation as an ideal type for community foundations, then its recent history suggests that a foundation's relative capacity for developing diversity policy depends, rather ironically, on the relative power of a White male elite. On the one hand, this elite appears to be translocal in character, since a national foundation was responsible for the foundation's redesign into a vehicle for strategic philanthropy and federal programs have provided much of the financial resources fueling the implementation of those race-related initiatives. On the other hand, it has been the availability of local elites for foundation partnerships that has strongly motivated the selection of the Cleveland Foundation as the "local office" for national philanthropy and policy. Predominantly White male leadership in the early twentieth century created the foundation and many other civic institutions that have become part of the Greater Cleveland toolkit for social policy. Since then, a predominantly White male upper-class board of trustees has facilitated personal and organizational ties with local and national elites. During Norton's directorship, the presence of a united White business front permitted the creation of an interracial group with financial and social clout. During Wadsworth's directorship, the victory of the corporate leaders over the progressive mayor allowed the Foundation to create a new version of the earlier interracial group. During Minter's directorship, the support of local conservatives has enabled the Foundation to remain entrenched in translocal policy networks in spite of a rightward political shift across the nation. In sum, it is a predominantly White male corporate power that empowers the Foundation's role as the local community bridge between otherwise highly segregated ethnoracial groups.

The impressive capacity of the Cleveland Foundation, however, does have certain limitations. First, its successes in convening core civic leaders and strengthening the role of middle-class Blacks contrast with its relative failures in the policy domains of education and housing. Second, although its directors wield considerable power, they do so within the limits and expectations of their trustee boards. To the point, had Norton not altered his management style in response to their advice, I suggest that his board would have set a less activist example for future directorships. Third, as will be especially evident in comparison with the San Francisco Foundation, its central place in its region has come at the cost of an exclusive, nondemocratic process for civic decision making. Because the region possesses the capacity for large-scale coordination and action, it also possesses the capacity for significant exclusion. In one instance, according to Bartimole (1996), when a parents association breached protocol by delivering demands to Mayor White through his woman friend, "the action cost them heavily with the loss of $85,000 each in funding by the Cleveland and Gund Foundations . . . and the Joyce Foundation in Chicago which had pledged $160,000 but withdrew its funding." Fourth, the predominantly White composition of corporate leadership in Cleveland makes the Foundation vulnerable to the charge of promoting a version of the paternalism prevalent in the pre–civil rights South, where Black leadership arose from the sponsorship of White elites instead of the mass support of African Americans.

In the next chapter, I turn to an examination of racial philanthropy in the San Francisco Bay Area, which possesses the ethnoracial demographics anticipated by diversity policies but not the political geography that magnifies the impact of philanthropy in Cleveland.

4

Progressive Philanthropy in
the San Francisco Bay Area

As goes California, so goes the nation.

A staff member at the San Francisco Foundation made the above quip, echoing an idea popular in California that the Golden State had surpassed its earlier status as the nation's frontier and become its cutting edge instead. Not surprisingly, this status is often associated with the state's demographic heterogeneity. As the state librarian, Kevin Starr (2001), has noted, "In demographic terms, the salient feature of California is its diversity. One out of every four Californians has been born outside the United States. Into California has come the human, racial, ethnic, linguistic, and cultural richness of the planet itself. There is no people, no race, no cultural or linguistic tradition that is not in some way represented in California."

Trustees, staff, and grantees in the San Francisco Bay Area share the belief that their demographic composition and the resulting intergroup dynamics can only foreshadow the future of the United States, if not also the globe. Sometime just before the twenty-first century, Whites became a minority of the population in California, and "Americans elsewhere have grown to realize in the past few years that what is happening in California is their future as well" (Maharidge 1996, xvii). Or so Californians tend to assume.

In philanthropic policy, insofar as it is a gauge for other promising examples of California leadership, the reality is more complex and arguably even refutes the ideal. Many years in advance of diversity's appearance in the national magazine for the foundation field, the San Francisco Foundation did expand the scope of its race-relations philanthropy beyond a Black-White focus. However, the Foundation largely did so via a traditional, now archaic approach to grant making, that is, through the support of an unco-ordinated assortment of what I have termed good causes and good works. In fact, the Foundation's first major use of strategic philanthropy in race rela-tions did not occur until 1991, the year after *Foundation News and Commen-tary* published articles on philanthropic pluralism. Instead, the Foundation sought to intervene in racial issues through largely symbolic, albeit rhetori-cally sophisticated, commitments to "empower" minority communities.

The Bay Area adoption of a more diverse scope in the mid- to late 1970s was associated with the new directorship of Martin Paley, and the adoption of strategic philanthropy in the early 1990s coincided with the Foundation's participation in a Ford Foundation diversity initiative. Three of its major race-relations projects since the 1960s suggest an evolving organizational culture suddenly jolted in recent years by national attention. As in Cleve-land, each project figures strongly in the racial objectives of distinct and successive executive directorships. In the three directorships spanning 1960–1990, these race-related programs consisted of two awards programs and a professional fellowship program.

Over this period, race policy generally meant awards to, as a staff mem-ber stated, people who had "made differences helpful rather than hurtful." Since the organization's first directorship under John May, the San Francisco Foundation Award has annually recognized notable *individuals* whose lives reflected that early expression of valuing diversity. Second, although the Koshland Awards Program preceded the start of Paley's directorship in the mid-1970s, it exemplified his ideal of multiracial community in its identifica-tion of *neighborhoods* in need of "community," or what sociologists presently term social capital. The Koshland Program has pursued its goal of, as a trustee quipped, "turning residents into neighbors" by identifying unsung neighborhood heroes, convening them, and giving each a personal award and the discretion to direct a small grant to a community-based organiza-tion. The Foundation's third director, Robert Fisher, significantly updated its individualistic focus in 1990 with the Multicultural Fellows Program. Foster-ing the supply of what I termed inclusive expertise, the program seeks to improve the pipeline for people of color into professional philanthropy by recruiting activists into one-year internships, where they directly assist the Foundation's program executives and learn about the practice of philan-thropy. Despite the organization's innovative diversity programming, how-ever, its focus on entry-level inclusiveness and group empowerment regret-tably suggests how removed the San Francisco Foundation has been from the major institutions in its local political system.

This chapter examines the development of foundation policy in a high-immigration metropolitan region on the West Coast and tells the story of how the San Francisco Foundation chose to gingerly handle its local non-profit sector as a wild garden. Without significant local allies, the San Francisco philanthropy responded to the sudden population changes mainly by encouraging its grantee organizations to adopt inclusiveness as a value. I discuss the Foundation's evolving culture, racial/ethnic priorities, relations with grant-seeking nonprofits, and *distance from* local politics by comparing the administrations of its first three executive directors: John May, Martin Paley, and Robert Fisher, all White males. This chapter relies on in-depth interviews in the San Francisco Bay Area; transcripts of oral history interviews (History 1974) with May and Foundation trustees, archived at the Bancroft Library of the University of California–Berkeley; and thirty years of the Foundation's annual reports.[1]

First, I introduce the San Francisco Bay Area by outlining its historically recent demographic characteristics, economic fortunes, and the racial/ethnic character of its neighborhoods, especially in the city of San Francisco. Second, I introduce the San Francisco Foundation by discussing its origins and the changing ethnoracial composition of its staff and trustees. In brief, the Foundation staff shifted from White and Black men to include Asians, Latinos, and, as in Cleveland, a female majority. Meanwhile, the trustees shifted from exclusively White with a minority of women to include Asians, Blacks, and Latinos in an equally balanced trinity of White men, White women, and people of color. Third, I discuss in turn the three directorships, highlighting, on the one hand, their respective managerial styles and racial priorities and, on the other hand, their relations with external actors and the local events that informed their decisions and dispositions. I argue that local circumstances limited the Foundation's range of predictable and reliable allies and inhibited the attention of national foundations and federal actors. Over the course of three decades, the Bay Area's continual flux of insurgent politics has produced an urban antiregime in San Francisco and modeled a hyperpluralist culture for the rest of the metropolitan area. By curbing corporate power, these political trends ironically have also reduced the Foundation's leverage in addressing socioeconomic strains and improving civic participation and intergroup relations. I close with a discussion of how a locally high level of political democracy has unfortunately underdeveloped the foundation with the greater demographic opportunity for diversity policy, pressuring the organization to accommodate rather than reshape its urban setting.

The San Francisco Bay Area

In the popular imagination, the San Francisco Bay Area is the leading edge of political innovations, lifestyle diversity, and race relations. By contrast, Cleveland is viewed as a midwestern backwater. Few representations of this alleged difference are as direct as Armisted Maupin's *Tales of the City*, a multivolume chronicle of fictional lives in San Francisco in the late 1970s and early 1980s.[2] In the first volume, a major character arrives from, in fact, Cleveland. Like the western frontier, San Francisco invites her to project dreams of a brave new future. After many weeks of difficult adjustments, this White female transplant almost returns home but changes her mind when her mother calls as her new friends are pleading with her to stay. Her mother becomes outraged at hearing a male voice answer the phone and promptly lectures her grown daughter, "You shouldn't let strange men answer your phone, Mary Ann!" In a declaration of independence that ends the first volume, Mary Ann retorts, "He's not a stranger, mother. He's a homosexual!" She resolves to begin her new life, still ambivalent about San Francisco's apparent lack of social rules but feeling more sure of her new aversion to the intolerant and unexciting milieu of Cleveland, Ohio.

While the Cleveland economy was losing jobs, the San Francisco Bay Area economy was benefiting from the post–World War II population movement from the East and Midwest to the West and Southwest and the associated economic shift from manufacturing to services (Mollenkopf 1983; DeLeon 1992). In particular, San Francisco became a national center for advanced corporate services, and San Jose became a major capital for the high-technology industry. Located on a peninsula, the core city of San Francisco experienced in a distinctive fashion the national phenomena of urban renewal, suburbanization, and White flight. In brief, the White middle class has held the city by effectively dislocating the poor to Oakland and other cities in the metropolitan area, while suburbs have also emerged *between* San Francisco, Oakland, and San Jose rather than only *outside* city centers as spreading rings of settlement. As a "community of communities," therefore, the region combines not only many ethnoracial groups but also multiple and intersecting political centers and peripheries.

Although the region is now perceived as synonymous with the celebration of ethnic, racial, sexual, and lifestyle diversity, intergroup conflicts also pervade the region's history. Like the state of California as a whole, the San Francisco Bay Area has long been imbued with a reputation for racial tolerance and yet has also witnessed episodes of intense racial conflict. Because of

TABLE 9 Nativity and Ethnoracial Characteristics of the
San Francisco Bay Area, 1960–2000 (U.S. Census)

SAN FRANCISCO BAY AREA					
	1960	1970	1980	1990	2000
Total population	2,783,359	3,109,519	3,250,630	3,686,592	4,123,740
Percent foreign-born	**10.8**	**11.0**	**15.7**	**21.1**	**56.0**
Percent White[1]	**87.5**	**82.8**	**66.1**	**58.9**	**49.0**
White	2,436,665	2,574,802	2,150,136	2,172,251	2,021,516
Black[2]	238,754	330,107	385,410	415,292	382,195
Native American[3]	3,883	12,011	18,136	16,911	13,315
Asian American and Pacific Islander[4]	98,897	164,627	325,619	582,823	807,722
Other[5]	5,160	27,972	19,631	6,298	165,648
Hispanic[6]	n/a	n/a	351,698	493,017	733,344

SAN FRANCISCO CITY					
	1960	1970	1980	1990	2000
Total population	740,316	715,673	678,974	723,959	776,733
Percent foreign-born	**19.3**	**21.6**	**28.3**	**34.0**	**36.8**
Percent White[1]	**81.6**	**71.4**	**52.3**	**46.8**	**43.6**
White	604,403	511,186	355,161	338,917	338,886
Black[2]	74,383	96,078	84,857	76,944	57,819
Native American[3]	1,068	2,900	3,548	2,621	2,054
Asian American and Pacific Islander[4]	58,236	95,095	147,426	207,457	241,976
Other[5]	2,226	10,415	4,609	1,380	26,433
Hispanic[6]	n/a	n/a	83,373	96,640	109,565

OAKLAND CITY					
	1960	1970	1980	1990	2000
Total population	367,548	361,607	339,337	372,242	399,477
Percent foreign-born	**9.6**	**8.9**	**12.5**	**19.8**	**26.6**
Percent White[1]	**73.6**	**59.0**	**34.8**	**28.5**	**23.4**
White	270,253	213,512	118,088	105,927	93,613
Black[2]	83,618	124,710	157,314	160,640	139,254
Native American[3]	1,166	2,890	2,199	1,695	1,475
Asian American and Pacific Islander[4]	11,676	17,373	26,341	53,818	62,227
Other[5]	565	3,076	2,903	895	15,465
Hispanic[6]	n/a	n/a	32,492	49,267	87,443

TABLE 9 (continued)

1. Whites are "non-Hispanic Whites" only for 1980, 1990, and 2000.

2. Blacks were reported as "Negro" in the 1960 and 1970 censuses.

3. Native Americans were reported as "Indians" in 1960 and 1970, as "American Indian" separately from Eskimo and Aleut in 1990, and as "American Indian" in aggregate with Alaskan Natives in 1990 and 2000. Alaskan Natives were reported as "Eskimo" and "Aleut" separately in 1980 and in aggregate with American Indians in 1990 and 2000.

4. Asian Americans were reported separately as Japanese, Chinese, or Filipino in 1960 and 1970; as those three categories plus separate categories for Filipino, Korean, Asian Indian, and Vietnamese in 1980; in aggregate with Pacific Islanders in 1990; and in aggregate but separately from Pacific Islanders in 2000. Pacific Islanders were reported separately as Hawaiian, Guamanian, and Samoan in 1980; in aggregate with Asian Americans in 1990; and in aggregate but separately from Asian Americans in 2000.

5. Multiracials are aggregated with "Other" because they were enumerated separately only in 2000.

6. Hispanics were not enumerated separately in the 1960 and 1970 censuses and were reported as "Spanish Origin" in the 1980 census. As a result, the 1960 and 1970 statistics for the "Other" category may include significant proportions of Hispanics.

Sources: U.S. Bureau of the Census 1964a, 1964b, 1964c, 1964d, 1973a, 1973b, 1973c, 1973d, 1981a, 1981b, 1981c, 1981d, 1993a, 1993b, 2000a, 2000b, 2000c. For metropolitan area data, I employed the San Francisco–Oakland Standard Metropolitan Statistical Areas for 1960, 1970, and 1980; the combined San Francisco and Oakland Primary Metropolitan Statistical Areas (PMSA) for 1990; and the combined San Francisco and Oakland PMSAs of the San Francisco–Oakland–San Jose Consolidated Metropolitan Statistical Area for 2000. For city data, I employed the San Francisco and Oakland Urban Places for 1960, 1970, and 1980 and the San Francisco and Oakland city components of the above PMSAs for 1990 and 2000.

a century of federal restrictions on immigration, the consolidated population of San Francisco and Oakland was only 10.8 percent foreign-born in 1960, only 1 percent more than Cleveland's 9.7 percent foreign-born population. By 1990, however, while the midwestern metropolitan area had fallen to 5 percent foreign-born, the Bay Area had risen to 21.1 percent (U.S. Bureau of the Census 1964a, 1964b, 1973a, 1973b, 1981a, 1981b, 1993a, 1993b). Table 9 details the shifts in nativity and ethnoracial composition for the San Francisco–Oakland metropolitan area and its respective major cities from 1960 to 2000. Although its current diversity is a relatively new phenomenon, demographic transformation is not new in the state's history. Indeed, the regional population was far more foreign-born just a century earlier, when U.S. settlers engulfed native Mexicans at the close of the U.S.-Mexican War (1846–1848).

Although the region's major community foundation has sought to cope with interracial and interethnic tensions, the scale of its efforts has been surprisingly modest given the region's quite positive economic fortunes of recent decades. One might argue that the Foundation's emphasis on changing cultural values is a unique mission that cannot be measured in monetary terms. Furthermore, the relative success of the regional economy and its reputation for social tolerance may have undermined the popular imperative (and even the "objective" need) for coordinated action on race relations.

The continuing racial and ethnic character of its neighborhoods, however, suggests the inadequacy of an economic attitudinal explanation for the Foundation's chaotic ethnoracial priorities. San Francisco and Oakland are not as residentially segregated as Cleveland and other eastern cities, but their neighborhoods do exhibit moderate to very high levels of segregation. The segregation of local Blacks, Asians, and Latinos all rival or surpass the highest levels historically experienced by European ethnics in northeastern cities (Massey and Denton 1993). More recently, over 60 percent of Blacks and Whites would have to move to another neighborhood to achieve an equal distribution with each other—61 percent in San Francisco and 63 percent in Oakland—in contrast with 77 percent in Cleveland. For Latinos and Whites, the Bay Area figures are 54 percent in San Francisco and 48 percent in Oakland, somewhat less segregated than Cleveland's 58 percent. For Asians and Whites, however, the regional difference is reversed, with lower segregation in Cleveland, where only 38 percent of Asians and Whites would have to move in comparison with 49 percent in San Francisco and 42 percent in Oakland (Lewis Mumford Center 2002b, 2002c).

That said, most levels of group isolation are less extreme and more moderated in the Bay Area. Measures of Black isolation from non-Blacks and White isolation from non-Whites are both dramatically lower in the Bay Area. The average Black person lives in a neighborhood that is 23 percent Black in San Francisco and 35 percent Black in Oakland, whereas the average Black Clevelander lives in a 71 percent Black neighborhood. Similarly, the average White person lives in a neighborhood that is 65 percent White in San Francisco and 61 percent White in Oakland, whereas the average White Clevelander lives in an 88 percent White neighborhood. By contrast, Latino and Asian isolation from other groups is higher in the Bay Area than in Cleveland. The average Latino individual lives in a 34 percent Latino neighborhood in San Francisco and a 30 percent Latino neighborhood in Oakland, whereas her counterpart in Cleveland lives in a 17 percent Latino neighborhood. The average Asian individual lives in a 40 percent Asian neighborhood in San Francisco and a 29 percent Asian neighborhood in

Oakland, whereas her counterpart in Cleveland lives in a 5 percent Asian neighborhood (Lewis Mumford Center 2002b, 2002c).

In optimistic terms, Bay Area Blacks and Whites have more opportunities for cross-racial interaction, and their fellow Asian and Latino residents have more opportunities for coethnic community. Indeed, every group in the Bay Area is less isolated from others than Whites and Blacks in Cleveland, and every group is less isolated from coethnics than Asians and Latinos in Cleveland. More pessimistically, though, the self-segregation of Whites remains high, especially in certain neighborhoods. Indeed, affluent Whites are perhaps the most residentially isolated group; as in other parts of California, certain Whites have constructed "islands" such as gated communities (Davis 1990; Maharidge 1996), with demographics widely variant from the broader metropolitan area. In brief, beneath the reputation of an integrated region (in an integrated state) lies evidence of continuing segregation, whether of a social nature amid relative residential desegregation or of a neospatial "fortress" version of eastern residential segregation.

Instead of interpreting less ambitious diversity policy as reflecting less need, I advance an institutional account for the culturally sophisticated but substantively shallow character of the San Francisco Foundation's policies. Despite the extensive and complex balkanization within the region, its institutional and political environment has diminished the availability of reliable allies with whom the Foundation could pursue citywide initiatives addressing its surrounding demographic diversity.

The San Francisco Foundation: From Predominantly White Male to Predominantly White (1948–1997)

Three major actors are credited with creating the San Francisco Foundation: two local foundations, the Rosenberg Foundation and the Columbia Foundation, and one individual, Daniel Koshland of the Haas family, the heirs of Bavarian immigrant Levi Strauss, the founder of the apparel giant still headquartered in San Francisco. In 1948, Koshland chaired the Exploratory Committee, whose members prepared the Foundation's incorporation, hired John Rickard May as the new Foundation's first director, and created a Distribution Committee that made disbursement decisions. In later decades, the Distribution Committee would rename itself the board of trustees.

Koshland and his Exploratory Committee founded the organization largely in the mold pioneered by the Cleveland Foundation, with a seven-member board, each appointed by the head of a major local institution: the president of the United Community Fund of San Francisco, the president of the San Francisco Chamber of Commerce, the president of the University of California, the trustee banks, the president of Stanford University, the chief judge of the 9th Judicial Circuit, U.S. Court of Appeals, and the president of the League of Women Voters of San Francisco. As modeled by the Cleveland Foundation, their appointments were formally for five years but usually ran ten years, since they could be renewed once. Two major divergences from the Cleveland model would foreshadow significant differences between the foundations: the single appointment, instead of multiple, controlled by the banks in which the philanthropy invested its endowments and the absence of a mayoral appointee.

Like the Cleveland Foundation, the San Francisco Foundation also started with primarily White male leadership. During the 1970s, however, organizational expansion resulted in dramatic changes in the racial, ethnic, and gender composition of foundation staff, paralleling the geometrically increasing presence of post-1965 immigrants in the Bay Area. By comparison, similar shifts in trustee diversity did not begin until the mid-1980s, as the larger foundation field was consolidating its reaction to the conservative climate heralded by the Reagan administration. Tellingly, the appointment of non-Black non-White trustees started even later, in the 1990s, during and after the publication of the special issue on philanthropic pluralism. Ironically, the rising ethnoracial diversity among the staff and trustees did not encourage the Foundation to become in the 1970s and 1980s the source of the strategic interventions promoted by the field magazine as philanthropic pluralism. Instead, the San Francisco Foundation's racial policies developed in ways corresponding to its early prediversification tendency for making niche contributions rather than seeking to lead its region. Not until much later did the Foundation begin fostering the style of bicultural leadership among non-Whites, termed inclusive expertise in chapter 2 and favored by the Cleveland Foundation since the 1960s.

1948–1973: AN EARLY MODEL FOR FEMALE AND BLACK INCLUSION

In its initial decades, the San Francisco Foundation remained a small philanthropy in comparison to its eventual potential and growth. The first trustees endeavored to train their new director because he had little familiarity with the philanthropic world in San Francisco. John R. May directed the organization with administrative support staff but no program staff until 1968, when he hired Llewellyn ("Lou") White to be his associate director. In 1971, he hired Rudy Glover to be his assistant director; Glover became simultaneously the first person of color, man of color, and African American to join the Foundation staff. By contrast, the Cleveland Foundation in 1973 had a staff of thirteen, eight of whom were dedicated to program activities but only one of whom was non-White.

Impressively, the first Distribution Committee in 1948 included two women, both White. By 1960, three White women sat on the seven-member board, including its chair, Helen Russell, who is noted in the annual reports as Mrs. Henry Potter Russell. Stanford University appointed Ira D. Hall, the board's first African American member in 1971, the same year May hired Glover. By then, female representation on the board had dropped to one, Mrs. Charles Kuhn, the appointee of the League of Women Voters. Thus, it was not until the early 1970s that the staff and trustees would begin to resemble the model of diversity that the Foundation would come to symbolize for the foundation field.

1974–1985: NON-BLACK, NON-WHITE, AND NONBANK DIVERSIFICATION

Both Lou White and Rudy Glover would remain on staff after May retired in 1973. The trustees subsequently hired Martin Paley to be executive director. After Glover retired in 1976, Paley hired Bernice Brown as a program executive; she became the first African American woman to join the staff. The subsequent incorporation of very large trusts in the late 1970s, most notably the Buck Trust, provided Paley the opportunity to expand his staff tremendously. In 1979, he hired an assistant director, three additional program executives, including the first Latino and the first Asian American, and two program associates. Within a single year, Brown went from being the only woman and only person of color on a staff of three to a member of the female majority of a staff of nine with three people of color. Before 1980, both the San Francisco Foundation and the Cleveland Foundation had thus transitioned to a largely female professional staff. As an indication of foundation leadership in professional integration, Paley brought the first Asian and the first Latino professionals to the national meetings of the Council on Foundations. He continued to expand his staff to its peak in 1985 with sixteen directors and program executives in addition to eleven program associates, a total program staff of twenty-seven, including Paley.

During Paley's directorship, the trustees experienced changes as their appointments ended or as they retired, in addition to a significant structural change. In 1974, the University of California appointed Rhoda Goldman, who became the first female trustee to have her own first name listed in the annual reports and whose presence lifted White female representation on the board back to two of seven members. In 1976, the same year Paley hired Brown, Stanford replaced Ira Hall with Charles ("Chuck") J. Patterson, another African American man. In 1979, the League of Women Voters replaced Mrs. Charles Kuhn with Mrs. Lawrence Metcalf, whom the annual reports changed to Susan S. Metcalf in 1982. Later, in 1984, the University of California replaced Rhoda Goldman with Joan F. Lane, keeping two White women on board. Last but hardly least, by 1985, the trustee banks gave up their collective appointing authority to the Distribution Committee, which then brought on its second African American trustee, Robert C. Maynard. By contrast, the trustee banks of the Cleveland Foundation have retained not one but multiple appointment positions on their Foundation's board.

In 1986, the departure of the enormous Buck Trust to its separate existence as the Marin Community Foundation was also the occasion for Paley's retirement and the departure of many other staff. In the late 1970s, the arrival of the Buck Trust had made the Foundation the second-largest community foundation in the United States; however, it carried the provision that its grants had to be made in Marin, which was reputed to be one of the richest counties in the nation. In the mid-1980s, when the Foundation attempted to change the bequest in court and distribute a fraction of the trust to the other four counties within its definition of the San Francisco Bay Area, Marin County officials took them to court and fought them to the settlement that created the Marin Community Foundation.

1986–1997: TRUSTEE DIVERSIFICATION

After making Associate Director Mort Raphael the acting director for 1986, the trustees hired Robert Fisher as Paley's replacement in 1987. Fisher's initial staff was significantly smaller than Paley's peak staff but also larger than Paley's initial staff: six of Paley's program executives plus a promotion of one of the former program associates to the seventh program executive position. By 1989, five of these executives had left the Foundation (two Whites, two Latinas, and one Asian American). By 1990, Fisher had replaced them with three executives (two Whites and one Asian American), three program coordinators (two Whites and one African American), and four program associates (two Whites, one Latino, and one Latina), a total program staff of thirteen, including Fisher.

In 1988, the seven-member Distribution Committee became the seven-member board of trustees. The representation of women remained at two members, who were then joined by Mary Lee Widener, the first African American woman, whom the board appointed to replace Robert Maynard in 1988. By that time, Charles Patterson had completed his ten years, and Stanford University had replaced him with Leonard Kingsley, a White male. In 1990, the 9th Circuit would replace Peter H. Behr with Herman Gallegos, the first Latino ever appointed to the board.

Gallegos's early and controversial resignation in 1992 would provoke significant changes in the organization. In 1993, the 9th Circuit gave up its appointing authority to the board of trustees, who appointed David J. Sanchez Jr. to replace Gallegos. In addition, the board added an eighth position to itself and appointed Roland C. Lowe, the first ever Asian American trustee. A year later, the board increased its membership again with a ninth position and appointed Leslie F. Hume, a White woman.

Over the history of the San Francisco Foundation, a majority of White males on the board of trustees has been replaced by a majority of Whites. In 1948, the Distribution Committee had been five White men and two White women. In 1994, the board of trustees was three White men, three White women, a Black woman, an Asian American man, and a Latino man. As on the Cleveland board, White trustees have remained in a significant majority, falling only from all seven members to six of nine. In contrast with Cleveland, however, White male trustees are no longer in the majority.

The May Years (1948–1973): Constructing a Niche for the "Pure" Foundation

A lot of people were changed by the war, got new directions. I could never have been happy going back into the area of sales management and that kind of thing . . . because of [my wartime experience with] doing a job that had to be done. After all, what is it if you're selling something [vacuum cleaners]—what real good does it do? . . . I came into this job not knowing—practically not knowing—what the word "philanthropic" meant. I had a good deal of learning to do, and that took quite a long time.—John May, History 1974

When Dan Koshland considered candidates for the Foundation's first executive directorship, he initially sought Frank Sloss, an attorney who "could relate to the big shots" in the city. Instead of accepting the offer, Sloss referred him to his friend John May, who had worked in the Office of Price Administration during and after World War II. May accepted the eventual offer in order to move back to the Bay Area, where he had grown up, and to avoid returning to the sales work he had done before the war. May knew that he wanted socially meaningful work but was unfamiliar with not only the concept of a community trust but also the philanthropic infrastructure of San Francisco. Perhaps because of his inexperience with philanthropy and local elites, his board treated him mainly as a custodian of numerous bequests to come. As a result, the Foundation's initial decades involved philanthropic interventions that were rarely strategic; although individual grants were notable, in the aggregate they appeared quite inchoate.

MANAGEMENT STYLE

May's directorship was largely passive in style, centering on proposal review and response, with the important exception of mission development. He devoted significant energy to defining a "good" grant or trust in contrast to a "bad" grantee that already had sufficient backers. The San Francisco Foundation was to be a "pure" foundation, in contrast to the private family and corporate foundations, that is, "looking for the best place to put its money regardless of whose back gets scratched" (May, History 1974). For advice, he first relied on an advisory committee that would meet for dinners at the homes of trustees, though later he cultivated his own pool of experts and professional colleagues. In one special instance, a trust required the San Francisco Foundation to study how best to address the financial needs of cancer patients and even to start up the program to receive the grants; however, such hands-on grant making seemed rare.

Over time, as he added White and Glover to the staff, May spent less time on proposal review and more on "working with the banks and the potential donors and with tax matters and lawyers and with accountants and all that kind of thing" (History 1974). He and the board dealt with the Foundation's relatively small resources by frequently dipping into the principal of the endowment for grants. Asset development was likewise passive, mostly waiting for potential donors to pass away and their bequests to mature. Not surprisingly, his management style fit with a regional philanthropic preference for reaction and response instead of setting agendas for others, a notion viewed as ethically unacceptable.

RACIAL PRIORITIES

During May's directorship, the San Francisco Foundation adhered to an informal racial policy of passive exceptionalism. He took pride in "taking risks" with minority organizations whose proposals, in his estimation, were objectively inferior to most other grant proposals except for those in the arts. That his donors were idiosyncratic in their orientation to minorities hardly facilitated a more proactive stance. The fund that established the Western Office of the NAACP Legal Defense and Education Fund (the Inc. Fund) arose from motives that might be described as bizarre: the donor identified with the situation of Negroes because he felt he had been discriminated against as a landlord who had to confront rent control codes. Otherwise, the San Francisco Foundation followed national trends in providing funding for the Urban League, who in 1953 was the recipient of its first grant for racial minorities.

Relatively speaking, the San Francisco Foundation was quite insulated from racial politics. May mentions one incident (during a visit to a Black-run nonprofit) in his directorship that frightened him but that made no real impact on his policies. The Foundation simply responded to the flow of grant proposals by organizations working for antidiscrimination in housing, promoting minority businesses, and surveying ethnic relations. Rarely did the Foundation act in a concerted and strategic way about race or any other priority; however, it provided long-term operating support for the Inc. Fund, and, in a rare proactive instance, May asked Glover to identify the best sickle cell anemia research projects in the area.[3]

The most prominent of its racial programs was in fact the aforementioned awards program, which also possessed idiosyncratic donor origins. The San Francisco Foundation Award was a present to Daniel Koshland from his wife, though he declined to have the program bear his name. Though the San Francisco Foundation Award is only one program, it crystallizes the Foundation's goal for race relations as a matter of "getting along" and "valuing difference," a conception that is both more sophisticated and less substantial than the Cleveland Foundation's goal of strengthening the role of the Black community.

RELATIONSHIPS WITH EXTERNAL ACTORS

With respect to the foundation field, May maintained three relationships: (1) an identity differentiation that righteously marked the San Francisco Foundation as a "pure" foundation; (2) knowledge sharing among the profession, especially locally; and (3) a sense of California marginalization from the regional core of the field in New York. In terms of the San Francisco Foundation's identity, he strongly distinguished, on the one hand, the "self-interested" private and corporate foundations and, on the other hand, the "pure" national and community foundations, in which he included private foundations such as the local Rosenberg Foundation because of its community focus. As a "foundation man," May saw himself as something of an eternal student because he believed that one could never know enough about a subject: "You find somebody who will know where to go to ask the right questions about a particular proposal and if possible, even who are the people to ask them of" (May, History 1974).

Especially in relation to racial priorities, he distinguished the role of the San Francisco Foundation from the role of corporate philanthropy, even in the personal activities of himself and his board. He acknowledged that a racial policy slowly did emerge, in that "an overwhelming proportion of our grants goes to support efforts to try to equalize opportunity in every way" (May, History 1974). Furthermore, he asserted that the board's willingness to deal with gross social inequalities should have been seen as even more courageous because they would not do so in their professional lives. "I don't think you ought to take stockholders' money and put it into risk capital kind of ventures. On the other hand, I think real foundation money ought to do just that . . . And the reverse of that: 'oh, I don't think this is anything for the foundation to look at at all, but I'm going to go home and write them a check.' " In brief, foundations should support *cutting-edge* efforts such as those addressing race and inequality, whereas corporate and personal philanthropy should stay in *stable organizations.* By differentiating rather than connecting these two forms of philanthropy, May created an ideological niche for the San Francisco Foundation. Either unable or unwilling to take leadership of San Francisco philanthropy, he revealed the absence of a broader consensus around the place of racial philanthropy in San Francisco.

Even without a broader consensus among the donors, May shared professional relations with fellow grant-making staff in both the region and the nation. His familiarity with the professional literature of that time demonstrated his connection to the field's debates. Regionally, the San Francisco Foundation would collaborate with other foundations, albeit primarily to share foundation staff expertise rather than to pool grant dollars. Because the Babcock Endowment was dedicated to health in Marin, May claimed he would "invariably go to [Babcock's director] Julie for advice [for evaluating related projects]. So she has a very substantial effect on our grants in Marin, whether it's health, mental health, or anything allied" (History 1974). He especially cited the Rosenberg Foundation as the other philanthropy with which the San Francisco Foundation had done the most mutual consulting. And May cited the meetings of the National Council on Community Foundations as a regular source of updates on specific community issues for himself and even individual board members who occasionally attended.

Although he could not be sure whether the San Francisco Foundation's involvement in community development ever affected federal discourse or how federal monies affected Foundation priorities, he felt sure that the Foundation's experiences with that field had been added to the foundation field's debates and that the latter had shaped the San Francisco Foundation's priorities in return. Professionalism was nearly synonymous with the knowledge distributed and debated at the regular field conferences.

By the 1970s, his relationship with the Council on Foundations appeared strained, ironically so, given that he claimed to be a founding member of the original association and its oldest living board member. He had been present in three important moments in the Council's history: when it began as the National Committee on Community Foundations, when it expanded to the National Council on Community Philanthropy by including locally oriented foundations such as the Rosenberg Foundation, and when it finally expanded to include all foundations who adhered to particular professional standards. When he began his directorship, he found other organizational practices tremendously useful for the San Francisco Foundation, but by the end of his San Francisco Foundation career, he found himself outside "the inner circle in the foundation world . . . [which he attributed to] . . . Partly geography, and partly because I'm a little bit inclined not to take the party line" (May, History 1974). In the 1970s, the COF lobbied to have the 6 percent payout requirement reduced to 5 percent. May opposed such efforts, although he agreed with the Council's other lobbying effort to obtain a reduced tax on foundation income. Asked whether Californians in the foundation world felt cut off in comparison to New Yorkers and those in Washington, D.C., May emphatically agreed: "We get damned little service out of the Council in proportion to the very large budget on which they operate. I think most of us think that if we were in Pennsylvania or Boston or New Jersey or somewhere close, we'd get a hell of a lot more attention" (May, History 1974). Despite the admittedly "helpful exchange of ideas, papers, project ideas, and success" (May, History 1974), something seemed to be missing.

In light of May's perception of a neglect of attention from the COF, the San Francisco Foundation's relative distance from the major national foundations is not surprising. On the one hand, May identified the San Francisco Foundation with the national foundations as the grouping of pure foundations. On the other hand, Ford chose to make grants in Oakland, not San Francisco, during the 1960s with its Gray Areas Program. Gabrielle Morris (History 1974) asked May, "Were there any negotiations with Ford as to which community they would pick?" May replied, "I'm sure there were, but I wasn't in on it. We weren't in on it; the foundation wasn't in on it. I think they had people out across the country to pick them, and I suppose many communities were fighting for the chance" (History 1974). In sum, the San Francisco Foundation was left out of the loop for the grants Ford used to promote its brand of community philanthropy during the 1950s and 1960s.

On occasion, the San Francisco Foundation did collaborate with Ford on projects that Ford would initiate and request local contributions. In actuality, May experienced these "collaborations" as impositions, observing that grantees would approach him saying, "Look, give us $20,000; you're giving us $100,000 in effect. We can't get the rest without you. How can you turn it down, if it's a good program" (History 1974). Asked how he responded to such pressure, May replied, "You give up. You turn up your toes and roll over on your back. Wave your paws in the air" (History 1974). When grantees used Ford's legitimacy against the San Francisco Foundation, May and his board felt greatly pressured to conform, though they did not always do so. He pointed to one actual collaboration as proof of how Ford's "good program" might differ from what he would promote:

> I'm not very proud of that Black House [a grant that had already received Ford money and was anticipating federal HEW money in short order] . . . I went over to look at the Black House program with Dick, and I was really kind of appalled. I didn't think it was doing what it ought to do. I was really kind of dreadfully shocked, in my old, conservative, white man's way. I sat in the back of the room in a creative writing class, and to hear and see a perfectly charming, teenage girl get up and read her contribution to the class, which was poetry, and all the four-letter words and all the rest of it tumbling out, and not just the words, but the actions they implied. I just thought, in my view, that was doing at least as much harm as it was good . . . Not because it was revolutionary and that kind of thing, but because the deliberate obscenity of both the thought and the words I don't think add anything. I think they didn't want to be good. (John May, History 1974)

May would have preferred race-relations grants that were more genteel or at least whose style did not deviate substantially from his personal culture. He associated Ford support with a loss of local control, at least on the part of his foundation. He claimed to prefer in-house grants for their investment in staff time for researching and monitoring projects, though ironically, he did not have program staff for extensive proposal review until the early 1970s, toward the end of his directorship. The absurdity he associated with the procedures of national foundations is epitomized in his comments on the program areas (e.g., health, arts, welfare) employed by the nationals. He stressed that although the San Francisco Foundation employed the same language, it used them as categories, not separate programs, because in actual implementation the projects often crossed such professionally defined boundaries. If policymaking was really about restrictive classifications, he wanted no part of it.

The Foundation's relationship with the federal government was likewise passive under May's directorship. The Tax Reform Act of 1969 was a boon for the nation's many community foundations. Not only did it leave them free of the new restrictions placed on private foundations, but those new restrictions also encouraged many private foundations to give up their independent status to become trusts within community foundations. Although May was a senior board member of the Council on Foundations, he did not testify in Washington on behalf of the community foundation movement and thus did not directly contribute to federal discourse about regulating philanthropy. The San Francisco Foundation's subsequent absorption of former private foundations was largely exogenous to the Foundation's locally oriented priorities. On a similar note, May was skeptical of the presence of both national foundations and federal monies that seemed to pour into the San Francisco Bay Area in the late 1960s and early 1970s. He raised questions about who was in charge, who was responsible, and who would have to pick up the pieces after the money was gone. He recognized successful collaborations with national actors, but he dwelled on the unsuccessful ones, such as Black House. He observed that national legitimacy came with substantial dollars but much less quality, by his own admittedly "conservative white man" definition of quality.

If his relationship with national foundations and the federal government was passive, his relationship with local government seemed nonexistent. The San Francisco Foundation supported grantees who themselves worked with local government authorities, but it did not convene these actors under its own initiative. Its closest connection with local politics was through supporting the San Francisco Planning and Urban Renewal Association (spur) and its predecessor, the San Francisco Planning and Housing Association, which urban renewal advocates criticized as "completely inadequate." According to Mollenkopf (1983), the business leaders of the Blyth-Zellerbach Committee organized spur as a more powerful alternative to the older association, getting it named the official citizens advisory committee of the San Francisco

Redevelopment Agency. "SPUR helped build a middle-class, professional constituency on behalf of renewal" (168). May seemed aware only of its technical functions, partially because he "tried to stay out of any direct connection with any agency that would logically be expected to approach us for a grant" (May, History 1974). Indeed, unlike his Cleveland contemporary, he viewed his presence on potential grantee boards as distorting his objectivity and undermining his conception of pure philanthropy.

May later described the Foundation's involvement with SPUR quite at variance with scholarly accounts of its role in San Francisco urban renewal (Mollenkopf 1983): "We put quite a lot of money into quite a lot of SPUR neighborhood programs, but it wasn't only that . . . Some work done . . . was carried on by the Saul Alinsky method" (May, History 1974).[4] In sum, May attributed to SPUR the kind of activism that resisted SPUR's agenda in downtown development plans because their benefits did not trickle down to residential neighborhoods, because they destroyed neighborhoods near downtown, such as the predominantly Black and historically Japanese American Western Addition, and/or because their promised neighborhood investments never materialized or were insufficient (Mollenkopf 1983). Whether as a business whip for middle-class support of downtown development or as a neighborhood tool against further downtown development, SPUR seemed to possess a separate agenda from the San Francisco Foundation and whatever leadership the Foundation might have convened.

Whether his board members knew of SPUR's importance and central role in the dominant urban regime promoting renewal is not evident from May's oral history. Their ignorance of these developments seems unlikely, as they were among the social and economic elites of San Francisco. Regardless, it is clear that the Foundation was not the primary organization to convene civic leadership in the city.

THE URBAN CONTEXT

Under its first directorship, the Foundation made a virtue of its isolation from professional philanthropy, an orientation that may also have led it to isolate itself locally. On the other hand, May confronted in his region an extreme level of political instability, surpassing Cleveland politics. Given the environment, it is not surprising that May's board did not demand that their first director seek to tame the chaos outside. The San Francisco Bay Area of the 1960s occupies a legendary place in U.S. collective memory for the political activism and countercultures that seemed to erupt during the decade. If one recalls that the 1950s Beat movement also emerged in San Francisco, perhaps it is less surprising that the free speech movement, Haight-Ashbury, and People's Park acquired notoriety in the same region. In contrast to Cleveland's short-lived Black-centered movement of the 1960s, the social environment confronting May's directorship produced a more radical, nationally known, and diverse range of minority and other politics. Furthermore, the latter insurgency did not significantly wane in the late 1960s and was also accompanied by the rise of a local political infrastructure led by neither African Americans nor non-Black non-Whites but by White liberals.

As in other geographies at the time, moderate and radical factions seeking minority advancement were both present in the Bay Area. However, perhaps because San Francisco's at-large council structure raised the expense and effort threshold for political entry, many more political aspirants in the region than in Cleveland chose the route of insurgency over electoral entrism. Spurred by southern civil rights struggles and their revealed limitations for social change, Blacks in the Bay Area formed political vehicles, some of which were common across other northern and western cities and others of which were unique in the nation. Similar to Cleveland's United Freedom Movement, San Francisco produced the San Francisco United Freedom Movement, which worked for desegregation in neighborhoods, schools, and workplaces. Also similar to Ohio's 21st District Caucus, California produced the Black American Political Association of California (BAPAC), members of which some commentators (e.g., Richardson 1996) have characterized as the moderates who made sacrifices to work within "the system" and accomplished real victories. This conventional trope elevates their activities above those of the radicals who made "noise" but were ultimately inconsequential because they produced only short-lived or politically disengaged efforts.

Nevertheless, the Bay Area did produce notable radical efforts with broad and significant effects; perhaps the best known of these projects was the Oakland-based Black Panther Party (BPP). In 1967, the organization gained national notoriety for its trip to the state capital in Sacramento, where its members entered the state legislature carrying unloaded rifles, and for its shadowing of police officers to monitor their behavior in Black neighborhoods and their treatment of African Americans. Though usually identified as a primarily radical organization, the BPP actually combined cultural politics, most evident in its famous ten-point platform, with both social service programs and electoral candidacy. In addition, its formation inspired affiliated or similar organizations for other groups such as Chicanos, Chinese Americans, Puerto Rican Americans, White leftists, and even senior citizens (i.e., the Gray Panthers).

Although popular commentary about the 1960s typically has viewed the year 1968 as the collapse of the "movement," the Bay Area witnessed the continuation of organized, insurgent politics past this date, practically as a new cycle of protest. After the 1965 police beating of a Black man in the Watts neighborhood of Los Angeles, urban riots swept the nation and prompted federal expenditures creating numerous agencies and programs. These new institutions indeed absorbed many civil rights activists into a growing social services infrastructure. In the Bay Area, however, college students initiated mass campus strikes for even broader social changes, first at the predominantly working-class San Francisco State College and then across the Bay at the more middle-class University of California at Berkeley.

In the longest student strike in U.S. history, the State students shut down their campus for five months and demanded, among other goals, the creation of a parallel "school of ethnic studies" with autonomous departments for Black studies, American Indian studies, Chicano studies, and Asian American studies. Although many of the other demands were never met, the institutionalization of ethnic studies at both schools created the precedent for the proliferation of similar units across the country. In addition, the strikes pioneered linkages among the four major ethnoracial movements.

Although minority activism was reliably present, non-White leadership may have been unavailable as partners for the Foundation's initiatives. The intensity of insurgency may have been constantly present, but its cost may have been the consistency of leadership. As in insurgent politics, electoral politics also did not generate consistent local minority leadership. Despite the Bay Area's reputation for liberal-left politics, a Black mayor was elected in Oakland only in 1976 and in San Francisco only in 1995, well after May's directorship. Instead, White Democrats have long led the dominant liberal organization with connections to state politics, the so-called Burton machine, constructed by Philip Burton and maintained by his protégés, younger brother John Burton (also White) and a singular Black politician, Willie Brown. Although Brown received his initial political training in a Black church, he was actually the harbinger of a new form of political leadership, created and sustained by the attention of the media (Richardson 1996). Indeed, his contributions to the insurgent projects of the 1960s appear centered on protests in which he participated by calming activists or assuming leadership to negotiate concessions after activism had already been initiated.

In addition, his style of leadership and early ambitions for higher political office beyond the city would arguably have been incompatible with any citywide foundation initiatives.

Last, those African American leaders who were more entrist-oriented and less media-oriented may not have been in short supply, but rather unavailable to the Foundation because of its still relatively meager resources. Especially in Oakland, these more stable politicians and community leaders may have paid more attention to the dollars and staff of the national foundations, which had decided, as May recalls, to largely exclude the San Francisco Foundation from its deliberations. In brief, its professional and political isolation may have fed its own identity-oriented isolationism.

The Paley Years (1974–1985): Defining Empowerment as Noninterference and Reflection

For its second director, the San Francisco Foundation hired Martin Paley, a public health planner with no foundation experience, to be its first truly strategic leader. Only late in May's directorship had the Foundation amassed a sufficient endowment to permit its directors to conduct the organization in any way comparable to the Cleveland Foundation; however, Paley's Foundation did not follow in Norton's footsteps. The San Francisco Bay Area's changing environment and the Foundation's ideological response would put the organization on a distinct path. Paley used his directorship as an opportunity to *test out certain ideas*, especially about diversity. In particular, he directed the Foundation to encourage community empowerment in a region he viewed as a unique "community of communities."

MANAGEMENT STYLE

Paley saw the San Francisco Foundation's reputation as the most prominent foundation in the Bay Area as an opportunity to be creative and make it a place for people to come and explore ideas, especially problem solvers and artists. He focused on the organization's internal culture, developing an institutional concern with racial and other inclusiveness and an ideological sense of itself as an exception in the foundation field.

Under Paley, the Foundation emphasized the values of leadership development, community-specific needs, and, following May, an aversion to directing others according to its agenda rather than theirs. The Koshland Civic Unity Awards epitomized its stance on race relations under Paley. These awards were both small prizes given to the unrecognized leaders in a community and small grants, which the awardees could direct to favored nonprofit organizations. The 1983 annual report identifies the purpose of the program: "The Koshland Awards Program honors individuals who and organizations which may not be well-known beyond a neighborhood, but who have contributed greatly to help their neighbors in need." Both the San Francisco Foundation Award and the Koshland Awards are connected to Daniel Koshland, the foundation's first chair of the Distribution Committee and a member of the prominent Haas family in the Bay Area. Ironically, the report also reveals the original target of the awards to have been the Western Addition neighborhood, "an area in transition from a predominantly Black working class neighborhood to a more racially and economically diverse community" (1983 Annual Report). The report does not note that the "transition" was the result of an earlier decade's policies of urban renewal, known in some circles as "Negro removal," nor that "more racially and economically diverse" meant White gentrification of the heart of Black San Francisco.

Under Paley's directorship, the Foundation began a series of initiatives that convened other funders and nonprofit agencies on a variety of projects. In fact, collaboration was touted as the preferred way the Foundation would intervene, and Paley delegated most of the efforts to individual staff members, who convened the appropriate actors. In general, Paley began with an explicit commitment to a value such as diversity and then informally allowed that value to inform policy and projects. Although his projects and initiatives maintained a consistency with his lofty values, however, they seemed relatively uncoordinated at a citywide level, much less a regional level.

The Foundation might have eventually begun this greater level of coordination but for the growing complexities of administering the new gargantuan Buck Trust. Prior to the arrival of the Buck, the Foundation received a $30 million trust from Dan Koshland's will, the largest completely unrestricted trust in its history. Though the Buck was originally similar in size, it was donated in the form of stocks which then multiplied in value within scant years. By 1980, the Buck had become the majority of the Foundation's endowment, and yet its trust restrictions limited its grant making to a single county, Marin, at the time one of the wealthiest counties in the entire country. The Foundation responded by making, for the first time, large capital investments, such as the Bear Valley Visitors Center. However, given the "progressive" culture of the San Francisco Foundation, its personnel did not perceive these investments as the best that could be made. One program officer stated quite simply that although the Foundation created some important institutions for middle-class people in Marin, many of those projects would not even have been "competitive" for foundation support in any other county. When the Foundation's board decided to ask the court to change the provisions of the trust, Marin authorities began legal proceedings to remove the San Francisco Foundation from its status as distribution trustee.[5] To prevent further damage to its reputation, the Foundation proposed a settlement to establish an independent community foundation in Marin and transfer the Buck there. Finally, its board asked Paley to resign for the good of the organization. However, even a decade later, past board members praised him for doing the right thing and regarded the court as having been wrong not to accede to their request.

Throughout Paley's directorship, his board supported his management style and objectives. In words very close to Paley's beliefs, Rhoda Goldman wrote in her 1983 statement as chairman of the board for the 1983 annual report: "The basic principles that characterized Dan Koshland's work—a concern for nourishing a commitment to civic unity, a respect for the capacity of people to identify and resolve their own problems, a caring for the enrichment of the individual and a pride in the traditions of the foundation—motivate each current and past member of the Distribution Committee." Whereas a Cleveland trustee had advised his director not to make appeals to values to his board and not to speak as if from a position paper, Goldman's board took pride in such things. Indeed, Goldman asserted in the 1984 annual report, "Position papers were developed on subjects as diverse as public interest law, health education, and the Bay area arts economy. Every other month, the Distribution Committee had the luxury of giving in-depth consideration to major policy issues."

Notwithstanding their expressed passion for meetings, Paley's board members seemed to limit their responsibilities to official Foundation business. One senses in the warning to program executives not to impose their agendas a boundary drawn to protect board members from nonobjective involvement: "Program executives must be out in the field observing, not telling; helping, not directing. The foundation should convene small group discussions to focus on needs in specific areas and members of the Distribution Committee should regularly attend these meetings to better understand the problems and agencies involved" (1984 Annual Report). Through external participation, program officers were to learn the lay of the land, and through selective convening, create situations for trustees to learn the main points of their research. Neither board nor staff, however, were to impose their will directly on the field of nonprofits and social needs itself.

My interviews suggest, however, that Paley perceived the restraint of his board as reluctance "to go out on a limb." Despite their explicit interest in diversity, he felt they resisted his attempts to truly diversify the organization. Considering their decision to bring aboard a "less radical" Black trustee than the candidate he supported, he noted that another trustee of color appointed well after his directorship was also "safer." Although the recent trustee was a recognized leader in his ethnic community, he was also the head of a professional association, whereas Paley's candidate had been the president of a political advocacy organization.

RACIAL PRIORITIES

Overall, Paley's racial priorities were more developed in rationale and mission than in scope and coordination. In his capacity as director, he had less influence with his board than over his staff, with whom he administered grants that focused strongly on low-income people, a priority that he acknowledged as somewhat tangential to racial and ethnic concerns. Instead of developing "ghettoized" racial initiatives, he favored "across the board" consideration of race and ethnicity in all grants. In addition, he implemented a fellowship program to hire individuals in midcareer, who were mostly people of color, to share new perspectives and insights with the Foundation. Finally, he brought his diverse staff with him to foundation field events. In the context of an East Coast– and Midwest–dominated Council on Foundations that conceived of race in terms of Black and White, he felt that his Asian, Latino, and Black staff impressed their counterparts by their intelligence, contributions, and very presence. In sum, Paley significantly built on May's earlier commitments to minority empowerment and internal diversity. Whereas empowerment meant support of civil rights litigation in May's day, in Paley's it meant a broader range of technical attention and assistance and a renewed emphasis on self-help, as epitomized by the Koshland Awards. While internal diversity for May meant one Black male trustee and one Black male staff member, Paley's staff was far more diverse, with Black, Latino, and Asian personnel and a female majority.

RELATIONSHIPS WITH EXTERNAL ACTORS

Although Paley's directorship was more focused and active than May's, its relations with external actors continued the tendency for professional and political isolation. According to my interviews, a strong sense of San Francisco exceptionalism permeated his opinions about foundations and other established private institutions in general. He felt that most foundation actors were "in denial" about the scope of their power and potential for making social change. He observed that although the field shared his foundation's values concerning diversity, other philanthropies were more apt to diversify the issues they handled while resisting the diversification of their staff and boards. He criticized foundations for a host of shortcomings, including being risk-averse and interested in only incremental change, faults that he saw as sins given foundations' relative freedom and lack of formal control by any constituency. He observed that staff were often more conservative than their boards or were too timid to ask their trustees to take risks. Ironically, he also criticized foundation boards for "boring" themselves by staying uninvolved. Most harshly, however, Paley claimed that "the idea that foundations develop ideas for the federal government hasn't been accurate for twenty years" precisely because they had been too risk-averse. By the time Paley had begun his directorship, the San Francisco Foundation was too large for the national foundations to ignore; nevertheless, their collaborations tended to be on a program-by-program basis rather than the extensive effort that launched the Greater Cleveland Associated Foundation in the 1960s.

Despite the sudden election of a conservative Republican president in 1980, the Foundation seemed preoccupied by growing pains associated with its enlarged endowment. With respect to local politics, its five-county focus insulated it from being directly affected; however, its relations with any city hall appeared to be quite distant. Program officers might have had contacts with city department heads, but Paley's directorship did not seek the kind of relationship that the Cleveland Foundation had initiated earlier in the 1960s, all the more surprising given the number of social movements erupting in their environment. However, the passage of California State Proposition 13 in the late 1970s did have a large impact, with the Foundation scrambling to identify its role amid grant recipients in danger of losing government funding and even dying out. Because of the tax revolt and other political upheavals during this time, the Foundation brought in consultants "to tap the wisdom in the community." That the organization sought the input of consultants rather than representatives of civic institutions speaks to its perception of chaos in the region.

THE URBAN CONTEXT

During the directorship of Martin Paley, the San Francisco Foundation elaborated May's concern with foundation purity into an organizational mission to respect the autonomy of the communities within its region. In addition, Paley initiated a value commitment to becoming a more accurate mirror of its increasingly heterogeneous region. In spite of these ultimately lofty and externally oriented missions, the Foundation concentrated its activities on internal diversity and the evaluation of proposals. This relative restraint between its values and actions reflected the Foundation's powerlessness in the face of a persistently unpredictable urban environment. On the one hand, the Foundation succeeded in supporting politically marginalized or disempowered groups (most notably, Asian Americans) and in developing nonprofits to address their respective needs. On the other hand, the Foundation did not attempt to participate in the chaotic events that, beyond the Buck controversy, included the emergence of a broad-based progressive political movement, its culmination in an antiregime united primarily by opposition to corporate control of urban space, and the surprising ascension of a Black politician, Willie Brown, into the speakership of the state legislature, perhaps the most powerful political position in the state. Although the Foundation can take credit for the creation of many local nonprofit institutions, some of which have become national models, it is not central to the history of nonprofits or minority politics in its region in the way the Cleveland Foundation has been.

During Paley's years, the Foundation provided important grants to individual nonprofits that have become major institutions in the Bay Area and even national models. It was the major source for organizations like BRIDGE Housing Corporation and also contributed significantly to the growth of others, like On Lok Senior Health Services and the public broadcasting station KQED. In distinction from national trends constructing race-related philanthropy in Black and White terms, the San Francisco Foundation enabled its local Asian American movement to construct a pan-Asian nonprofit infrastructure of social service and advocacy organizations.

The social history of Asian American nonprofit organizations pivots around the Asian American movement of the late 1960s and 1970s. Long delayed by anti-Asian exclusion in U.S. immigration law, the first sizable U.S.-born generation of Asian Americans started organizations that challenged older, ethnic-specific community leadership. Inspired by the coalition nature of the Third World Student Strikes, the new organizations tended to have a strong commitment to panethnicity among Asian Americans. Also, whereas the older generation of leaders related to the wider community by protecting the "respectability" of their groups in mainstream eyes, the new organizations were more confrontational, demanding "social justice" from the same mainstream. A significant factor in favor of leadership succession by the more assertive 1970s generation was its effort to apply for federal dollars and attract external funding for Asian social needs, which, unlike the older leadership cohort, they did not seek to hide. In fact, the newer generation came to perceive the older generation's preservation of respectability as complicit with the new stereotype of Asian Americans as a model minority, a perception that both undermined the newer generation's alliances with other people of color and delegitimized Asian social needs from the attention of policymakers.

Although similar to their Black counterparts of this era, Asian American organizations encountered a different political and institutional reception. Whereas Black organizations built themselves using federal programs, these sources of support had largely waned by the time the Asian organizations incorporated in the 1970s. Because the expansion of Black agencies was closely tied to local electoral politics, to which Asians remained outsiders until the 1990s, policymakers also had greater stakes in Black social needs.[6]

Into this funding and political gap stepped the San Francisco Foundation, which played a pivotal role in the emergence and development of the local Asian American organizations. In many cases, the Foundation was the funder that supported organizational startups and even the subsequent development of new programs. As one agency director recalled in our interview: "We had a great relationship with San Francisco Foundation because many of the program officers have been great supporters of us. They played a key role in developing key areas and programs. And we were able to use San Francisco Foundation's money to leverage money from other funders. It's really [sic] for program staff there to approach their colleagues at other organizations. The initiative to make contact has gone both ways [between the Asian organizations and the Foundation]. It made a big deal to connect with people there. San Francisco Foundation really promoted [our] rise in San Francisco."

Furthermore, as immigration began to increase the local Asian population, especially with the poor refugees and immigrants of the 1980s, the philanthropy supported the organizational inclusion of the newcomers in an even broader panethnic infrastructure. Given the reportedly central role of the program officers, Paley's diversification of the professional staff beyond Black and White paid off significantly. By the 1990s, many major Asian American organizations in the Bay Area were celebrating their twentieth to twenty-fifth anniversaries. Nevertheless, even though the Foundation did help "outsiders" become "challengers," it did not become the primary bridge by which organizations gained access to local elites or dominant political coalitions.

As during the first directorship, the continuing instability of local politics during Paley's directorship may have motivated the continuing hands-off approach of the Foundation with regard to shaping its local environment. In San Francisco, the rising minority bloc was not Black, as it was in Cleveland, but gay and lesbian. The city became the unofficial capital of the gay liberation movement, which, like the earlier racial/ethnic movement, branched into camps of older institutional entrists and younger radicals. In the 1980s especially, the latter established organizations like AIDS Coalition To Unleash Power (ACT-UP), Queer Nation, and Bad Cop, No Donut, which, like the Black Panthers, inspired a national wave of local chapters and imitators. During this time, although the African American population had the second-highest rates of political participation after gays and lesbians, non-Black non-Whites had not translated their growing demographic presence into political power. Thus, when liberals, environmentalists, and populists first came to power through the 1975 mayoral election of George Moscone, the emergent progressive coalition was characterized more by gays and lesbians than racial/ethnic minorities (DeLeon 1992).

San Francisco also experimented with district-based elections for the board of supervisors, resulting in a tragedy that would distinguish the region's progressive movement from its counterpart in Cleveland: "Many [candidates] lacked the financial backing or name recognition usually required to win an at-large election. One who succeeded was Harvey Milk who won in his district as the city's first openly gay elected official; another was Dan White [a straight White male] who won in his district on a wave of anti-gay sentiment and conservative resentment toward the new liberal mayor" (DeLeon 1992, 23).

While Cleveland lost its progressive mayor, Dennis Kucinich, in a power struggle with business elites that culminated on December 15, 1978, San Francisco lost its mayor to an assassin's bullet. On November 27, 1978, less than a month before Kucinich's political fall and hundreds of miles away, Dan White shot and killed both George Moscone and his fellow supervisor, Harvey Milk. While Cleveland's movement was defeated by business leadership, San Francisco's movement was cheated of its progressive regime. Recovering from the assassinations, the progressive coalition returned in the form of San Francisco Tomorrow, the slow-growth association that would succeed in 1987 with the mayoral election of Art Agnos.

More than vengeance, however, characterized the resurgence of the progressive movement. The strength of business leadership present in San Francisco in earlier decades had declined as corporate takeovers and mergers pushed corporate headquarters to the South Bay and "overgrowth" divided the interests of landlords and builders (DeLeon 1992). Furthermore, not only were local elites drained and divided in leadership, but they were also relatively privileged in comparison to midwestern elites, whose local economies were hemorrhaging population and capital to other parts of the nation. Faced with extraordinary political insurgency and a weak, yet perhaps content business elite, the San Francisco Foundation might have regarded any search for citywide alliances to be simply a waste of time and effort.

The continuing condition of political instability is yet again well illustrated with the unique career of Willie Brown. From his initial political training in the Black church and the San Francisco NAACP, Brown had been elected to the California Legislature at the age of thirty in 1964 during May's directorship. Subsequently, not only would Brown become a leader in the Negro (later Black) Political Action Association of California, but he would also attain during Paley's directorship the most powerful position in the California Legislature. Brown's ascension in 1980 to the office of speaker of the California State Assembly is remarkable given the state's proportionately small Black population and the reluctance of even White Democrats to elect non-White politicians. His achievement is even more unusual considering that the Assembly bloc that gave him the position was not only majority White but also majority Republican—in the same year that former California governor Ronald Reagan took the White House. In brief, when trustees and staff at the San Francisco Foundation looked up from their chaotic locale and the rising controversy surrounding the Buck Trust, they would hardly have regarded themselves as located on an island of political anarchy within a more politically predictable state. Instead, they would have witnessed the rise of a liberal-left, albeit not radical, political operative by means of an alliance with statewide conservative forces against his own party.

The Fisher Years (1986–1997): Professionalizing Empowerment, Confronting Progressivism

Robert Fisher implemented some of the most extensive racial priorities his foundation had ever seen; however, he relegated them to secondary importance behind donor development and set the stage for tensions with a board whose proportion of White men decreased more than at any other time in San Francisco Foundation history. Though Fisher was hired to restore donor confidence in the philanthropy, I suggest that significant numbers of trustees themselves viewed Paley's departure mainly as a necessary evil and resented the very respectability they sought. Indeed, Fisher's tumultuous directorship reveals the strong external tension between the philanthropy's dependence on local elites and its region's emerging antielite political culture.

MANAGEMENT STYLE

Fisher's directorship continued many elements of Paley's contributions but also introduced an equal number of elements. In continuity with the Paley years, Fisher's staff was majority female and had a slight majority of Whites, despite the departure of many of Paley's staff after his resignation. Fisher also selected program officers from the nonprofit and government sectors rather than from purely corporate or academic backgrounds. Following in a long tradition since May, the San Francisco Foundation carried out its work in friendly distinction from the United Way: the San Francisco Foundation handled improvement or startup of organizations and focused on "significant public issues," while the United Way granted current operating support. The Foundation took pride in the increasingly professional nature of the proposals to which it responded, as an indication of the growing sophistication of the Bay Area's nonprofit sector.

Unfortunately, Fisher's interest in professionalizing the organization was viewed as conflicting with the board's interest in diversity. Fisher introduced a communications department and a development department into the Foundation's staff structure, pulling its major attention away from grant making to donor solicitation and relations. His hiring policies also changed, favoring older candidates for staff positions, albeit the same current age as the staff who remained from the Paley years, "the Sixties Generation," as one staff member quipped.

In addition, the grant review process changed, again reflecting the director's style. When Paley began, he inherited a loose system of grant categories from May, who pointedly distinguished them from the divisions used by national foundations. As the organization grew, Paley institutionalized teams of officers, with particular officers as designated facilitators for categories that now came with set budgets. When Fisher entered, he decided that the teams were too cumbersome and institutionalized the very departments that May despised, though he tried to maintain staff collegiality in select programs rather than across the board, as Paley had done. While Fisher was making the Foundation more like a traditional business organization, the composition of his board changed to include trustees who looked askance at his seeming deprioritization of the surrounding "communities." Ultimately, a nationally recognized board member would resign, and the resulting upheaval resulted in the creation of a new program department largely for immigrant needs and eventually the resignation of its third director.

Despite these tensions over Fisher's relative inattention to communities, his directorship radically transformed how the Foundation prioritized race. Fisher continued the organizational priorities in empowerment and internal diversity and added two entirely new components: institutional pressure for grant-recipient organizations to diversify themselves and a Multicultural Fellows Program to put young people of color in the pipeline for diversifying the foundation profession.

Along with increasing the average age of new staff, Fisher systematized the Foundation's affirmative action efforts. Whereas Paley simply recruited from a pool that one program officer described as the "people he saw," Fisher pushed extensive advertising for candidates, especially in ethnic presses, formalizing the process significantly. Simultaneously, the board chose to add additional minority and women trustees. Following the trustee banks' surrender of their aggregate appointing authority, the federal judge followed suit; furthermore, the board increased its membership from seven to nine trustees. At this point, Fisher felt he could encourage grantees themselves to become more diverse. By "more diverse," the Foundation meant that a grant recipient's staff and board should not be exclusive of the diversity in its client population and should even aim for a more equitable representation. Fisher also created a new fellows program that was more formalized, larger, and oriented not only to bringing fresh perspectives into the organization but also to training future professional practitioners. To coordinate these programs, Fisher relied not on across-the-board values but on assigning a staff person with oversight responsibilities for diversity policy. Within this new context, a new program officer initiated the "little d" committee, a regular group for both program and nonprogram staff to discuss internal diversity in the context of their work. Ironically, Fisher's policy of racial institutionalization would be interpreted as hand-washing to others, especially as he apparently rarely attended little d meetings.

RELATIONSHIPS WITH EXTERNAL ACTORS
During Fisher's directorship, the Foundation's relations with external actors experienced uneven change. On the one hand, federal policies seemed not to take center stage, local mayors remained distant from foundation priorities, and program officers, on their own, could maintain or not maintain rela-

tions with city department heads. On the other hand, the arrival of a Ford Foundation grant in the early 1990s for diversifying the Foundation's donor pool changed its position in the foundation field. The Ford grant also sparked a reconsideration of the Foundation's mission statement regarding diversity, providing the context in which the little d committee and the new program area created after Gallegos's resignation played important roles. The Foundation's relationship with the Cleveland Foundation became more noticeable in its longevity. As a source of technical assistance, the Cleveland Foundation provided a computerization model for the San Francisco Foundation, ironic considering the latter's proximity to Silicon Valley. The initial discussions between Paley, Wadsworth, and Minter became discussions between Fisher and Minter. Furthermore, the organization's directors and board chairs regularly met at professional meetings, both those for all foundations and those for large community foundations in particular, effectively exposing the Foundation to a national level of collegiality beyond the regional networks on which it had relied since May's directorship.

THE URBAN CONTEXT

Ironically, in the aftermath of its bruising during the Buck controversy, the Foundation became available as an institutional vehicle for the national foundations that the Reagan revolution had shut out from their valued place in public policy networks. Like the Cleveland Foundation, the San Francisco Foundation continued its race-relations philanthropy despite the federal retrenchment against race-based policies. Unlike the attention given to the Cleveland Foundation, however, the foundation field began paying attention to the San Francisco Foundation more for its demographic context than for its regional clout or record as a local convenor.

Lacking significant leverage over the city of San Francisco, much less the Bay Area, the Foundation remained mainly in its historical role of modeling either "progressive" intergroup relations or, more narrowly, the potential productivity of a diverse workforce. Although its continuing inertia may be attributed to the internal conflicts between Fisher and his trustees, the latter struggle also echoed a broader political contradiction in the region. During this period, the Foundation faced an urban context struggling to reconcile competing interests in economic development and equality—once again, hardly a situation where reliable corporate and minority allies could be found, much less united. The result was the Foundation's continuing accommodation to a hyperpluralist political environment that included the election of a moderate "law and order" mayor in the liberal Democratic city and facilitated the use of neighborhood philanthropy to simplify the potential welter of demands for group-specific philanthropy.

Although local politics during Fisher's directorship did not reach the criminal extremes of the 1970s, the mayoralties from Agnos to Willie Brown reflected continuing social transformations, and as such did not provide stable partnerships for the Foundation. The left had returned to power with Mayor Agnos in 1987, but the same progressive movement that brought him to power would also turn against him. Beneath the progressive impulse for radical egalitarianism, like any other movement, some members of the coalition were more equal than others. Despite the San Francisco Foundation's efforts to encourage the civic participation of politically marginal groups, Asian Americans remained noticeably absent from the new ruling coalition, especially in comparison with their demographic presence. Though the Foundation had assisted the new insurgent generation in establishing a non-profit basis for community leadership, this did not translate into holding political offices. One Asian American community leader directly attributed the absence of Asian Americans to the deliberate exclusion of the same insurgents by the liberal Democratic organization associated with the Burton brothers. Pointing to the similarly noticeable absence of non-Chicano Latinos, he argued that the organization's larger political ambitions marginalized groups that were insignificant on the statewide level. Because Chicanos and Blacks were the best organized and largest non-White populations in California, only they were groomed for leadership in the local "machine."

Another possible explanation comes from DeLeon's (1992) analysis of the progressive movement as distinct from simply an extension of liberal or Democratic politics. In his analysis, the inclusion of Blacks and Chicanos was more as "ornaments of social diversity" (148), little better than the exclusion of Asian Americans. As a strategic unity between the "red" (or materialist) and the "green" (or postmaterialist) wings of the left, progressivism in San Francisco was unified solely and primarily by its critique of the pro-growth business coalition that had overbuilt its downtown during the 1960s and 1970s. Although they agreed to curb corporate development projects, the coalition members did so for distinct reasons. Whereas the traditional liberals based in working-class and ethnic minority populations opposed the destruction of low-income housing, they were also motivated by their disappointed hopes in the promises of the pro-growth machine to deliver jobs and affordable replacement housing. Their orientation to corporate development was thus more ambivalent than that of their more powerful environmentalist and populist allies, who were more focused on "quality of life" concerns, more popular among those already possessed of middle-class footing or at least homeownership. The result was an increasing disunity after Agnos's installation as a mayor: "The political carrying capacity of the progressive movement's governing coalition appear[ed] quite limited relative to the inclusive sweep of the electoral coalition that . . . put Art Agnos in power" (148). In brief, the marginalization of non-Whites in the progressive coalition contributed to its relative weakness postvictory.

Furthermore, as the movement's unity waned, so did the affection of its more powerful middle-class members for their new mayor. Ultimately, Agnos lost his reelection in 1991 to Frank Jordan, "a pro-business moderate who had little sympathy for growth controls, social reform, or left-wing progressivism" (DeLeon 1992, 159). Rather than employ the same progressive strategy in governance that won in his campaign, Agnos had sought progressive goals through closed-door dealings with established downtown interests. His core constituents experienced his governing strategy of "right-wing progressivism" as a betrayal, and the relations between the new mayor and his electoral base steadily worsened. In almost any other city, mayoral attempts to develop working relationships with corporate leaders would be regarded as normal politics, but after a progressive electoral victory, such behavior was vulnerable to being seen as "selling out the revolution." And if the mayor did not possess the legitimacy to build even an informal relationship to business elites, one might question whether the Foundation could really have gone even further to develop institutional bridges comparable to those in Cleveland.

In retrospect, Willie Brown's return to the city of his political beginnings as its new mayor seems preordained, if not by his personal political clout, then by the region's internal contradictions. Whereas those tensions complicated Fisher's directorship as it did Agnos's mayoralty, Brown benefited from them, casting himself as simultaneously "homegrown," an outsider with statewide influence, left-liberal, and experienced with corporate political lobbies. Since the older Burton's passing, Brown had created his own electoral organization and successfully shifted it to the Bay Area (Richardson 1996). His record fourteen years as speaker of the Assembly had left him with tremendous influence among state Democratic Party leadership, but also a very specific set of political skills. On the one hand, he was too much of an insider to become a voice of moral authority, and on the other hand, he was too flamboyant and controversial to run for statewide, much less national office. "To serve as Assembly Speaker required taking the heat for deals with unsavory lobbyists and boorish legislators" (384); even his personal charisma was better suited to deal making than mass mobilization.

Ironically, then, San Francisco would elect an exceptionally skilled right-wing progressive to replace the pro-business mayor who had benefited from the progressives' rejection of an earlier right-wing progressive. Such a conclusion, however, was not foregone. In fact, Jordan's campaign successfully cast Brown as a crooked politician, more interested in political survival and notoriety than the politics he espoused. As little as ten days before the first election, Brown's campaign faced the possibility that he would lose in a three-way race between Jordan and Roberta Achtenberg, who was trailing but also rising in the polls. Her national celebrity among gays, who numbered 20 percent of the city electorate, and her past experience as President Clinton's chief of fair housing in the Department of Housing and Urban Development made her an extremely strong contender for unifying the progressive coalition. Then Mayor Jordan posed in the nude with two radio personalities for a picture published on the front page of the *San Francisco Examiner*. It was a gaffe that convinced enough of his own supporters that he was not a good fit for the sophisticated city, no matter how grating they found its constant insurgency. When Achtenberg finished third to Brown's first in the no-majority first election, she and other progressives were faced with the prospects of replicating in the runoff election the results of the Agnos-Jordan election four years before. Loath to repeat history, Achtenberg persuaded her supporters to vote for Brown, a pragmatic strategy for an ideological coalition to elect its city's first African American mayor, nearly two decades after Carl Stokes became Cleveland's first Black mayor.

San Francisco's political instability not only made reliable allies difficult for the Foundation to find, but it also subtly effected a cultural hurdle for coalitional efforts. I suggest that the steady stream of social protest fostered a way of thinking about insurgency that cast any form of institutional continuity as a latent and undesirable political conservatism. Because of the continuous cycle of protests, San Franciscans (and the Bay Area more broadly) came to expect insurgency as a legitimately permanent feature of local politics, in contradiction to conventional theoretical expectations. In political theories of urban politics, Browning, Marshall, and Tabb's (1984) classic theory of minority political success features protest as a temporary stage, a necessary precursor to electoral mobilization, incorporation to insider coalitions, and government responsiveness to group demands. Building on this model, Hero (1992) validates its procession as necessary for gaining certain formal political powers, in particular, the capacity to address police-community relations, make appointments to boards and commissions, increase minority contracting, and increase minority city employment. However, he also expands the conventional conception of racial politics beyond the search for a larger and fairer piece of the pie to encompass the "higher" decision-making aspects of city politics associated with corporate economic development. In fact, the business dependence of local government underlies the theoretically expected direction of non-White political participation from outsiders to insiders with the ear of the corporate leadership on whose taxes city governments depend.

In San Francisco, though, a business victory did not occur as it did in Cleveland, and political challengers were not directly required to work with big business. Instead, the progressives made an art of using city bureaucracies to frustrate corporate development initiatives. Ruling, however, means more than the capacity to say no, especially when a significant fraction of the progressive coalition would prefer to approve any development that provides jobs and housing. DeLeon (1992) notes the numerous contradictions that emerged in the process of governing without a coherent agenda and instead by means of an oppositional identity. The postmaterialist leaders of the movement tried to direct the materialists' desire for development to small business mainly because it was small and without an understanding of that sector's dependence on big business. At least rhetorically, they tried to secede as an autonomous city-state even from the surrounding metropolitan region without recognizing its dependence on state and even national politics. Rather than selectively creating one agenda out of the plethora of single interests that constituted the coalition, they sought a charismatic leader, who would somehow by herself or himself "forge new solidarities across the divisions of race, class, and turf and resolve disharmonies among competing values within a singular vision of progressive reform" (174). In brief, they sought to remain in permanent revolution without ever having to actually govern. While progressives could have indicted Agnos for a lack of imagination in courting the usual suspects to pursue progressive goals, his critics did not provide a feasible alternative.

In a political environment where core membership was persistently unpredictable and challengers devalued insidership, the San Francisco Foundation somehow arrived at pursuing the same kind of community philanthropy pursued in Cleveland: grant making directed at neighborhoods. On the one hand, neighborhood philanthropy has genealogical roots in long-standing place-based federal policies and in a national culture that "remembers" and valorizes small-town life. On the other hand, the contemporary and practical meaning of such philanthropy varies at the local level. Unlike in Cleveland, place-based policy in the San Francisco Bay Area does not ameliorate the partisan tensions between place- and identity-based policies and constituencies. Because of the Bay Area's lower level of residential segregation, the emphasis on place is not a de facto concern for race, ethnicity, or other identities, no matter how they are construed. Segregation in the Bay Area is instead a matter of social segregation amid spatial *non*isolation, as it is in much of the surrounding state. Since the immigration waves revived by the 1965 Immigration Act, intergroup relations in California have been characterized in contradictory fashion by regular interaction across racial lines for most Californians, gated islands of class and/or racial homogeneity, and the popularity of state initiatives against repeat offenders, undocumented immigrants, racial preferences, and bilingual education (Maharidge 1996). Anticipating the state's millennial transition to a majority non-White population, many White Californians were possessed of both a far greater familiarity and association with non-Whites than most White Americans and an intense, racialized fear of a displacement that would reverse their own engulfment of native Mexicans after the U.S.-Mexican War, 150 years before. Between this climate of ethnoracial fear and an unstable and oppositional local politics, neighborhood policy serves the San Francisco Foundation not as a mechanism for bipartisan accord but as a prophylactic against anarchy. Though this attempt to simplify and thereby manage the local chaos may be laudable, Bay Area neighborhoods do not "build up" to a mechanism for addressing citywide or regional intergroup relationship, as they do in Cleveland's hypersegregated metropolitan area. The effect is that the Foundation may have unintentionally neglected group-based issues in its effort to find neutral common ground for the many groups sharing each piece of Bay Area geography.

Conclusion

The San Francisco Foundation eventually secured national recognition in its institutional field, but only in the fifth decade of its existence. During the 1990s, it would become a model for the philanthropic conception of diversity policy, even though its record for regional or even citywide initiatives has never approached that of the Cleveland Foundation. Although the San Francisco Foundation confronted greater levels of immigration and more complex race relations than did its Cleveland counterpart, its relative restraint from attempting citywide projects arose primarily from the unstable nature of its political environment. Instead of recreating its local nonprofit sector, the foundation treated it as a wild garden, calling attention to notable innovations and encouraging promising startups. Instead of becoming the institutional bridge between different communities in the region, the Foundation became a model for intercommunity relations, seemingly with the hopes of inspiring the changes it could not create by itself.

During each of the Foundation's first three directorships, internal decisions and external circumstances barred the organization from widening the scope of its racial and ethnic initiatives. First, John May chose a strategy of organizational purity that made a virtue of his professional inexperience, the Foundation's relatively small endowment, its exclusion by national philanthropies, and the unavailability of local allies. Second, Martin Paley elaborated May's tendencies into a philosophy of noninterference and started an organizational mission to reflect its region's growing demographic diversity: internally oriented policies that insulated the Foundation from its unstable political environment but did not protect it from the controversy over the Buck Trust. Third, Bob Fisher finally extended its internal diversity policies in external directions by creating a training program to racially integrate the philanthropic profession and requiring grantees to report on the relative diversity of their own staff and trustees in comparison with their clients or community of interest. Although these initiatives fit well within his efforts to restore the respectability of the Foundation, his greater emphasis on the donor community ran afoul of an emergent antielitism not only in the surrounding region but also from his own trustees. As in Cleveland, the faith of the Foundation's trustees was crucial to the survival and thus effectiveness of the executive director.

Immigration and race relations complicated the San Francisco Foundation's pursuit of its long-standing goal of "making differences helpful rather than hurtful," but the more significant cause of its more limited diversity policies was its local political environment. When the percentage of immigrants soared in the Bay Area population, the Foundation responded well before non-Black non-Whites achieved local political incorporation and fostered nonprofit development for those communities. However, these nonprofits failed to become central to the progressive coalitions that ascended in San Francisco politics. The newcomers also reshaped the local racial and ethnic landscape so that regular interracial and interethnic contact occurred for Whites with increasing frequency. On the one hand, their presence instigated conflicts over cultural differences and the identity of a "real" San Franciscan, but White and Black progressives were already challenging older conceptions of local culture and identity. On the other hand, the greater receptivity of San Franciscans to each other as neighbors undermined the traditional tool for dealing with Black-White relations, neighborhood policies, and diffused its intended consequences for building cross-racial community. Though this complexity suggests a greater need for citywide instead of subcity projects, the nature of local politics has stymied the Foundation's capacities for building coalitions.

The absence of predictable, recognizable, and securely powerful allies left the San Francisco Foundation without partners with whom to reshape its local civic arena. This chapter has primarily emphasized the explanation that this unavailability was the result of political instability. Rather than presiding over a stable and cohesive local regime, Bay Area politics were hyperpluralist, characterized by a shifting plethora of insurgent movements, divided business leaders, and an electorally successful anticorporate coalition. On the other hand, one might argue that such reliable actors were actually present but remained uninterested in the Foundation as a vehicle. Similarly, one might object that the Bay Area is incomparable to the Greater Cleveland Area because reliable partnerships would have had to be negotiated within each major political jurisdiction: San Francisco, Oakland, and San Jose. And yet, if political contests are a valid indicator, these actors never showed their hand, even when we limit our attention to San Francisco, the home county of the Foundation.

San Francisco is indeed an international and national corporate headquarters, but only the Haas family and its Levi Strauss corporation appears to have made itself consistently available to the locale's premier community foundation. If we assume that reliable allies must include business leadership, the above account of race-relations philanthropy cannot distinguish whether corporate leaders were too divided to be stable partners or were uninterested in exercising civic leadership on race relations. With respect to the former, the Haas origins of the Foundation suggest the possibility of a local philanthropic "feudalism," even though the philanthropy is ostensibly a community rather than a family foundation. On the other hand, the relative economic health of the Bay Area suggests a reason for elite disinterest. Without a significant threat to the local economy, business leaders may feel little imperative to control its civic life. In fact, the translocally oriented members of the business community may have focused their attention on other, "needier" localities.

Regardless of whether a general political instability or a more specific elite distraction explains the Foundation's inertia on diversity policy, I argue that the San Francisco Foundation would face more difficult challenges learning from the Cleveland Foundation than vice versa. To directly shape intergroup relations, the San Francisco Foundation would have to build a political regime capable of supporting the citywide bridges that, even then, could only attempt to achieve its goals. Also, to forestall progressive revulsion at the prospects of such a philanthropic greenhouse, the Foundation might have to develop within the progressive coalition reliable institutions with the legitimacy to broker their participation in initiatives of scale. By contrast, the Cleveland Foundation could more easily become a comparable model for productive intergroup relations and for a cross-racial sense of community by altering internal organizational policies or creating community awards. The major challenge for the Cleveland Foundation would be to locate non-White males acceptable to the heads of local corporations, a task arguably less formidable than the transformation of Bay Area urban regimes.

In sum, local factors explain why the San Francisco institution has made diversity policy on a smaller scale than the Cleveland institution. However, all is not local; there was a crucial extralocal factor in the Cleveland Foundation's leverage of its local advantages: the Ford Foundation. In the next chapter, I explore the singular role of this national institution in shaping the racial rhetoric and practices of the foundation world.

5

Elite Visibility in Institutional Racial Formation

When the Ford Foundation talks . . .

In the 1980s, the investment company E.F. Hutton commissioned a memorable series of television commercials, each of which highlighted a public conversation between friends. When one friend confides, "My broker is E.F. Hutton, and he says . . . ," the larger gathering of people falls silent, each individual straining to hear the presumably valuable financial advice. A disembodied voice would then end each commercial with the signature statement, "When E.F. Hutton talks, people listen." In brief, the commercials sought to associate the company with authoritative expertise not by offering any particular evidence but by claiming a reputation that transcended the need for evidence.

Similarly, the Ford Foundation enjoys a name recognition rivaled by few other philanthropies and nonprofit organizations and possesses a reputation whose basis has arguably transcended the need for specific evidence. By contrast, Dean Rusk, the president of the Rockefeller Foundation from 1951 to 1961, characterized the Ford Foundation in an earlier decade as "the fat boy in the canoe" (quoted in L. Gordon 1997, 111); the metaphor communicates an exceptional status premised less on expertise or proven experience than on being an inherent danger to others in the same boat. In fact, Ford's notoriety has arguably made the organization both a unifying presence for the foundation world and a threat to the political legitimacy that governs the field's very existence. After all, it was Ford philanthropy, arguably its support of voter-registration campaigns during the 1960s, that triggered the congressional investigations of foundations resulting in the Tax Reform Act of 1969 (Ostrander 1999). In turn, the passage of the act led to the ascension of the Council on Foundations as the "prime spokesman for foundations"

(Frumkin 1999), a process that included its transformation of the newsletter originally published by the Foundation Center into the trade magazine now titled *Foundation News and Commentary*.

With respect to the philanthropic adoption of diversity policies by the early 1990s, I argue that the Ford Foundation has played a central role in race-relations philanthropy and influenced other foundations to follow suit. The instrumental nature of Ford's role suggests that the apparent independence of foundation discourse from racial politics is not an innate property of the organizational field but is instead the strategic response of a singular elite organization to shifts in the political climate for racial policies. Generalizing beyond philanthropy, what is "institutional" about diversity policies may be not only the existence of field-specific cultural logics but also the centrality of elite field members in those very logics.

In this chapter, I revisit the local construction of foundation policies and the national-institutional discourse on race and ethnicity to tell the story of how the Ford Foundation influenced both levels of philanthropic diversity. I compare the Ford Foundation's early involvement with the Cleveland Foundation since the 1960s with its absence from the San Francisco Foundation's activities until the 1990s and introduce Ford's association with the major ethnoracial themes published in the national magazine. Most of this chapter, however, is dedicated to reviewing the scholarly literature on the Ford Foundation, placing the organization in the history of foundations and identifying its racial and ethnic agenda in the decades surrounding the civil rights movement. In brief, I reveal the role of the Ford Foundation in Cleveland, the San Francisco Bay Area, and the national discourse before examining the history of the national organization that connects the three cases.

As the preceding three chapters demonstrate, the trajectories of the respective local foundation practices in the Cleveland and San Francisco Bay areas and of the racial discourse in *Foundation News* do not suggest a simple relationship wherein the institutional field leads its organizational membership. On the one hand, one can recognize in their respective racial priorities the institutional cultural logic of identifying talent instead of the federal discourse of protecting victims from discrimination. On the other hand, the recognizable racial and ethnic themes do not follow the same historical progression in both regions, much less follow the progression expected from the national discourse. In fact, the national seems to mimic the local instead of vice versa, reversing the expected pattern of institutional isomorphism (DiMaggio and Powell 1991).

Both foundations eventually instituted a form of strategic diversity policy, but their paths suggest that local foundations can actually *lead* the larger institutional field. In the national magazine, foundations appear to shift over three decades, from looking for good causes until the mid-1970s, to good works until 1980, to, finally, good strategies.[1] However, local priorities start instead with a form of good works and proceed to diverge. Both organizations begin the 1960s with passively custodial directorships—Kimball Johnson's in Cleveland and John May's in the Bay Area—that supported an uncoordinated assortment of good works. The Cleveland Foundation skips the stage of good causes in the early 1960s to pursue good strategies under Dolph Norton's directorship. Therefore, it is the Cleveland Foundation that pioneers philanthropic diversity policy's content of good strategies in the 1960s. By comparison, the San Francisco Foundation does not shift to actively looking for good strategies until the early 1990s, during Robert Fisher's directorship. However, the San Francisco Foundation pioneers a post-Black scope to grant making in the late 1970s under Martin Paley's directorship. Thus, diversity policy does not arrive whole cloth in 1990, raising the question of how the parts became a whole.

I argue that the Ford Foundation is the missing link in the historical synthesis of these elements into the theme of philanthropic pluralism propagated by *Foundation News and Commentary* in 1990. First, I summarize how Ford magnified the Cleveland Foundation's already greater resources and entrenched the philanthropy in national private-public policy networks, while the San Francisco Foundation experienced an exclusion and isolation from the national networks. Second, I trace the increasing visibility of the national foundation in the philanthropic discourse about race and ethnicity, in particular the post-1980 ascension of strategic philanthropy in foundation rhetoric. Third, I employ the historical and sociological literature on the Ford Foundation to explain how its activities have provided a certain unity to philanthropic participation in racial formation. These accounts of its belated emergence in U.S. foundation history and its involvement in urban policy, international development, and social movements explain its preference for Cleveland over San Francisco in the 1960s and suggest that the apparent autonomy of the field's racial rhetoric is quite dependent on the relationship of the Ford Foundation with the federal government. I argue that Ford's search for new allies during the conservative 1980s facilitated its attention to the new demographic shifts and provided the template for the foundation field's construction of philanthropic pluralism. I close by discussing the implications of Ford's centrality among foundations for (1) the relationship of racial discourse with actual practices, (2) the specific character of philanthropic pluralism, and (3) the dependence of racial social change on institutional structure.

Ford Effects on Local Philanthropy

In 1990, the trade magazine *Foundation News* published a special issue reporting the increasing tendency of foundations to adopt the philosophy and practices characterized as pluralism in philanthropy. Like other diversity policies, philanthropic pluralism gave equal attention to the four major non-White groups in the United States—an important deviation from the magazine's earliest racial focus on Blacks. Though the issue focused on efforts to connect affluent people of color with worthy projects, the magazine had consolidated a broader diversity policy since the mid-1980s. Repudiating earlier rhetoric advancing philanthropy for good causes and good works, the foundation discourse promoted instead the support of efficient organizations with clear and specific plans for affecting broader social relations. Furthermore, it associated this *strategic philanthropy* with a new model of racial talent: the combination of group culture and mainstream success, or what I have termed *inclusive expertise.* Significantly, the magazine broke with its tradition of modeling minority discourse on philanthropic experience with Blacks and instead drew this new diversity policy from its discourse about Native Americans. In addition to efforts to integrate what insiders call "the donor community," foundation discourse also exemplifies philanthropic pluralism in community development corporations, community foundations, and voter registration organizations.

At the local level, however, the adoption of diversity policy varied in surprising ways from the national discourse. Given the focus on the post-1965 immigration from non-European parts of the globe, one would reasonably expect local demographic heterogeneity to have differentiated the adoption of this policy. In other words, the San Francisco Foundation should be a pioneer, well ahead of the Cleveland Foundation. In actuality, the Cleveland Foundation appears to have pioneered the use of strategic philanthropy and inclusive expertise in the 1960s, whereas the San Francisco Foundation does not adopt these elements until the 1990s. Both organizations begin the 1960s in a custodial mode, serving largely as instruments for either the passive evaluation of uncoordinated grant proposals or the fulfillment of idiosyncratic donor wishes. But it is in Cleveland that the inertia associated with this kind of philanthropy breaks first—not because of immigration but due to the involvement of the Ford Foundation.

In chapters 3 and 4, I stressed the importance of local conditions for distinguishing the paths taken by each foundation. Each organization has been enabled or limited by the availability of allies, whatever its surrounding racial and ethnic demographics. With reliable allies, the Cleveland Foundation has implemented philanthropy of great scope with citywide partners, focusing on connecting Black and other non-White leaders with White CEOs. The organization pioneered strategic philanthropy decades before it dominated the field discourse about race and ethnicity. Without reliable allies, the San Francisco Foundation innovated various ways of doing philanthropy, albeit with smaller scope: from supporting idiosyncratic donor causes to empowering ethnic nonprofit development. In other words, despite the region's growing Asian and Latino populations, the organization did not become the source of the strategic philanthropy that the field magazine promoted when it adopted diversity policy.

However, although local conditions have been crucial, the intervention of a singular national actor has also been significant. Organizations change infrequently because the existence of "a way" to pursue their respective missions discourages innovation; already organized social relations operate as a package of elements that presuppose the existence of all the others, making it easy "when you choose any one of them . . . to take everything that comes with that choice, and [making it] enormously difficult to make any substitutions" (Becker 1995, 304). Change occurs only when people are willing to pay the price of innovation involved in creating a new package or in realigning the relationships among all of the preexisting elements to accommodate the new element. In the early 1960s, certain actors in Cleveland persuaded the Ford Foundation to pay that price for them, whereas no national actor offered to do the same for the San Francisco Foundation until decades later.

However, paying the price of introducing innovation to an organization does not automatically lead to its survival within the broader social system, which had legitimized the previous package. And yet the Cleveland Foundation not only adopts the elements of philanthropic pluralism decades before the 1990s but also does not revert to its custodial mode after the 1960s. The local foundation maintains sufficient momentum from Ford involvement to influence its local environment to view the new mode as legitimate. From the perspective of organizational ecology, institutional environments select not for efficiency or quality but for reliability and accountability, that is, the ability to reproduce results and reasonably explain their attainment (Hannan and Freeman 1984). In the 1960s, the Ford Foundation participated in the creation of a new entity, the Greater Associated Cleveland Foundation, which consolidated local civic leadership and eventually took over the Cleveland Foundation. Indeed, the inertia that impedes the San Francisco Foundation before the 1990s also characterizes the Cleveland Foundation after its successful reorganization.

Cleveland possessed a relatively stable urban regime before the 1960s, but the unity of its corporate, political, and African American components was not a given. Nor was their coherence around the specific organization of the Cleveland Foundation foregone as an outcome. Instead, the Ford Foundation played an important role in facilitating both the unity and the coherence that permitted the Cleveland Foundation to develop strategic racial philanthropy in the 1960s. It provided the "neutral" external resources to fund the civic leadership study resulting in the broadly supported proposal to Ford itself for a grant to start the Greater Cleveland Associated Foundation, which remade the Cleveland Foundation into a strategic philanthropy decades before the formal emergence of diversity policy.

The creation of the Associated Foundation facilitated the alliance of corporate leadership with African Americans into an urban regime that has proven to be a reliable partner in the Cleveland Foundation's citywide initiatives addressing race relations and racial inequality. In addition, its early relationship with Ford permitted the local philanthropy to develop special access to federal policymakers during a time when national foundations and the federal government initiated regular collaborations. Consequently, external actors of all sorts have been more available for the Cleveland Foundation than for the San Francisco Foundation, with the result that the Cleveland institution has long had a place in national social policy networks. An example of its continuing stature is the Hope VI federal program to transform public housing, which lifted language directly from the Cleveland Foundation–commissioned studies of local poverty and made its first grant to the midwestern city.

By contrast, the San Francisco Foundation has long operated without the benefit of an available coalition of interests, much less the mandate to maintain that unity and act as its master tool. The organization came to age during the rise of a local antiregime, making it hard to discern whether there was a "there" there in both city politics and business leadership from which to locate consistent partners for broad initiatives. Such a "turbulent and uncertain" environment may favor not reliable or accountable organizational policy but "organizational forms that can take quick advantage of new opportunities and the appearance of new habitats" (Hannan and Freeman

1984, 163). Not surprisingly, the San Francisco Foundation has prioritized the empowerment of outsiders, not elite involvement or even the familiarization of challengers to any local elites.

Furthering the local foundation's isolation, the Ford Foundation ignored the nascent San Francisco philanthropy during the 1960s, when it chose to target the city of Oakland for its urban initiatives. Only decades later did Ford engage the San Francisco Foundation in its initiative to diversify the donor base of community foundations nationwide. As a result, in the 1990s the local foundation shifted how it prioritized race relations from general cultural values guiding the staff to specific programs for which specific personnel were accountable. Time will tell whether these innovations survive, much less transform the organization's weak relationships with the local political regime, the comparatively smaller scope of its racial philanthropy, and its status in national policy networks as a unique laboratory for interesting but nonreplicable ideas.

Nevertheless, it is questionable whether, without Ford Foundation intervention, the Cleveland Foundation would have followed in the same footsteps as its Bay Area counterpart. Another metropolis might have become the first major U.S. city to elect a Black mayor, but it is doubtful that Ford's absence would have resulted in the emergence of a midwestern hyperpluralism comparable to San Francisco's antiregime. Even before Ford's involvement, a significant fraction of Cleveland's corporate and political elites had already united for the purpose of soliciting the national foundation to sponsor an institutional unification of civic leadership. If Ford had declined to make the grants that initiated the Greater Cleveland Associated Foundation, the effort at unity might have lost steam, for it had been premised on using Ford's national clout to legitimize the local leadership of those specific elites. Alternatively, the same group could have sought the external legitimacy of another national actor and won its support, though the result might have been a new institution other than the Associated Foundation. But even without Ford's involvement, the Cleveland Foundation would still have had more reliable allies in the corporate and political spheres than did the San Francisco Foundation.

Where Ford support was much more critical was for the inclusion (or cooptation) of local African Americans into the dominant coalition. Ford grants and legitimacy sustained the Associated Foundation of the 1960s and the varied activities of its Businessmen's Interracial Committee on Civic Affairs (BICCA). White business leaders and middle-class Blacks developed working relationships and new cultural precedents on committees examining how race and racism related to youth, employment, desegregation, housing, and police-community relations. Furthermore, Ford support of the Associated Foundation connected Cleveland with the federal government and helped define the local foundation as a trusted partner for federal projects. As in many other U.S. metropolitan areas of the period, many Black Clevelanders secured middle-class careers in federal employment through funding from the War on Poverty and other urban policy initiatives. Without Ford involvement, these federal programs may not have been as generous to Cleveland and its Black residents. More important for local political coalitions, the association of federal resources with the Cleveland Foundation may have encouraged the leaders of the new Black middle class to distinguish the Foundation's corporate allies from the Whites visibly resisting Black social and political advancement.

Ford's role in Cleveland suggests the effects that its early intervention on behalf of the San Francisco Foundation might have had. On the one hand, Ford would have had a more difficult and complex task of fostering an institutional vehicle for corporate and city hall unity. In comparison with Cleveland, the business community was more dispersed and conflicted, and increasingly so. Additionally, political officials were divided into multiple cores despite their increasing economic integration within the same metropolitan area. In any case, it does not seem that Daniel Koshland attempted to unify the local business community around the San Francisco Foundation, as Harold Clark did in Cleveland. On the other hand, Ford could have played an instrumental role in building an interracial coalition that would have altered the Bay Area's culture of activism, either tempering its extremes with institution building or perhaps further dividing moderates and radicals. In brief, though not all-powerful, the Ford Foundation could have significantly influenced the political conditions in the Bay Area for organizational reliability and accountability, as it certainly did in Cleveland.

At the very least, the attention of a national actor like Ford might have ameliorated the community foundation's sense of alienation from the eastern establishment. In turn, an early relationship would have discouraged its first executive director from fostering an exceptionalist identity in opposition to the foundation field and its second director from defining empowerment to exclude any form of interference with local communities. In contrast, the Cleveland Foundation has benefited from its early acceptance of the authority of the national foundation. Unlike the San Francisco Foundation, it did not experience Ford officials or other national actors as threats to local authority. Instead, the director of the Associated Foundation and later the Cleveland Foundation saw them as the legitimate intellectuals of the field: "One of the primary people in the field of philosophy of philanthropy in the 1960s was Paul Ylvisaker of the Ford Foundation. Paul used to talk about using social jujitsu, jujitsu being the form of self-protection that uses an opponent's weight against him . . . Essentially that's what you try to do in philanthropy" (James Norton, Families 1982–85).

Ford Visibility in Foundation Rhetoric about Race

Further evidence of the significance of the Ford Foundation for the emergence of diversity policy is its organizational visibility in the foundation rhetoric about race and ethnicity. I define organizational visibility generally as the relative association of an organization with discourse bounded within a specific scope, for example, the articles in the total rhetoric about race and ethnicity, the discourse about Latinos, or the thematic shift from good works to good strategies.[2] With respect to the discourse promoted in *Foundation News* articles about race and ethnicity, I measure visibility as the count of unique articles that mention an organization by name. This operationalization provides rough approximations of both the relative importance of a given organization as a carrier of discourse and the institutional structuration of a given scope of discourse. By comparing visibility counts (per organization) within a scope of discourse, I distinguish the more central carriers among the mentioned organizations. In addition, I interpret discourses with more uneven visibility distributions as more structured than the more equally carried discourses. By these indicators, the Ford Foundation is a central player in both the racial discourse of foundations and the field shift to philanthropic pluralism; furthermore, it is the primary organization among the elite foundations whose gravity gives structure to philanthropic race talk in aggregate.

In the total racial rhetoric from 1960 to 1989, before the publication of the special issue on philanthropic pluralism, the Ford Foundation is by far the most visible organization and shares an elite position with the foundations associated with the Rockefeller and Carnegie names. The forty-five articles constituting the magazine's racial discourse mention in aggregate 114 organizations, including 99 foundations, 7 other philanthropies such as the United Way and corporations, 6 federal and state government agencies, and 2 professional associations, the Council on Foundations and the Association of Black Foundation Executives. The racial discourse mentions these organizations a total of 211 times, excluding multiple references within the same article, and of those 211 mentions, an overwhelming 192 are to the foundations. The magazine references 80 of 114 organizations, including 68 foundations, in a single article and never again. Of the remaining 34 organizations, including 31 foundations, the magazine mentions 13 twice, 11 three times, and the remaining 10, foundations all, in four or more articles.

Of the forty-five articles in question, the Ford Foundation appears in twenty-one, over twice as many as the second and third most-mentioned foundations, the Carnegie Corporation of New York and the Rockefeller Foundation, each mentioned in nine articles. However, the fleet of Rockefeller foundations appears in nineteen articles, rivaling the visibility of Ford, while the foundations associated with the Carnegie name appear in eleven articles in total (table 10). The fourth through tenth most-visible foundations are the Rockefeller Brothers Fund (6 articles), the New York Foundation (5), the Southern Education Foundation (5), the William H. Donner Foundation (5), the Alfred P. Sloan Foundation (4), the John F. Slater Fund (4), and the Rockefeller General Education Board (4).

Across individual decades, only the Ford Foundation among the "Big Three" consistently remains distinctly visible in the racial discourse. During the 1960s, three articles mention Ford, whereas no other foundation is mentioned in more than two articles. Over the 1970s, ten articles mention Ford, whereas no others are mentioned in more than five. In the 1980s, eight articles mention Ford; others are mentioned in no more than four. By comparison, the Carnegie Corporation is distinctly visible only in the 1970s and the Rockefeller Foundation only in the 1980s. As with the total discourse, if we aggregate the foundations associated with the Carnegie and Rockefeller names, then their visibility again becomes distinct, but only in specific decades. During the 1960s, the magazine mentions the Rockefeller fleet in one more article (5) than the Ford Foundation, and the Carnegie name just as frequently as Ford. Over the 1970s, the discourse mentions the Rockefeller name in ten articles, as many as Ford. However, by the 1980s, Ford is clearly the leading organization in foundation racial discourse.

In all three core subdiscourses—about Blacks, Native Americans, and non-Whites in general—the Ford Foundation is the most visible organization. Over the 1960s and 1970s, the discourse about Blacks provides the model for foundation rhetoric about race and ethnicity. *Foundation News* publishes eighteen articles about African Americans, among which eight articles mention the Ford Foundation. In comparison, the magazine mentions only once another thirty-five foundations, including the Carnegie Foundation for the Advancement of Teaching. In addition, the discourse about

Blacks mentions only twice nine foundations, including the Carnegie Corporation of New York; three times, five foundations, including the Rockefeller General Education Board; four times, the John F. Slater Fund and the Rockefeller Brothers Fund; and five times, the Rockefeller Family Foundation. Once again, although the Ford Foundation is the core organization, it shares core status with the Rockefeller fleet.

Among the other group-specific discourses, Native Americans are unique. During the 1980s, the magazine turns to the discourse about Native Americans to provide a new model for racial rhetoric. Although only five articles constitute this group-specific discourse, all but one mention the Ford Foundation. Also, the magazine mentions only once eleven foundations, three other philanthropies, and one government agency and mentions twice the Rockefeller Foundation. However, three articles do mention a non–Big Three organization, the William H. Donner Foundation.

By comparison, the two marginal subdiscourses about Asian Americans and Latinos include no mention of the Ford Foundation. Perhaps not surprisingly, it does not appear that these discourses possess much institutional structure. Among the small set of three articles about Asians, the magazine mentions only once ten foundations, including the San Francisco Foundation, and one government agency. Among the set of six articles about Latinos, the magazine mentions only once two foundations, including the Carnegie Corporation, two other philanthropies, and four government agencies.

Ultimately, it is the general discourse about minorities from which *Foundation News* directly launches philanthropic pluralism. In these thirteen articles, the Ford Foundation appears in eight; the second most-visible organization, the Carnegie Corporation, trails with mentions in five articles. By contrast, this general discourse mentions only once forty-two foundations, including the Carnegie Foundation for the Advancement of Teaching and the Rockefeller General Education Board, two other philanthropies, two government agencies, and the Association of Black Foundation Executives. These articles mention twice seven foundations, including the Rockefeller Brothers Fund, the Rockefeller Family Foundation, and the San Francisco Foundation, and mention three times the Council on Foundations. The Carnegie organizations and the Rockefeller fleet garner six and five mentions, respectively. In this especially important subdiscourse, therefore, the Ford Foundation is the most visible institution both as an individual organization and as a name among the Big Three.

Interestingly, the magazine associates the Ford Foundation before the 1980s with articles sharing themes that one might characterize as pragmatism

TABLE 10   Organizations Mentioned in
Philanthropic Discourse about Race

Organizations	Number of Times Mentioned in Distinct Articles
Top Ten	
1. Ford Foundation	21
2. Carnegie Corporation of New York	9
3. Rockefeller Family Foundation	9
4. Rockefeller Brothers Fund	6
5. New York Foundation	5
6. Southern Education Foundation	5
7. William H. Donner Foundation	5
8. Alfred P. Sloan Foundation	4
9. John F. Slater Fund	4
10. Rockefeller General Education Board	4
All Other Organizations	
Aaron E. Norman Fund	1
Akbar Fund	1
American Can	1
Arizona Community Foundation	1
Arthur Vining Davis Foundation	1
Association of Black Foundation Executives	1
Astor Foundation	1
Atlantic Richfield Foundation	1
Avalon Foundation	1
Booth Ferris Foundation	1
Bush Foundation	2
Carnegie Foundation for the Advancement of Teaching	2
Charles Steward Mott Foundation	2
Chicago Community Trust	1
Commonwealth Fund	1
Cooperative Assistance Fund	1
Council on Foundations	3
Cowell Foundation	1
Cummins Engine Foundation	3
Dade Community Foundation	1
Danforth Foundation	3
Daniel J. Bernstein Foundation	1
Eastman Kodak	1

TABLE 10 (Continued)

Organizations	Number of Times Mentioned in Distinct Articles
All Other Organizations	
Edna McConnell Clark Foundation	3
Edward Elliott Foundation	1
El Pomar Foundation	1
Ernest and Mary Hayward Weir Foundation	1
Eugene and Agnes E. Meyer Foundation	1
Field Foundation	3
Florence V. Burden Foundation	1
Fund for the Advancement of Teaching	1
Fund for the City of New York	1
General Mills	1
George F. Peabody Fund	1
Grant Foundation	1
Greater New York Fund	1
Hall Family Foundation	1
Hartford Foundation for Public Giving	1
Hattie M. Strong Foundation	1
Hispanic Development Fund—KCCF	1
Irwin-Sweeney-Miller Foundation	1
Ittleson Family Fund	1
J. N. Pew Charitable Trust	1
Jeanes Fund	3
John Hay Whitney Foundation	2
Johnson Foundation	1
Joint Foundation Support, Inc.	1
Josiah Macy, Jr. Foundation	1
Julius Rosenwald Foundation	3
Kaiser Family Foundation	1
Kansas City Community Foundation	1
Lilly Endowment for Religion	2
Louis Calder Foundation	2
Louis W. and Maud Hill Family Foundation	1
Luke B. Hancock Foundation	1
MacArthur Foundation	1
Markle Foundation	1
Mary Reynolds Babcock Foundation	1

TABLE 10   (Continued)

Organizations	Number of Times Mentioned in Distinct Articles
All Other Organizations	
Merck Foundation	1
Merrill Trust	1
Mervyn's	1
Monadnock Fund	1
Muskiewinee Fund	1
National Council of Churches	1
National Endowment for the Arts	2
National Endowment for the Arts' Expansion Program	1
New World Foundation	3
New York City's Cultural Affairs Commission	1
New York Community Trust	1
New York State Council on the Arts	2
Norman Foundation	1
North Dakota Foundation	1
Northwest Area Foundation	1
Old Dominion Foundation	1
Peabody Education Fund	2
Peninsula Foundation	1
Phelps-Stokes Fund	2
Robert Sterling Clark Foundation	2
Robert Wood Johnson Foundation	2
Rosenberg Foundation	3
Rosenwald Fund	1
Sachem Fund	2
Samual S. Fels Fund	1
San Francisco Foundation	3
Schubert Foundation	1
Smithsonian Institution	1
Spelman Fund of New York	1
Stern Family Fund	1
Taconic Foundation	1
Third World Fund	1
Twentieth Century Fund	1
Twenty-First Century Foundation	1
U.S. State Department	1

TABLE 10   (Continued)

Organizations	Number of Times Mentioned in Distinct Articles
All Other Organizations	
United Jewish Appeal	1
United Way	1
Veatch Foundation	1
Victoria Foundation	1
Virginia Randolph Fund	1
W. K. Kellogg Foundation	1
Waterman Foundation	1
William and Flora Hewlett Foundation	3
William Nelson Fund	1
William Penn Foundation	1
Zellerbach Family Fund	1
Total number of mentions	211

Source: *Foundation News* 1960–1989 (45 articles; 114 organizations)

averse to controversy, but during the 1980s with articles carrying the themes that become diversity policy. During the 1970s, the Foundation is present in all three articles promoting the Black professionalism that repudiates as impractical an earlier theme of Black nationalism, which ironically mentions the Foundation in one article. Soon after, the magazine also begins publishing articles promoting technical assistance for minority nonprofits, philanthropic attention that steers clear of substantive issues related to their societal goals. This technical assistance theme mentions the Ford Foundation in more articles, three out of a possible four, than any other organization, and again, repudiates an earlier theme promoting radical Black organizations as the vanguard for other minority movements, including again one article that mentions the Ford Foundation. During the 1980s, however, the Ford Foundation, along with the Carnegie Corporation and the Rockefeller Foundation, appear centrally in articles promoting minority self-reliance and new kinds of leadership among people of color. Crossing six articles about Asians, Blacks, Latinos, and Native Americans, the self-help theme mentions three times the Ford Foundation and the Rockefeller Foundation, twice the Edna McConnell Clark Foundation, and once eleven foundations,

Institutional Racial Formation   165

including the Carnegie Corporation. In a small set of three articles immediately preceding the promotion of philanthropic pluralism, the leadership theme references the Ford Foundation in every article and mentions twice the Carnegie Corporation and once twenty foundations, including the Rockefeller Foundation and the Rockefeller Brothers Fund, one other philanthropy, and the Council on Foundations.

The Ford Foundation becomes especially visible in foundation rhetoric about race in its broad shift from philanthropy motivated by good causes or good works to strategic philanthropy. Of the fifteen articles that focus on good causes for foundations, only five articles mention Ford, although this figure still defines it as the most visible organization; in comparison, these articles mention fourteen other organizations more than once and thirty-four organizations only once. Of the nineteen articles that focus on philanthropy for good works, seven articles mention Ford, albeit again as the core organization, though the Rockefeller Foundation is a rival with five articles. These articles mention twelve other organizations more than once and thirty-three organizations only once. The visibility of the Ford Foundation leaps in the articles that focus on strategic philanthropy, where it appears in nine of the eleven articles, in comparison to three articles each for the Carnegie Corporation and the Rockefeller Foundation. This time, the foundation discourse mentions only three other organizations more than once but forty-five organizations just once.

The foundation world includes several thousand organizations, many of which are concerned with race and ethnicity. Of this large number, field media like *Foundation News and Commentary* can recognize only a subset of organizations; however, within this subgroup, three names have dominated since the 1960s. Although some commentators have criticized the tendency to focus on the Carnegie, Ford, and Rockefeller institutions, my audit of field media demonstrates that, since the civil rights movement, they have become the leading foundations concerned with race relations in the United States. By the 1970s, the renown of the new Carnegie, Ford, and Rockefeller projects had eclipsed the traditional philanthropy benefiting the historically Black colleges. And during the 1980s, the Ford Foundation rose to become the singular institution most identified with racial philanthropy and, indeed, the new approach of diversity policy.

How first the large foundations and then the Ford Foundation in particular became such central actors in the foundation field is intimately related to the question of what one means by categorizing foundations as a field. Until now, I have largely referred to the foundation field as synonymous with the organizational population of foundations. In actuality, it is arguable that the foundation world started forming an institutional field only in the 1970s, with full institutionalization only during the 1980s. Frumkin illustrates this shift in his article examining "how and why foundations transformed themselves from private institutions guided by the values of the donor [during the first six decades of the twentieth century] into public institutions governed by grantmaking professionals [from the 1970s to the present]" (1999, 70). His answer is that foundations responded to the 1969 Tax Reform Act and the controversies leading to it by seeking ways to defend themselves from further government investigation and regulation. Institutionally, the Council on Foundations ascended as the main spokesperson for foundations, taking over *Foundation News* from the Foundation Center, which instead focused on brokering information to grant seekers researching sources of funding. The Council's main rival, the National Council on Philanthropy, merged with the Coalition of National Voluntary Organizations to become Independent Sector, which would represent all nonprofits, not only philanthropic organizations. In time, the Council encouraged the recruitment of "professionals" who embraced a new sense of public responsibility and also doubled the percentage of foundation budgets dedicated to administrative expenses. Of course, the Carnegie, Ford, and Rockefeller foundations had already adopted complex staff structures, which the Cleveland Foundation mimicked in its 1960s reorganization.

In sum, regulatory shock encouraged the foundation world to seek organizational identities and practices that would appear reasonably accountable to other actors who could become their future allies: the government, the donor community, their own grantees, and the larger public. Ironically, they found their new model among themselves in the largest foundations and especially in the Ford Foundation—the very organization that had drawn the political lightning of congressional investigation and regulation. It is no real mystery, then, how the core elements of the philanthropic diversity policy of the 1990s went back in time to appear in the innovations of the Cleveland Foundation of the 1960s. Ford's own inertia between the 1960s and the 1990s explains the diffusion of the strategic philanthropy, which it helped birth in Cleveland, into the rhetoric of a later institutionalizing field modeled heavily on the national philanthropy. In other words, institutional isomorphism does not occur in reverse from local to national but from elite to both local and field apparatus. Ford resources and legitimacy mediate the common dependencies driving the convergence of foundation rhetoric and individual foundations toward diversity policy.

I now turn to an organizational history of the Ford Foundation to identify the factors that caused Ford itself to innovate twice: initially to develop strategic philanthropy and later to adopt a post-Black policy breadth to racial policies.

Historical Disposition of the Ford Foundation

If Ford involvement was critical for the directions taken by both foundations in their convergence to diversity policy in the 1990s, what explains its early and intensive involvement in Cleveland and its comparatively late association with the San Francisco Foundation? At present, there is no comprehensive historical monograph about the Ford Foundation beyond its origins (Magat 1999). Unfortunately, my analysis provides only an indirect history of Ford through a wide-ranging but undoubtedly incomplete review of the scholarly literature about the Foundation. What I found of the historical and social science literature on the institution is uneven in coverage, focus, and quality; nevertheless, these accounts suggest an explanation for why Ford treated the two community foundations differently.

Recent commentary on foundation scholarship replicates the traditional divide in organizational studies between the manager centrality promoted in business schools and the environment-centered approaches favored in the social sciences.[3] The specific literature on Ford reveals both tendencies to privilege the roles of "great men" (and occasionally women) and structural forces, respectively, sometimes in the same work. Founded in 1936, the Ford Foundation did not begin operating outside of Michigan until the early 1950s, by which time older organizations like the Carnegie, Rockefeller, and Russell Sage foundations had already created the founding practices and myths of institutional philanthropy. Within one decade, however, Ford had gained a reputation for drawing political lightning and had established key elements to U.S. policy discourse about the "race problem."

During the early 1960s, the Foundation developed domestic programs that had an enormous impact on federal urban policy; in other words, Ford appears to have created ad hoc the very resources and legitimacy that it was providing the Cleveland Foundation. Its ability to command the attention of Cleveland elites and federal actors alike was probably rooted not in its domestic reputation but in its notable international activities and their unassailably anticommunist goals. Indeed, the foundation's cold war interest arguably motivated its extensive engagement with domestic social movements from the late 1960s onward. I suggest that the Ford Foundation supported the Cleveland Foundation because the community foundation had access to local leadership, not unlike the elite allies abroad on which Ford international programs relied. Unfortunately, significant events in the 1980s severely diminished the power of the institution's allies and encouraged it to seek new coalitions to maintain its organizational stature. Not surprisingly, its "new" diversity strategy had less to do with addressing the new immigration than with updating its "old" approach to race relations for a new political climate.

STUDYING FOUNDATION BEHAVIOR

As a selective history of the Ford Foundation, this chapter focuses on the interaction among internal objectives, external relations, and culture of the organization and considers its multiple roles (1) with respect to specific policy formations, (2) in relation to social movements, and (3) in the foundation field itself. These foci converge with directions in current scholarship toward analyzing foundations as socially embedded organizations rather than presuming their power or agency. Recent commentaries on the methodology of foundation scholarship share the argument for formal organizational analysis to replace more conventional approaches that are unequivocally self-congratulatory or critical.

A senior Ford Foundation staff member, William S. McKersie (1999), combines an obvious personal investment in the honor of his occupation with an outline of the flaws in the literature and a persuasive argument for examining how foundations are embedded in organizational fields and possessed of a coherent and dynamic professional culture. Building on a criticism of nonprofit studies as overly national in focus, he calls for scholars to consider local philanthropy, arguing that most studies improperly use nationally aggregated data to observe organization-level priorities. Beyond grants, McKersie also cautions against relying entirely on archives to study internal processes; recommends a neoinstitutional consideration (DiMaggio and Powell 1991) of the external environment of a foundation, in particular its *local* peer institutions, nonprofits, businesses, and government; and highlights the rise of a strategic philanthropy not specific to race as the major post–World War II development in the foundation world. One senses an earnest desire to improve the standards of foundation scholarship mixed with a self-interested assumption about their good intentions. Ironically, his call for more formal analysis undermines the latter assumption, as most nonmanagerial organizational studies treat the behavior of staff and trustees as acting out the imperatives of external conditions rather than vice versa.

Though also a Ford Foundation officer, Lucy Bernholz explicitly observes that most foundation histories "presuppose that the foundation's work did, in fact, make a difference" (363). She singles out for praise the small amount of research that places foundations and their grantee organizations in the larger historical context surrounding a social movement, ethnic group, or city so that their social role rather than their impact can be more even-handedly assessed. She recommends to foundation scholars nine questions that fall into three associated aspects of foundation behavior: (1) the development of their objectives, (2) their external relations, and (3) their professional culture.

Even more broadly than Bernholz, Ellen Condliffe Lagemann (1999) urges foundation scholars to examine the social role of foundations through three distinct subjects of study: (1) foundation behavior in the aggregate, (2) foundations' role in specific developments in U.S. history, and (3) their relationship with social movements. Agreeing with McKersie and Bernholz, she recommends more "fully rounded evaluations that take into account all sides" (xv). All three statements argue for exploring complexity in foundation behavior; in doing so, they also raise a critical question about whether the internal and external processes that enable foundation effectiveness might also be associated with the very organizational conditions that limit the scope of, and indeed define, managerial discretion.

SETTING THE FORD FOUNDATION IN THE HISTORY OF FOUNDATIONS

By the time of Ford's beginnings in 1936, foundation work was already decades old. Andrew Carnegie had launched the Carnegie Corporation of New York, the largest of his philanthropic institutions, in 1911 (Nielsen 1972). In 1913, John D. Rockefeller Sr. began the largest of his fleet, the Rockefeller Foundation. Indeed, given the start of the Cleveland Foundation in 1914, the local organization is actually more senior than Ford.

In the early years of foundations, most philanthropy was heavily identified with the charitable interests of affluent individuals and families whose fortunes were created during the U.S. industrial expansion of the preceding century. Many of the leading foundations today established their institutional reputations during the early period, setting precedents that defined the scope of legitimate foundation activity and raising issues that continue to confront the field. Indeed, critics of the Ford Foundation sometimes take the organization to task for problems more accurately ascribed to the entire philanthropic enterprise than to the otherwise singular institution.

David Hammack argues that the most significant action of foundations during the early twentieth century was the successful efforts of a select group of foundations to reorganize the scope and control of nonprofit activity in the United States: "In some cases—higher education before the 1960s, the evaluation of college applicants, education for African Americans in the segregated South, establishing the teaching hospital-medical school complex in the 1920s and 1930s, creating the institutions of nonsectarian private social welfare between 1905 and 1930—foundations played a more important role than federal or state governments, the courts, religious denominations, or other previously existing organizations" (1999, 59). Before, in the nineteenth century, religious communities were the primary providers and coordinators of most educational, health care, and social services in the United States. In response to both increasing conflicts between Protestant sects and the massive immigration of Catholics, Jews, and Orthodox Christians at the turn of the century, certain general-purpose foundations supplied new sources of nondenominational financial support, "enabling many nonprofits to shift from a Protestant denominational basis to non-sectarianism and science" (53). In the course of reorganizing the provision of social services, they also created "a new set of nonsectarian coordinating organizations for nonprofits" (53). In the early twentieth century, foundations legitimated this trend toward secularization by supporting the development of the social sciences within universities as an alternative to the research conducted by theologically trained men in independent asylums, hospitals, clinics, and other institutions (Hammack 1999). Furthermore, "many colleges ended their formal relationship to a Protestant denomination to make their faculties eligible for [the] pensions" (55) offered by the Carnegie Foundation for the Advancement of Teaching, which later became the present-day Teachers Insurance and Annuity Association (Nielsen 1972).

In curbing traditional religious authority and replacing it with secular rationality, however, foundations raised "the central paradox of American life [between] the . . . ideals of political equality . . . and the realities of unequally distributed wealth, influence, and talent" (Hall 1999, 3). Although secularization challenged traditional barriers to equality, its agents—the new class of businessmen and professionals, and the foundations that legitimated them—were themselves the beneficiaries of an emerging social hierarchy. From the outset, foundations were mired in the contradiction of employing the profits of inequality to promote greater democracy.

Not surprisingly, retrospective considerations of early foundation projects reveal a blatant paternalism, what we might describe as an authoritarian reformism, a charge that critics have also leveled against the later activities of the Ford Foundation. While current criticisms may be accurate regarding the desirable degree of paternalism in a given foundation initiative, its presence has been endemic to foundation work since its beginnings. For example, Toon (1999) demonstrates how two foundations earnestly sought in the 1920s to improve community health but measured the success of their programs by the ability of local communities to recognize the wisdom of foundation expertise.

Besides possessing the authority to dismiss local alternatives as provincial, foundations have also influenced the magnitude of social improvements. Biographies of White female philanthropists in the early period are particularly suggestive of how foundations accommodate prevailing societal conventions and thus the scope of the proposals they are willing to support. Crocker's characterization of Margaret Olivia Slocum Sage reveals the privileges and constraints that shaped her philanthropic activities: "Mrs. Russell Sage, as she was now called [after marriage], constructed a separate identity for herself as one of that 'New York type of well-to-do committee-working church women'[4] . . . When Russell Sage died in 1906 at the age of ninety, he left her virtually all of his $75 million. Olivia had had to watch every penny during her thirty-seven year marriage, but now she launched into an astonishing philanthropy . . . [Of particular note], she gave $10 million to set up a foundation with the broad goal of 'social betterment,' naming it the Russell Sage Foundation, and thus erasing her own name as she commemorated the husband who had despised charitable giving in a gesture that we probably should see as ironic" (1999, 318–319). Thus, the principal U.S. foundation in supporting social science research into the present has its origins in the philanthropy of a White woman who only belatedly gained the financial power to do so, at the age of seventy-eight.

The career of Mary van Kleeck, director of the industrial studies program for, again, the Russell Sage Foundation, is similarly telling. On the one hand, during the 1930s, "she was the only prominent American who could claim, for better or worse, a simultaneous and leading reputation in the worlds of social science, Christian social action, and Communist fellow-traveling" (Alchon 1999, 158). On the other hand, prevailing gender restrictions also channeled her public service. Her studies of women workers in New York City facilitated the passage of protective legislation and attracted the attention of the Foundation. As the United States entered WWI, "van Kleeck was . . . managing much of the nation's women war workers, a job which led to her becoming the first director of the new Women's Bureau of the Department of Labor . . . in 1919" (157). Indeed, although U.S. women's labor force participation has grown geometrically since the early twentieth century, it remains, as then, a heavily sex-segregated phenomenon, so much so that it still has had no effect on rates of White male unemployment (Hudson and Carter 2002).

In the present, foundations are more cognizant of the criticism of paternalistic authority, and anecdotal evidence suggests that many philanthropic personnel even regard arrogance to be an occupational hazard. Likewise, they are also more sensitive to the charge that they quash the potential for "real" change by funding incremental innovations or "safe" proposals. Anecdotal evidence also suggests that foundation actors are more aware that a course of pragmatic reformism can have unintended political and substantive consequences. Nevertheless, the paternalism critique has remained a risk in most foundation activities simply because foundations decide what to fund and whom to exclude in order to supply limited funds to efforts with at least a minimal prospect of success. Within limits, they construct and finance the definitions of authority and possibility.

Ford did not invent the affection of foundations for demonstration projects or, more generally, the process of *benchmarking* social phenomena for the nation. In facilitating the rise of secularism over tradition, foundations also promoted a faith in the ability of science to identify universal truths that would be persuasive to rational actors. Demonstrations of scientific truth therefore played a central role in foundation efforts to improve human society. Grant's (1999) examination of the Rockefeller experience in child welfare reveals how "demonstrating truth" has long been a complex process that is hardly universally persuasive to other actors. In brief, the early efforts to benchmark childhood proclaimed the philanthropic intention to demonstrate truth to society, but the process exposed foundations to a wider range of responses than simple rational persuasion. Initially, foundation efforts focused on ameliorating inequalities and defined truth as the value of health exams, infant care, and bacteria-free milk, demonstrated by their provision to poor families. Though White middle-class families were the benchmark for truth, other actors understandably did not object to this demonstration. Subsequently, however, when the foundations focused on improving parenting behavior and defined truth as expert knowledge suggested by child development researchers, the targeted mothers questioned the expert advice. Their resistance led the foundations to cease funding the educational programs and shift focus to supporting basic research on child development, insulated from public sanction, and defining truth as standards of normality useful for medical assessment.

Notwithstanding the early precedents of foundation secularization, paternalism, and benchmarking, Edsel Ford started the Ford Foundation "in a small way [with an] original endowment [of] $25,000 [and] articles of incorporation [running] just three typed pages" (Macdonald 1955, 130). "It had been conceived as a device [in part] to avoid the necessity of selling control of the company in order to pay estate taxes after the death of the donors" (Nielsen 1972, 79). Until the 1950s, the Foundation operated exclusively as a tool for family charity to favored local institutions in Michigan, principally Detroit. This "provincial period" came to an end only after the founder's wife, Eleanor, and her young son Henry Ford II forced old Henry Ford from control of the Ford Motor Company, after his "paranoia and arbitrariness" had almost destroyed it, having already harassed his only child, Edsel, to death (Nielsen 1972). Following the settlement of the estates of both Edsel and Henry I, the Foundation endowment ballooned to an estimated asset level of $474 million (Magat 1979).

Under the direction of Dr. Karl Compton, a nonfamily member of the Foundation board who was also president of the Massachussetts Institute of Technology, the trustees appointed a study committee headed by H. Rowan Gaither Jr., a San Francisco attorney and banker. Besides being the chair of the Rand Corporation, Gaither was also Compton's friend from his years as assistant director at MIT's Radiation Laboratory during WWII (Macdonald 1955; Nielsen 1972). In two years, the committee produced "what remains the most exhaustively researched and explicitly stated blueprint for a foundation's operations" (Raynor 1999, 196). After the resulting reorganization, the Foundation sought to attain national and even international preeminence by prioritizing five "areas for action":

1. Activities that promise significant contributions to world peace and to the establishment of a world order of law and justice.
2. Activities designed to secure greater allegiance to the basic principles of freedom and democracy in the solution of the insistent problems of an ever changing society.
3. Activities designed to advance the economic well-being of people everywhere and to improve economic institutions for the better realization of democratic goals.
4. Activities to strengthen, expand, and improve educational facilities

and methods to enable individuals more fully to realize their intellectual, civic, and spiritual potentialities; to promote greater equality of educational opportunity; and to conserve and increase knowledge and enrich our culture.

5. Activities designed to increase knowledge of factors that influence or determine human conduct and to extend such knowledge for the maximum benefit of individuals and of society. (Magat 1979, 18)

Through the 1950s, the Foundation made uneven progress toward its heady new ambitions in world peace, democracy, the economy, education, and the behavioral sciences. More to the point, historians of the Foundation disagree about the relative cohesion and depth of its programs during this period. O'Connor characterizes the young foundation as quickly building "a substantial international grant portfolio and a strong overseas presence" (1996, 171). Ford owed its strong start to the connections of its first president, Paul Hoffman, who was still the leader of the Marshall Plan to rebuild Europe when the Ford board hired him in 1950.

However, it is arguable that Ford's considerable international impact occurred without the benefit of a coherent agenda from its headquarters. Within three years, political controversy and personal differences with the board resulted in Hoffman's "resignation" and the trustees' replacement of him with Gaither. Unfortunately, the Foundation became occupied with more controversy, and Gaither's illness in 1956 prompted trustees to promote him to chairman. The board replaced him with Dr. Henry Heald, then head of New York University, who, according to Nielsen, promptly put his "intellectually narrow and desiccated stamp" on the Foundation (1972, 90), de-emphasizing its international programs and reallocating its funds toward college education and educational television.

Aside from its educational investments, O'Connor describes Ford's domestic programs as "weak, directionless, and unable to take on the major issues of the day" (1996, 171). Sutton (1987) agrees and attributes the Foundation's slowness in responding to the rise of civil rights concerns to its caution in engaging in controversial domestic matters at a time when it felt ill understood and attacked by conservatives. On the other hand, Raynor (1999) argues that its national urban initiative in the 1960s was an outgrowth of earlier involvement during the 1950s in minority education and desegregation experiments in the South and school-community relations in New York City. Like its international programs, however, these early domestic impacts also occurred without the direct sanction of Ford headquarters.

During Hoffman's short presidency, the Foundation had established three quasi-independent funds, including the Fund for the Advancement of Education (FAE). It was this intermediary organization, not the Ford Foundation itself, that became active in civil rights before the 1960s.

Despite its uneven impact in both international and domestic arenas, once the Foundation raised its aspirations beyond tax relief and family charity, it began to follow the early precedents for foundation philanthropy and contributed its own unique precedents to the field: the provocation of political controversy and the expansion of race-relations philanthropy. The outbreak of the Korean War in 1950 bound the Ford Foundation's bid for philanthropic stature to a cold war context, wherein two congressional investigations would subject its domestic programs, racial and otherwise, to charges of communist subversion (Nielsen 1972; Sutton 1989). The first investigation in 1952 "charged that America's largest private philanthropic foundations had been infiltrated by communists who funded subversive activities" (Raynor 1999, 200). The Select Committee to Investigate Tax-Exempt Foundations chaired by Representative Eugene Cox (D-Georgia) was the culmination of opposition to a little more than one year of FAE grants to support desegregation campaigns and college scholarships for Blacks. Though the Cox Committee did not result in legislation, its hearings and the antecedent boycotts of Ford Motor Company products by segregationists provided the political opportunity for Ford trustees dissatisfied with Hoffman to replace him with Gaither (Raynor 1999).

The second investigation in 1954 "kept the staffs of Ford and FAE busy responding to punitive congressional audits and official questionnaires . . . for nearly a year" (Raynor 1999, 204). The trigger for the new inquiry, chaired by Representative Carroll Reece (R-Tennessee), was again FAE involvement, this time in a public schools initiative in "impoverished multiracial neighborhoods blighted by white flight, destabilized by urban renewal, and besieged by rural migrants and minorities" (203). The Reece Committee charged the Foundation with attempting a communist subversion of U.S. education and produced a blacklist of associations and organizations, including civil rights groups, as unfit for philanthropic support. While the investigation was directed at FAE educational activities, it also gained legitimacy from the outrage of Senator Joseph McCarthy at the Foundation's establishment of another intermediary organization, the Fund for the Republic, "to concentrate on problems of civil liberties in the United States" (Nielsen 1972, 84). And again, although no legislation emerged from the Reece hearings, Foundation trustees decided to reabsorb the FAE and directed the Foundation staff to make "a half billion dollars in unassailable grants to private universities and private hospitals in 1955–56" (Raynor 1999, 205). Judging from a Ford-commissioned opinion poll, the public relations campaign worked.

Burned early and twice by racial philanthropy, Ford nevertheless established in the 1950s and early 1960s "an intellectual linkage between race, inequality of educational opportunity, and poverty in America" (Raynor 1999, 196). How the Foundation continued to return to (and retreat from) a concern for race relations was the result of two factors. Internally, although its third president, Heald, considered civil rights leaders like Dr. Martin Luther King to be "propagandistic politicians" (Nielsen 1972), he apparently permitted his staff sufficient latitude to develop significant urban affairs and international development programs on its own. Indeed, it was during Heald's narrow presidency that his Public Affairs Division facilitated the grants that started the Greater Cleveland Associated Foundation, supported its new strategic racial philanthropy, and precipitated its capture of the Cleveland Foundation. Externally, Foundation personnel with political connections regarded the forces of McCarthyism as misguided and destructive but essentially correct in their belief of the threat posed by global communism. "They assumed that America had to achieve a modicum of improvement in domestic race relations in order to protect its international image and secure its place as leader of the free world" (Raynor 1999, 195). Although domestic efforts at desegregation remained tainted by the charge of communist subversion, they had also gained political currency as evidence that the United States might prove worthy of the allegiance of the newly independent former colonies.

THE URBAN POLICY CONTEXT FOR STRATEGIC PHILANTHROPY IN CLEVELAND

The Ford Foundation's interest in Cleveland occurred simultaneously with major urban initiatives led by its public affairs director, Paul Ylvisaker. From 1960 to 1966, the Foundation made $30.9 million in grants to address "problems of the urban poor" through its Great Cities and Gray Areas programs (Magat 1979, 169). A major focus on the Gray Areas Program prevails in the existing scholarship on Ford's involvement in urban affairs, though some studies also explore its later support of community development corporations starting in the late 1960s. The literature reveals the ambitions and assumptions that motivated the Foundation and also suggests the nature of its underlying ambivalence with race and politics. In particular, the design of Ford urban policy significantly reflected a gap between an aspiration for influencing federal policy and the fear of political controversy, mostly among the trustees.

The Gray Areas Program bears the significance of providing the blueprint for the federal urban policies of the mid-1960s: the Community Action Programs (CAP), Model Cities Programs, and more broadly, the War on Poverty (O'Connor 1999; Raynor 1999; Sundquist 1969; Yarmolinsky 1969). Initially, Ford awarded $12.1 million to demonstration projects in six places, mainly cities: starting with Oakland, then New Haven, Boston, Philadelphia, Washington, D.C., and the state of North Carolina. The purpose of the grants was "to develop and coordinate programs in areas such as youth employment, education, and expanded community services" (Kravitz 1969, 55). Specifically, "each grant was made to a new corporation[5] designed to coordinate all agencies in the community, public and private, whose activities impinged upon the poor. The specific activities to be financed were agreed upon by the community sponsors and the foundation staff" (Sundquist 1969, 13). As in the Greater Cleveland Area, Ford resources provided some actors with opportunities for policy innovation; however, as in the San Francisco Bay Area, its involvement also provoked charges by other actors of arrogantly ignoring local experience, tradition, and wisdom.

From his Public Affairs Division, Ylvisaker succeeded in his aggressive bid to fulfill the desire of the Foundation for national stature, defined as influence and regular consultation in domestic policies, albeit with mixed results in policy effectiveness. "In retrospect, it is not difficult to find flaws in the Gray Areas vision, with its too-narrow focus on social-service systems reform and its naïve hope that it could sidestep the problem of race" (O'Connor 1999, 189). Evaluating the community action programs modeled on the Ford vision, Kravitz (1969) characterizes them as modest successes for narrowing the gap between the poor and nonpoor and in improving the quality of social services. However, he and other scholars voice the criticism that both the Gray Areas Program and the federal programs imitating it were insufficiently attentive to larger social forces and structures. In particular, Ford philanthropy did little to reverse the more macrolevel trends of the disinvestment in central cities and the ghettoization of non-Whites in them (Raynor 1999). In fact, it is arguable that for philanthropic and federal urban policies to have been more effective, certain even more dramatic policy initiatives needed to have been present: a national income redistribution program, a large-scale public employment program, and the construction of housing for low-income individuals and families (Kravitz 1969).

Besides making the short-sighted assumption that community participation in social services reform would leverage the elimination of poverty, Ford personnel also evidenced an elite-directed approach to addressing social problems, which undermined its rhetorical commitments to community autonomy and expanding the reach of democracy. While successful at attracting federal funding to expand the demonstration programs, Ford's social engineers were increasingly confronted by the very citizens that the urban experiments sought to empower. No longer satisfied with resident participation that could be characterized as simple input, neighborhood residents and non-White community leaders raised trenchant critiques of the contradictions between welfare dependence and human dignity. These criticisms were ironically epitomized in a Ford-funded book charging the Gray Areas Program and its federal imitators as agents of "welfare colonialism" that regularly made residents feel like "guinea pigs in sociological experiments" (Silberman 1964, 317). As O'Connor succinctly observed, the Ford Foundation made the mistake of assuming "that a smooth-running foundation-government partnership would—or should—displace political struggle, ideological conflict, and grass roots organizing as a means of influencing social policy" (1999, 189).

It is possible to attribute the shortcomings of the Gray Areas Program to the characterization of Ylvisaker and his Public Affairs staff as White liberal do-gooders who ignored how residents experienced their policies. In actuality, the design of Ford's urban programs reflected more than simply personal naïveté, White ignorance, or even an elite culture that infantilized the predominantly non-White and poor city residents. Instead, the flaws in the demonstration grants resulted from strategic decisions to persuade, circumvent, or appease other actors.

First, although the charge of elitism may have been valid from the perspective of residents, it was possible only because Ford personnel had chosen to leave their foundation offices to more directly engage urban reform. Indeed, within the Foundation, the Public Affairs Division was attempting a shift between paradigms of how foundations, Ford especially, conducted their philanthropy. Ylvisaker and his staff introduced a new activist style of grant making that would attract the attention of federal policy. The new style favored applied expertise and social action over detached academic research and shifted the role of program officers from sober masters of esoteric philanthropese and foundationese (Macdonald 1955; Sutton 1989) to skilled, politically astute negotiators (O'Connor 1999). They modeled for the other Ford divisions a more engaged form of philanthropy, even though it fell short of resident expectations.

Second, Ford personnel were not blind to the structural context for the Gray Area vision. Indeed, they hoped that a system of community action projects and improved juvenile services coordinated by a new agency might connect central city residents with the mainstream economy and prepare them for civic and political participation. Although the majority of Americans lived in urban areas by the early twentieth century, cities remained politically isolated from their rurally dominated state legislatures for decades (Anyon 1997). During the 1950s, urban renewal coalitions persuaded desperate city governments to try reviving central business districts through "slum clearance" or the destruction of deteriorating physical structures, a practice that had the consequence of displacing the low-income residents who relied on them for their basic housing needs. After reviewing cases of urban renewal, Ylvisaker concluded that it had the "weakness" of treating cities as if they were "bricks without people" and "did little or nothing for the displaced" (Sundquist 1969, 13). In brief, he perceived urban disinvestment as an unfortunate policy gap and directed his division to close the gap with new organizations.

A strong motivation for Ford to develop new intermediary agencies at the local level was to bypass the political actors who were ignoring urban concerns. Almost all state legislative districts were based on counties instead of population until before the one-man-one-vote rulings of *Reynolds v. Sims* (1964). As a result, state governments tended to be prorural and antiurban through the 1960s (Anyon 1997). Unfortunately, the Ford strategy provoked intense reactions from nonfunded local actors. Public Affairs tried to justify its demonstration grants as comprising an effort to fill gaps "between the job to be done and the capacity of our urban communities as presently structured to accomplish it" (Sundquist 1969, 13). Nevertheless, the new initiative effectively bypassed many local authorities, for whom it came to "represent a monstrous compound of evil, waste, and disrespect for experience" (Kravitz 1969, 58). In a less tactful fashion and resulting in even greater criticism, Ford intervened into the New York decentralization controversy in the late 1960s in a manner widely seen as siding with the claims of Black parents that the school system was actively resisting desegregation. Circumventing the Board of Education, Ford supported new Black demands for community-controlled schools and aroused intense opposition from the teachers union, which was eventually successful at blocking decentralization. In brief, Ford efforts to circumvent actors whom the Foundation regarded as hopelessly intransigent often incurred the opposition of yet other actors who considered urban reform to be their turf.

Third, and most important, it may be tempting to interpret the attempts by Gray Area staff to sidestep the issue of race as a harbinger of the more contemporary ideology of naïve colorblindness. Certainly, the Ford staff was hard-pressed to respond to the frustrated aspirations of Black and other non-White leaders and communities and was unable to do so in the early to mid-1960s. However, the design of gray areas philanthropy was arguably a deliberate though piecemeal strategy to address race relations without scaring or provoking the reaction of Foundation trustees.

Explicitly, the Gray Areas Program sought to ameliorate the impact of migration on urban areas, specifically the physically deteriorating inner cities "swelling" with Black, Latino, and White Appalachian newcomers from rural areas (O'Connor 1999). To redress the abandonment of cities by business and the White middle class, the new intermediary organizations would substitute coordinated social services that might connect inner-city residents with mainstream culture and upward mobility. Ylvisaker himself characterized the program as conceptually framed by, not race relations, but migration; in fact, his original intention was an international program focusing on rural-to-urban movements across the globe, rather than a domestic initiative (Ylvisaker 1991).

Beneath this race-neutral mission, however, the Gray Areas Program supported efforts that directly addressed racial concerns. In New York, it facilitated the organizational leadership of sociologists Lloyd Ohlin and Richard Cloward and the application of their opportunity theory, "that antisocial behaviors like gang formation were rational responses to foreclosed opportunities in an inequitable capitalist system characterized by institutional racism" (Raynor 1999, 213). While foundation headquarters spoke of reconnecting migration to its "traditional" outcome of assimilation, their intermediaries spoke of attacking problems produced by capitalism and racism. Historians regard these inconsistencies as a strategic legerdemain, rhetorically cloaking Ford's most direct involvement in racial liberalism yet in the guise of the traditional mission of charity to change the culture and behavior of the poor (O'Connor 1999). Although the Ford program proved in its execution to be quite flawed, the alternatives known at the outset to the Public Affairs staff were simply inaction or yet more college scholarships for minorities—options more detached, less structural, and more color-evasive than the actually implemented policies.

Beyond providing an ancillary anticommunist motivation for contorted racial and urban initiatives, the international context has had further significance for the Ford Foundation's design of domestic racial policy. As noted earlier, the stature with which Cleveland businessmen and politicians regarded Ford in the early 1960s could hardly have been rooted in its controversial domestic programs. Instead, Ford had established a new reputation through international activities and a renown that continued through the 1960s. From 1950 to 1975, Ford would invest $1.5 billion in international philanthropy, including over $1 billion specifically for development (Sutton 1977).

Perhaps not surprisingly, the elite orientation of its involvement in developing nations suggests a key reason for its early decision to include the elite-allied Cleveland Foundation in its community foundation initiative and not the San Francisco Foundation. By the late 1960s, however, Ford had witnessed the passing of its golden age of philanthropy in India (L. Gordon 1997). In subsequent years, Foundation personnel would interpret its decades of experience as providing lessons with which Ford would alter its development paradigm. And it was these new rationales and practices that the fieldwide foundation rhetoric adopted stateside to advance its conception of diversity policy. Indeed, Ford's declining confidence in Western modernization seems to have contributed to the postmodernist content of philanthropic pluralism, that is, preferences for cultural relativism and microenterprise projects. Ford involvement in foreign policy proceeded through three stages: an early heyday, a period of disaffection and criticism, and the emergence of a new paradigm with effects on domestic policy.

The Golden Age of Elite Philanthropy. Although wedded to U.S. interests in the cold war, the Ford Foundation sought to become more than simply a tool of its homeland politics and established for itself an international relations niche working toward long-term victory. In this ambitious pursuit, the Foundation could rely on impressive human and financial resources. Ford trustees had intimate personal connections with both corporate and governmental institutions. Besides already mentioned individuals, a rather singular trustee was John J. McCloy,[6] who served not only as chair of the Foundation's board of trustees but also in an enormous range of other capacities: he was assistant secretary of war during the internment of Japanese Americans, the creation of the Office of Strategic Services (later the Central Intelligence Agency), and the decisions to integrate Blacks into the U.S. armed forces and to drop the atomic bomb on Japan; high commissioner to Germany in the post–World War II period; president of the World Bank; chair of the Rockefellers' Chase National Bank, guiding its merger with the Bank of Manhattan; trustee of the Rockefeller Foundation; and "private unpaid consultant to the United Nations Secretary General," on whom U.S. President Eisenhower called to negotiate the resolution of the Suez Canal Crisis (Bird 1992, 452; Berman 1980). Furthermore, the relative magnitude of the Ford endowment in the 1950s can hardly be understated. Its "endowment exceeded the combined assets of the next two largest grantmakers, the Rockefeller Foundation and the Carnegie Corporation. It exceeded the combined assets of the nation's three wealthiest universities: Harvard, Yale, and Texas. And it exceeded the total budget of the United Nations by a significant margin" (McCarthy 1995, 294). By 1968, its assets would reach $3.7 billion dollars (Nielsen 1972).

The Foundation applied its elite connections and tremendous wealth to shape international affairs primarily in the newly independent Third World, starting with South Asia, Africa, and later Latin America. In the Third World, Ford hoped that its involvement would show the superiority of Western society over Soviet communism. Its first president, Hoffman, hoped that "assistance to India would demonstrate what free men with wealth and wisdom could do to help other men to follow them down the same or a similar path of development . . . [Hoffman] seemed to think that alleviating poverty in India would put Indians firmly in the Western camp and further democratic rights" (L. Gordon 1997, 111). Tellingly, Ford did not seem to make much distinction within the Western camp between technical expertise, capitalism, and democracy. In addition to major funding for development, the Foundation also made grants for cultural programs, especially in the 1950s with the mission of countering Soviet propaganda in the Third World (McCarthy 1987).

Though Ford shared a political mission with the U.S. government, its international programs built on precedents set by other large foundations, especially the Rockefeller Foundation, and even by its own early domestic philanthropy. Following other large foundations, Ford emphasized a research orientation searching for the roots of social problems and the means for dealing with them, over simple "open-hearted" generosity (Sutton 1977). Increasingly, it followed Carnegie and Rockefeller in pursuing "sectoral development" in the areas of agriculture, population, education, and health, working closely with "political leadership, bureaucracies, and professional specialists in developing countries" (98).

An especially important model was the extensive international portfolio of the Rockefeller Foundation; indeed, Ford followed Rockefeller into India (L. Gordon 1997), which eventually became the country of Ford's largest involvement. Leonard Gordon notes a friendly but revealing disagreement between Dean Rusk, the president of Rockefeller, who "felt that foundation funds should be used to bring some Indians and Indian institutions to world-class rank," and Moraji Desai, the finance minister, who, "looking at the many poor of India, wanted to spread the money to more than a few elite-of-the-elite institutions. Rusk's model had the best influencing the rest, while Desai wanted to help some of the rest before the best were pushed to an even higher plateau" (109). Ford activities during the 1950s and 1960s suggest an initial agreement with Rusk on the importance of fostering a national elite, whether through educating a predominantly White male managerial elite for U.S. government, foundations, and academia (McCarthy 1995) or "the recruitment and training of a national and international managerial elite, a diversified network of . . . experts with a strong commitment to . . . the local scene" (296) throughout India and Africa (Berman 1980).

By the mid-1950s, the international programs initiated by its first president had settled into three divisions: international training and research, international affairs, and overseas development. The first division began what became the Foreign Languages and Area Studies Fellowship program, the largest program providing U.S. citizens with extended periods of residence and study abroad (Sutton 2001). The second sought to advance "peace and order" through more direct means, such as fostering international exchanges motivated to counter Soviet programs in "iron curtain universities" (Berman 1982, 52) and modernizing European universities to ensure "the continent's democratic progress" (Sutton 2001, 89).

Ford's third and most extensive division, however, sought to wage a more long-term war against communism. Scholars have characterized the early overseas development paradigm as an era of technical assistance, wherein foundations brought U.S. technical knowledge to the Third World by importing foreign experts to advise the governments of developing countries to develop institutions in major sectors (L. Gordon 1997). In particular, Ford emphasized public management and economic planning over programs of outreach to the broader population (Sutton 1977).[7] Even in the area of population control, the Foundation instructed its staff to pursue only projects in which the national government was prepared to invest substantial manpower and other resources (McCarthy 1995). Ironically, its reluctance to engage the larger population and thus appear to intrude in "massive and deeply political matters where a legitimate role of outsiders is hard to find" (Sutton 1977, 77) did not spare the Foundation from similar criticisms of its collaborations with developing governments.

The preference for elite direction characterized not only the content of Ford's international programs but also their very administration and design. For its largest program in India, Hoffman selected Douglas Ensminger, an agricultural sociologist from the U.S. Department of Agriculture, to be the Foundation's representative. From the start of his leadership, "the India office [developed] extremely close and cordial relationships with figures in the highest reaches of government. Ensminger was a friend and confidant of Prime Minister Nehru and shared many of the Prime Minister's views" (McCarthy 1995, 300). Even after the FAE controversies of the early 1950s that removed Hoffman and undermined top-level support for international programs, Ensminger remained and benefited from "unusual ties to the trustees . . . that allowed him occasionally to go around administrators including the foundation's presidents in New York" (L. Gordon 1997, 111). These relationships may explain his program's continuance through Heald's dessicated presidency.

The elite sponsorship behind Ford's international philanthropy extended to its controversial relationship with the Central Intelligence Agency. "The Ford connection revolved around the Congress for Cultural Freedom and a few other organizations that received grants from the Ford Foundation and were also supported by the CIA" (L. Gordon 1997, 113–114). The later revelation of its cofounder's identity proved to be embarrassing to its reputation as an independent institution; worse were the joint operations that the intelligence organization continually suggested. To maintain a working distance from the CIA, Ford established ground rules that required proposals to obtain approval from trustee John J. McCloy and barred the agency from recruiting current Foundation officers and ongoing fellowship recipients (Bird 1992).

Finally, its preferences for elite action and independence informed its undertaking projects against the explicit preferences of the U.S. government. To circumvent a McCarthyite campaign characterizing modern art as communist subversion, the Foundation replaced U.S. State Department support for the inclusion of American paintings in an Indian art show to counter communist entries. To circumvent congressional censure of religious programming, the Foundation provided a $250,000 grant for the Sixth World Buddhist Synod in Burma, on the grounds that the religion was innately opposed to communism. Ford hoped that "the revitalization of traditional indigenous values [would] prove an even stronger barrier to the acceptance of Communism by Hindus and Moslems [*sic*] than imported Western ideals" (McCarthy 1987, 98).

From Criticism to the New Paradigm of NGO *Empowerment.* Over time, the early emphasis on technical assistance for developing governments receded in the face of a new international context. After 1965, the USAID, the United Nations, and the World Bank all began major programs whose expanded expenditures shuffled the Foundation from leading donor to junior partner (McCarthy 1995). A subsequent fall in the U.S. stock market reduced Ford's assets, driving down annual international expenditures to $46 million by 1980, in contrast with their peak of $122 million in 1966. Furthermore, many people, both in the West and in the Third World, had lost faith in the hope that Third World development could replicate the victories of the Marshall Plan in post–World War II Europe. In India, Prime Minister Indira Gandhi marked the end of an era by urging "her people to cultivate self-reliance instead of taking foreign gifts" (301). Her comments crystallized a worldwide wave of suspicions about Western assistance, including growing criticisms about the omnipresence of CIA operations (Berman 1982). Furthermore, accusations emerged in the Indian press of the Foundation's being a CIA front, as did claims that the Indian government collaborated with Ford in "planning and doling out aid from the top down or the center outward, so that the masses of India have never felt involved and hardly been assisted" (L. Gordon 1997, 106).

At the heart of these sentiments was the increasingly popular view that foundations like Ford hid and operated an agenda of domination behind their rhetoric of altruism. I argue instead that something other than neocolonial intent motivated the technical assistance era. Indeed, the belief in the efficacy of Western expertise and institutions was genuine, rather than merely a shield for advancing U.S. interests. The story of Ford's development policies in the 1970s pivots on the fall of that cultural hegemony that earnestly, though patronizingly, cast development as a "White man's burden" and identified the pursuit of certain U.S. interests as beneficial for all countries. Curiously, by the 1980s, the Foundation became associated with an emerging alternative to technical assistance—arguably its opposite: microdevelopment and microenterprise carried out by holistically oriented non-governmental organizations (NGOS).

Francis Sutton's 1977 evaluation of the history of foundation involvement in international activities is especially notable because the author was at the time an officer with the Ford Foundation. He defines development ideology as laudably egalitarian, materialist, and activist, but notes that developed countries are less sympathetic to developing countries because the recurring news of political instability, coups, and repression has created "new questions about the legitimacy of close cooperation with [these] governments" (110). Indeed, Sutton starkly asserts, "It is painfully evident that a great many of the domestic troubles of countries around the world derive from the malfunctioning or incompetence of governments, and these troubles provoke international tensions and disturbances" (117). Though he largely blames developing countries for the failures of private and public policies to close international inequalities, he does attribute to foundations a major problem within Third World countries: the increasing polarization between elites and nonelites. Implicitly critiquing Rusk's model of elite-targeted development, he warns future foundation efforts of the unintended consequences of international training, communication, and collaboration in tempting philanthropic recipients to maximize status and rewards without benefit to their fellow citizens, especially those in rural areas. In fact, he suggests drastically reducing programs for international training and instead localizing training programs within developing countries.

By contrast, Berman (1982) is critical of Sutton's claim that the Ford Foundation has not been officially committed to the advancement of U.S. interests and summarizes the new criticisms of international development that emerged over the 1970s. Analyzing its support of intermediary organizations, he argues that Ford's motivations have not been exclusively humanitarian or apolitical. Rather, he observes that Ford has supported educational programs that betray a particular ideology that Foundation personnel share with high-level State, Defense, corporate, and financial actors: "(1) Third World nations with holdings of strategic raw materials needed to be aligned with the United States; (2) Third World . . . markets needed to remain open to [U.S.] capitalist penetration; and (3) social change . . . should never be revolutionary in nature, and steps should be taken to insure the gradual, moderate, and controlled development of these nations" (49).

In an account of philanthropic support for education in Africa, Berman also indicts Ford's international activities as extending pre–World War II

Foundation projects to cultivate and recruit "the 'safe' African, . . . an individual who had accepted the necessity of incorporating into African educational systems American pedagogical principles, content, and socio-political perspectives" (1980, 220). Instead of facilitating political liberation, African universities fostered a cultural dependence on the West, and instead of transmitting proven expertise, foreign advisors used poor nations as laboratories for social science ideas untested and even opposed in Western nations (Berman 1980). Even after Foundation personnel "reluctantly accepted the development reality of the 1970s," Berman charges them with organizing an international conference and stacking the development country representatives with former recipients, trainees, informants, and trustees (1982, 62). Although his critiques possess an ideological consistency, its characterizations of the Ford Foundation drift from an all-powerful agent of imperial hegemony to a rather stupid and shortsighted entity that cannot help but pat itself on the back. In the end, he awkwardly fuses his evaluations of the Foundation as both productive of positive benefits for the United States and Third World nations and participating in a larger system of domination.

An alternative view of the Foundation arises from examining not only its political effects but also how its priorities actually shifted from the technical assistance paradigm. The appointment of McGeorge Bundy to the Foundation presidency in 1966 led some to anticipate a rejuvenation of Ford's international activities. After all, Bundy was arriving from Lyndon Johnson's White House, where, as an anticommunist liberal, he had been an architect of the Vietnam conflict (Bird 1998). These speculations, however, proved to be false, as the new president made clear his intention to devote his personal energies to domestic affairs, especially race relations (Sutton 2001). Nevertheless, Bundy sought not to reduce the international program in priority but rather to change its focus, turning away from the high political purposes that McCloy and others had encouraged.

When Ensminger stepped down in 1970 as representative to India, the Foundation replaced him with Harry Wilhelm, who created "a new emphasis on Indian institutions and indigenous research. 'Truly,' noted Wilhelm, 'there will be no foreign solutions . . . The best we can seek is to assist India to find an Indian solution . . . For we do not share our predecessor's faith that we know the way'" (McCarthy 1995, 301). These comments signaled a new sense of humility on the part of the Foundation as Americans and Indians both realized the dangers of extremely centralized grants, overambitious hopes for easy poverty alleviation, monocultural and monodisciplinary prescriptions, and imported definitions of freedom (L. Gordon 1997).

The initial effect of this change in personnel was the shift from providing foreign advisors to government programs to supporting new research conducted by Indians in indigenous research and planning institutions. The shift was the result of not only Third World desires for self-determination but also U.S. concerns about the assumptions of traditional development programs. Especially significant were the criticisms raised by U.S. demographer Kingsley Davis about how population programs were geared for "prescribing contraception" as if overpopulation were a disease instead of resulting from underlying socioeconomic factors shaping the decisions of individuals (McCarthy 1995). This initial "retreat" to a new research program recalls the direction taken by the Rockefeller Foundation in its early child welfare philanthropy; after incurring political controversy, the Foundation sought to reconstruct its programs through supporting insulated social science research. In a short period of time, Ford's international activities shifted from operating Western institutions for national governments to making grants to Indian experts and institutions (L. Gordon 1997). If the "insidious" introduction of Western institutions into Third World countries indicated that the purpose of development philanthropy was to maintain Western control of recently decolonized nations, then arguably, Ford had abandoned this purpose by the 1970s.

More broadly, its international development focus shifted because the institution itself lost confidence in the appropriateness of Western expertise premised on Western experiences with economic development. Starting in the 1960s and culminating in the 1970s, cultural relativism replaced liberal universalism as a reigning assumption in Ford's international activities. Not surprisingly, international cultural grants surged, albeit as adjuncts to economic development projects. Foundation personnel saw culture as an opportunity to fill multiple gaps in existing development programs; cultural grants were simultaneously a way of tailoring general development plans, a counter to the anomie that development created, a unifying symbol for nations increasingly fractured postindependence, and a strategy for protecting traditional legacies from Western contamination. Reflecting a bold change in attitudes toward developing countries, cultural relativism redefined "the past" from an obstacle to modernization into a source of dignity and worth that facilitated new manners of development (McCarthy 1987).

By the 1980s, the aversion to the earlier paradigm had grown from a retreat to indigenous social science to a new emphasis on an even more local recipient of philanthropy: the indigenous NGO. "By the end of the 1980s, programs to assist the informal sector in developing countries had become quite popular" (Tendler 1989, 1033). Although Tendler associates the popularity of microenterprise programs specifically with smaller donor organizations rather than large foundations, her examination of successful programs and their observable traits highlights six select grantees of a Ford Foundation program for Livelihood, Employment, and Income-Generation (LEIG).[8]

McCarthy's (1995) study of Ford's population programs suggests the earlier diffusion of successful experiences from that sector to the entirety of Ford's international activities. After Bangladesh won independence from Pakistan in 1971, Ford established an office in Dhaka, which "began by following the foundation's general drift toward social science research" (307). By the mid-1970s, the office started working with NGOs as an alternative to the internal rivalries that beset the social science institutes and achieved surprising results in family planning. "Unlike the government program or the foundation's ill-fated research and management grants, [it was grassroots organizations that] produced results" in reducing birthrates (307–308). A new rationale consolidated behind the successful grants: NGOs were effective because they were locally focused, regarded as more trustworthy than government, possessed a more flexible structure than government bureaucracies, and, especially significant, heavily run by local women, who could transform local traditions from within. By 1980, "communal self-help, rather than governmental expansion, now became the *leitmotif* of [Ford's] campaigns" (312).

In addition to the newly discovered efficacy of NGOs, Ford headquarters experienced a personnel shift that complemented and extended the new family planning paradigm throughout the foundation. In 1979, after Bundy's retirement, the trustees appointed Ford's first Black president, Franklin Thomas, the former head of the Bedford-Stuveysant Development and Services Corporation, an antipoverty organization launched by Senator Robert F. Kennedy with money partly from the Ford Foundation under Bundy (Bird 1998). "Under Thomas' direction, Ford increasingly began to explore new ways of working with grass-roots organizations as catalysts for reform" (McCarthy 1995, 306). In the following decade, as noted in chapter 2, the discourse of the foundation field singled out community development corporations (CDCs) like the Bedford-Stuveysant as important philanthropic recipients for developing "mature" minority leaders with both mainstream and coethnic credentials.

Notwithstanding the formal compatibility between an international focus on NGOs and a domestic focus on CDCs, Ford's experience with what we might term the *indigenous local nonprofit* has not been entirely positive. Just as NGO proponents have cast them as more effective than the preceding recipient of Third World governments, CDC proponents have cast them as more effective than the controversial community action programs (CAPS), themselves an earlier type of domestic NGO. Chafkin (1978) specifically uses Ford-supported CDCs to illustrate their advantages: the capacity to manage large sums of public and private monies, a record of producing local results, and the tendency to sidestep political entanglements and controversy. However, NGOs also possess limitations similar to those that Ford discovered in its experience with CAPS. Just as CAP attempts to circumvent state and local government inaction eventually provoked backlash, Ford decisions to support the more efficient NGOs have resulted in "distance and mistrust . . . between the governmental and non-governmental sectors, thereby reducing the possibility that governments will replicate successful NGO 'experiments'" (Tendler 1989, 1042). Furthermore, the same criticisms of CAPS as unable to effect the broader changes that might complement their highly local activities (Kravitz 1969) reappears in criticisms of the low impact, lack of broader replicability, and other "diseconomies of scale" prevalent among NGOs (Tendler 1989).

Additional complications are evident in the convergence of Ford's international and domestic programs toward local nonprofits. Domestically, Chafkin (1978) characterizes Ford CDCs as an institutional alternative to the belief that the effective delivery of social services requires revolutionary changes, including the adoption of a strong central government as in China and Cuba. Ironically, though Ford development policy had the high purpose of anticommunism, its technical assistance paradigm led it to encourage the centralization of planning in national governments for decades. Internationally, McCarthy (1995) views Ford support of Indian NGOs as empowering women leaders much as the Gray Areas Program developed African American leaders. Ironically, though Ford and War on Poverty CAPS started the political careers of many Black leaders, their controversial origins isolated them from mainstream politics. In sum, Ford's early race for the new paradigm appears to have suppressed the lesson that the autonomy of local nonprofits had both advantages and disadvantages.

By contrast, Ford's experience in Cleveland suggests that a crucial adjunct to expanding the impact of local nonprofits lies in forming alliances with elites. Indeed, the Foundation's subsequent experiences with NGOs suggests a relearning of why the Foundation chose to collaborate more with the Cleveland Foundation than the San Francisco Foundation in the early 1960s. Tendler (1989) argues that the six Ford NGOs in her study perform better than most other microdevelopment efforts for reasons counter to conventional philanthropic wisdom. First, the successful organizations were minimalist in their activities, whatever their often broader rhetoric, rather than actually "multiservice," holistic, and at risk of being stretched too thin. Alternatively, the organizations had begun minimalist and continued to conserve a core activity as a priority above expansion. Second, these NGOs were intimate with centers of power, having the support or at least tolerance of banks, municipal authorities, politicians, ministries, and departments instead of their opposition. Third, they provided products and services that simultaneously benefited both their direct clients and more powerful consumers. In sum, they possessed the local advantages of the Cleveland Foundation over the San Francisco Foundation: an already locally recognized niche, support from a broad alliance of elites, and a mission to integrate disparate factions into a larger public.

Unfortunately, this analysis of Ford's new paradigm suggests that the Foundation's successful transformation beyond its technical assistance era coincides with its increased isolation from the political and corporate centers that so empowered its early philanthropy. By the 1990s, projects promoting democratization bore striking similarities to earlier development projects: partnerships with national governments; provision of foreign expertise, in the form now of consultants instead of trainers; and an abstract concern with communism, such as village democracy in China (Shelley 2000) and "capacity building" for the exiled Tibetan government residing in Nepal and India (Fisher et al. 1996). In this new situation, other institutional actors have taken up and perhaps cornered the pursuit of U.S. interests through nongovernmental action. In fact, Shelley presents a new characterization of the Ford Foundation as a uniquely international and independent NGO in contrast with the more clearly partisan International Republican Institute and the Carter Center. And it is to these newer organizations that Shelley attributes the role of producing reports read by U.S. corporations and government elites. While Ford's financial resources remain considerable in comparison with other international NGOs, its political capital appears to have followed the descent of foundation rhetoric post-1980.

FORD AND SOCIAL MOVEMENTS: CRUCIBLE
FOR THE SOCIAL ROLE OF FOUNDATIONS

Like Ylvisaker and Ensminger, McGeorge Bundy became a metonym for the philanthropic institution that employed him. Unlike them, however, Bundy was its president and, indeed, the Ford Foundation's first president to be neither outshone by his staff nor outmaneuvered by his trustees. In the literature on foundations and their relationship with social movements, scholars have paid special attention to Ford, especially to activities attributed to Bundy or at least sponsored under his directorship from 1966 to 1979. I suggest that these programs are intimately associated with the decline of the Foundation's political clout and with the ascent of Republican presidents in the 1980s. The conservative movement that brought Reagan to power displaced the Eastern Establishment, whose "Rockefeller Republicans" had long provided impressive connections and influence for the Foundation. Indeed, in the wake of the terrorism of September 11, 2001, President George W. Bush would repudiate many of the foreign policies institutionalized by the internationalist wing of the GOP since World War II.

Even without this shift in political power, however, the Ford Foundation had become politically unpalatable to those members of the national elite that had long supported the philanthropy. Before Thomas assumed the Ford presidency, Bundy had already shifted institutional norms so dramatically that arguably even moderate Republicans may have regarded the Foundation as hopelessly tied to liberal Democratic policy assumptions. Over the course of the Bundy years, the Ford Foundation initiated a relationship with social movements that shifted its motivation for racial philanthropy from an ancillary anticommunism to a direct and outright liberalism. "The disadvantaged in American society—Blacks, Hispanics, American Indians, the poor in general—became the central domestic concern of the foundation in education, housing, urban neighborhoods, civil rights, and political participation" (Sutton 1989, xviii).

Although politicians and activists have criticized foundations, Ford especially, for excessive partisanship (Nicolau and Santiestevan 1991), scholars tend to criticize them instead for timidity, that is, their support of "safe" causes, organizations, and strategies. Over the 1960s and 1970s, however, the basis of these recurring criticisms shifted, revealing a politically leftward drift in foundation conceptions of safe grantees. Haines (1988) observes that until the 1960s, foundation contributions to Black causes were minimal and limited to the safest institutions and organizations, the earliest being Black education. During the nineteenth century, White foundations provided support for Black colleges with a focus on "separate but equal" institutions; not until the 1950s did certain smaller foundations make funding available for Black collective action. With respect to Ford, he disparages its aversion to controversy and notes that "congressional attacks . . . in the 1950s . . . tended to discourage what little initiative [Ford and other large funders] had been inclined to take in regard to social and racial issues" (114). Focusing on the subsequent Gray Areas and War on Poverty programs, Yarmolinsky (1969) praises their "pragmatic and eclectic" qualities but also emphasizes their ironic shortsightedness for not realizing that the organized urban poor would find little appeal in the efforts of planners to deracialize poverty as purely economic. Nevertheless, by the 1960s, Black poverty had become a safe philanthropic target.

With Bundy's presidency, the norm proceeded to drift into the support of political activism. Exploring patterns in the emerging social movement sector of U.S. philanthropy, Jenkins and Halcli criticize philanthropy for targeting the new professional advocacy organizations "based on paid staff who represent or act on behalf of groups" instead of the classical indigenous movement groups based on grassroots mobilization (1999, 244). Similarly, from an examination of Ford Foundation support for the women's studies movement, Proietto criticizes the philanthropy for facilitating the institutionalization of women's studies and mainstreaming the movement with the effect that it "increasingly resists reliance upon strategies and actions which risk alienation or stigmatization" (1999, 279). In brief, the political drift in foundation philanthropy since World War II has pushed critical scholars from questioning foundations for being aloof to social movements to questioning them for favoring types of political activism.

Remaining static, however, are the characterizations of the political orientation of the Ford Foundation as somewhere between the mass of foundations and the subgroup of avowedly progressive "alternative foundations." Even though Haines (1988) views Ford's 1950s efforts as minimal, he does view the Foundation as an exception (along with the Rockefeller Brothers Fund) among the larger foundations, likening it to the progressive Stern Family Fund and the Field Foundation, which made grants to civil rights organizations. Similarly, Jenkins and Halcli (1999) attribute the explosive interest in social movement philanthropy to Ford grants under Bundy's leadership, but also observe the succession of new alternative foundations, starting with the Vanguard Foundation in 1972, as the new leaders in the field. Ostrander (1999) more firmly draws the distinction between the alternative foundations like Vanguard and other funders, including Ford. From a study of the Haymarket People's Fund, she argues that grantee participation in grant-making decisions distinguishes the new progressive funders and is in fact the culmination of a tradition that began with the earlier Stern, Field, and Rosenwald institutions. In brief, the Ford Foundation has become politically "activist" but remains "elitist."

Theories of the relationship between foundations and social movements originate from the scholarly debate over whether conscience or social control is the primary sentiment motivating external patronage. A persistent problem in the debate remains the existence of "two versions of the social control thesis: control as the intention of patrons vs. control as the consequence of patronage" (Jenkins and Eckert 1986, 813). Indeed, the literature on foundations and movements has tended to conflate the motivations and effects of philanthropy, primarily by "reading" motivations from effects. I suggest that a better characterization of Ford's relationship with social movements comes from viewing foundation motivations and effects on movements as nonidentical and, furthermore, loosely coupled. In fact, when the goal of philanthropy is not direct influence but rather a reliable relationship, then both conscience and control are secondary considerations.

Proponents of the social control perspective argue that elites become involved only in reaction to mass mobilizations, which they then seek to direct into regular political participation. Notwithstanding the attribution to motivation, scholars have mainly elaborated the thesis by looking for the expected effects of movement demobilization after the provision of funding but have not explored the possibility that an intention to control may have other consequences than direct success. Jenkins and Eckert (1986) advance an alternative thesis that focuses on patronage effects and characterizes foundations not as transforming movement goals or tactics but as channeling them toward professionalization. However, they leave open the question of motivation, for instance, whether foundations seek to contain and moderate or to improve and expand movements.

Building on this control versus channeling debate, Proietto (1999) suggests an institutional mechanism for the channeling effects: programmatic alienation, which, over time, leads to the expected effects under the social control thesis. She argues that inherent in the grant-making relationship is the translation of a movement into a discrete fundable project with reasonable aims within a given time period and with proven technical competencies at hand. "The process of co-optation involves the extraction of dynamic elements of a movement through the funder's ability to privilege that element by providing funds, legitimacy, and other resources, with little or no reference to the whole political or social revolutionary vision" (283). She concedes that the resources provided have real and positive effects in the short term, but she also suggests that this type of deradicalization may eventually lead to demobilization.

The neocolonialism thesis links elements of social control and channeling perspectives with the unique characteristics of U.S. race relations. Focusing on the Black liberation movement of the 1960s, Allen (1969) adds foundations to the internal colonial theory of racial inequality, which emphasizes the parallels and connections between the domestic situation of non-Whites and the international position of their ancestral homelands. In both contexts, decolonization movements overthrew historical systems of oppression but then confronted new relations of domination or neocolonialism. In the international arena, economic dependence replaced coercive exploitation and resource extraction; meanwhile, colonial powers became "developed" countries assisting the formerly colonized in the process of modernization. In the domestic arena, the neocolonial critique suggests that the apparent "conscience" of foundations has been a cover for the control of movement goals and, even more profound, the maintenance of racial inequalities.

Though neocolonialism connects patronage with movement content, it does so through a theory of total domination that tends to reduce patronage to the "invisible hand" of an unequally structured society. At one point, Allen (1969) charges the Ford Foundation with funding all of the major Black protest groups in order to stall protests and urban revolts and to ensure the stability necessary for the expansion of the U.S. empire. At another point, he asserts the sincere desire of White businessmen to help the Black movement but attributes to the larger economic system the capacity to transform any expressions of conscience into instruments for control. Less expansively, Allen indicts efforts led by Bundy for channeling the call for Black power into programs promoting Black capitalism and aiding Black businessmen to engage in ghetto development. In addition, he characterizes community development corporations not as exceptional organizations but as neocolonial institutions serving corporate capitalism.

Like the neocolonial critique of development philanthropy, this perspective on movement philanthropy possesses more internal consistency than empirical validity. The decline of post–World War II Black insurgency had more sources than simply elite patronage. These well-documented factors include (1) the passage of the Civil Rights Acts of 1964 and 1965; (2) increasingly salient divisions between institutional entrists, socialists, and nationalists; (3) the erosion of Democratic Party support as the movement moved into northern and western cities; (4) the nationalization of White backlash; and (5) the federalization of state repression (Jenkins and Eckert 1986; Omi and Winant 1986, 1994). At its extreme, the neocolonial perspective on foundations and movements attributes the influence of these other dynamics entirely to philanthropy and classifies movement outcomes as patronage effects, interpreting foundation motivations post hoc. In sum, the theory grants the Ford Foundation an excess of agency for the persistence of racial inequalities.

A similarly incomplete perspective might view the Ford Foundation more positively as a unique catalyst for social change. As noted above, its support of notable organizations such as the Congress of Racial Equality (CORE), the Southern Christian Leadership Conference (SCLC), the National Urban League, and the National Association for the Advancement of Colored People (NAACP) dramatically expanded the social movement sector in U.S. philanthropy. Proponents of this catalyst thesis also focus on the role of the foundation in fostering new activist organizations that still exist into the present, especially the major Mexican American nonprofit organizations, including the National Council of La Raza, the Mexican American Legal Defense and Educational Fund, and the Southwest Voter Registration Education Project (Nicolau and Santiestevan 1991). However, this thesis commits the inverse error of reducing the foundation-movement relationship to merely interorganizational assistance abstracted from the political and historical context that informed philanthropic decisions. In brief, none of these theories account for why any foundation would make grants that controlled, channeled, subverted, or expanded movements that were lacking in, or had already lost, both significant popular support and internal cohesion.

Himmelstein's (1997) study of corporate philanthropy suggests that an adequate explanation would require a loosely coupled motivation that could generate all of the above effects. Examining why so much criticism of corporate giving tends to come from conservatives, he advances a theory of corporate pragmatism that "pictures corporations as situated in a society in which they face other social actors with interests different from theirs, but few real enemies. Securing corporate interests in this situation requires establishing relations with and gaining access to these interests" (8). I suggest that the many effects that foundations, especially Ford, have had on social movements are less compatible with narrow intentions to do harm or good than with the broader motivation to secure a particular type of relationship: *elaborating issues and piloting programs for eventual government adoption.* Demobilization, professionalization, local entrepreneurship, and nonprofit formation—all might be viewed as byproducts of initiatives to develop movements into potential public agencies or expand constituencies for existing public programs. In this light, the increasingly left character of the Ford Foundation reflected an organizational mission to secure its Gray Areas–War on Poverty relationship with federal actors engaged in liberal social reform. Ironically, by the end of Bundy's presidency, the Foundation had become highly relevant for a federal regime that soon evaporated with the ascension of Ronald Reagan to the U.S. presidency (O'Connor 1999).[9]

Conclusions and Implications

The omnipresence of the Ford Foundation complicates our main question: Why and how have foundations adopted diversity policy? By the 1980s, the national foundation had captured the field in terms of its discourse about race and ethnicity, and probably in more ways than can be shown in this book. In the process, Ford achieved a greater audience for the lessons of its experiences in urban policy, its renowned participation in international development, and its increasing association with social movements. Foundations, therefore, adopted diversity policy because their new field apparatus,[10] the Council on Foundations, and its magazine, *Foundation News*, modeled its racial rhetoric on the ongoing organizational trajectory of an elite member. During the 1980s, Ford programs became the foundation model for racial discourse, importing its international development experience first into Native American, then the general minority discourse. Consequently, philanthropic pluralism is more than strategic philanthropy, inclusive expertise, and a post-Black breadth. Arguably, it is motivated by the search of the Ford Foundation for new allies with whom to further racial liberalism in a politically conservative era. Foundations adopted diversity policy because one of its elite members found the policy useful for securing its institutional stature in the aftermath of losing significant political capital. Although foundations looked to Ford for solutions to prevent future sieges, it remains an empirical question how they actually adopted Ford's historical tendencies, indeed, which tendencies, and furthermore, whether at all.

The visibility of Ford in the foundation shift to philanthropic pluralism has significant implications for understanding the sociological nature of racial discourse, the general character of diversity policies, and racial social change within institutions. First, racial discourse is neither representative of universal practices nor merely random talk. Instead, it reflects the complex relationship within a field between nationally oriented elites and locally oriented nonelites. Elites possess a gravity that attracts the attention of field rhetoric and enables them to select local organizations to elevate as national models for racial discourse. The discursive shift to diversity policy may have signaled the rise of Ford visibility instead of a widespread shift in framing minority issues from taste combinations with Blacks to structurally equivalent food groups. In brief, racial rhetoric simultaneously reflects elite power and elite dependence on nonelites; therefore, it possesses sociological meaning only by reference to discrete institutions and other social actors.

Second, Ford's historic preference for elite-directed social reform results in specific divergences of philanthropic pluralism from the ideal type of diversity policy presented in chapter 1. By comparison with broader currents, foundation diversity policy is incomplete in a significant manner. It unevenly responds to the political experience of previous racial policies, possesses a post-Black scope of constituent groups, and introduces an international perspective; most of all, its primary attention to grooming non-White leadership falls short of reflexive and symmetric social relationships that treat Whites themselves as racialized actors. Without this fourth element, foundations continue conflating racial policy with minority policy and render diversity policy into yet another program to make non-White subjects more tolerable for White judgments. Ironically, this asymmetry may be rooted in the hierarchical assumptions of the elites on whose resources foundations depend to enlarge the scale of social policy impacts. The comparison of the local cases suggests that diversity policy might involve a trade-off between scale and democracy. Similarly, political events at the national level appear to have forced Ford to trade privileged membership in the design of primarily Black-related public policy for wider alliances with Asian, Latino, and Native leaders.

Third, because Ford activities provide racial and ethnic coherence to the foundation world, field cohesion is primarily systemic in nature, or largely constructed by the field apparatus, rather than cumulative, or related to the actual prevalence of corresponding practices in the field population.[11] Therefore, any field-to-member isomorphism would likely require direct Ford involvement, that is, interfoundation initiatives such as its major grants to community foundations. In institutions like the foundation field, racial social change may have an extraordinary dependence on the participation, preferences, and culture of its elites. Unlike the foundation "profession," true professions like medicine and law control the training and licensure of their practitioners; similarly, the sciences control the training and prestige of scholars. By comparison, organizational fields like foundations control simply the diffusion of ideas and, more loosely, the status of their members through the organizational counterpart to gossip. While the apparatus of fields might be more vulnerable to elite influence, these institutions also have less control over their membership. In brief, internal hierarchies deeply structure the direction and character of racial social changes through an institution.

6

Exploring the Validity of Diversity
Policy for Foundations Themselves

What's more important? That a trustee or staff have a Chinese
American face or that they have knowledge of the community?

A San Francisco Foundation trustee posed the above rhetorical question to
me during our interview; furthermore, he suggested that a non-Chinese
person from the city might know more about Chinatown than a Chinese
American from the suburbs. However, the trustee was *not* arguing that the
Foundation should be colorblind with respect to its personnel decisions.
Instead, he advanced the above issue as indicating the current challenge
facing the Foundation now that it had achieved "the right numbers" in
the ethnoracial composition of its trustees and staff. In other words, he
conceived of institutional diversity as possessing two distinct elements: an
emerging goal of cultural competence that *built on* an accomplished goal of
workforce heterogeneity. Of course, his conception of diversity policy, as a
natural supplement to affirmative action, diverges from the actual history of
how U.S. institutions adopted diversity policy in the wake of the political
backlash against affirmative action and multiculturalism.

Indeed, I have demonstrated in the preceding chapters that the strategic
value of diversity has been more important to policy adoption than the
appeal of the distinctive elements that set it apart from earlier racial policies.
Although the new policy explicitly invokes a post-Black constituency, the
internationalization of race relations, and a new symmetry in intergroup
relationships, its historical imperative has mainly been to respond to political conditions. As shown in chapter 2, the rise of philanthropic pluralism in
field discourse deliberately breaks from the national political retrenchment

during the 1980s against preexisting racial policies. Chapters 3 and 4 revealed how the organizational adoption of the new mode for racial philanthropy depended on the availability of reliable allies in their local political regimes. And Chapter 5 suggested how the 1980s decline of the Ford Foundation's political clout ironically underlies its rising visibility in the foundation field, which thus seems to construct diversity policy with the face of the San Francisco Foundation but the heart of the Cleveland Foundation. In brief, the motivations behind the new policy are only tangentially related to its distinct goals of building more symmetric communities, broadening the concerns of domestic race relations, or recognizing the demographic presence of non-Black non-Whites.

In this chapter, I move beyond my primary argument about foundations as shapers of racial policy and refocus on foundations as workplaces themselves to explore how well diversity policy accounts for actual organizational cultures. The question of policy accountability is important because its future existence depends in part on evaluations of its ability to reach its goals. Arguably, only its core proponents will evaluate the policy primarily on the basis of strategic purposes, whereas others will assess its legitimacy more by the relative validity of its intrinsic characteristics and expressed goals. Despite its strategic motivations, however, or in fact because of them, the adoption of diversity policy has shifted the basis by which institutions define and evaluate workplace heterogeneity. The older, justice-oriented policy of affirmative action focuses on the disparities experienced by members of specific protected categories; by contrast, the newer, productivity-oriented diversity policy focuses on the cultural competence of the organization. The former policy monitors and polices the exclusion of non-Whites, while the latter policy promotes their contributions to organizational culture. The value of "nontraditional" personnel shifts from evidence of nondiscrimination or even activist egalitarianism to being a unique resource for organizational performance. Therefore, the future persistence of philanthropic pluralism may rest in part on its relative success at pursuing not only its underlying affirmative action goals but also *its explicit mission to improve philanthropic effectiveness.*

I assess the latter issue by demonstrating how non-White foundation personnel both fulfill and fail to fulfill the promise of diversity policy rhetoric to make their organizations more culturally competent. As noted in chapter 1, during the 1990s, conservatives embraced diversity as an institutional good; however, they have also distanced their preferred policies from identity politics, or what they perceive to be a liberal-ideological association between an individual's cultural contributions and her membership in the federally protected categories. Taking the stated mission of diversity policy at face value, they argue that organizations can best achieve genuinely productive diversity by ignoring the race and gender "straitjacket" promoted by the more moralistic diversity consultants (Lynch 1997).

In this chapter, accordingly, I examine how well identity politics accounts for the institutional perspectives about race held by individuals in philanthropy. Do the "new insiders" voice unique and valuable perspectives on how foundations participate in race relations? To what extent does group membership make an individual more "talented" and the organization more "culturally competent"? In particular, I focus on the definitions and assumptions surrounding the most distinctive aspect of diversity policy: an institutional responsibility for symmetric intergroup relationships.

My answer is that racial membership does affect individual perspectives but does so less than proponents of identity politics assume and yet more than conservatives would expect. Specifically, I argue that race sometimes attains a secondary significance in characterizing philanthropic perspectives *mainly after* taking institutional and regional circumstances into account, by showing that:

1. Theories about how racial and ethnic diversity shapes organizational culture diverge in their expectations over how the institutional perspectives of the new foundation personnel might compare with those of both their White colleagues and their grantees.

2. Regarding the institutional responsibilities of grant-making foundations themselves, the non-White trustees *diverge* from their White peers to contribute uniquely reflexive, regionally specific perspectives, while non-White program staff *converge* with their White colleagues in regionally distinct standpoints.

3. However, both non-White trustees and staff assess the institutional responsibilities of nonprofit grant seekers (grantees) in the same way as their respective White peers—*converging* furthermore across the trustee and staff boundary into regional philanthropic "cultures" that confront their respective grantees.

4. By contrast, the concerns of grantees are far more similar across both regions and racial memberships, and their cohesive standpoint is both quite isolated from the foundation perspectives in their respective areas and more attentive to the external environments of organizations.

I close by summarizing the multiple positions of the new insiders, revisiting the theoretical debate on how diversity affects organizational culture, and suggesting how the "incomplete social change" of post–civil rights America explains the real but limited validity of diversity policy.

I have two ulterior motives: first, to convince students of organizational dynamics that race can influence how individuals understand and perform their institutional roles, and second, to convince students of race and ethnicity that the salience of race for institutions is a distinct phenomenon from the significance of race for personal experience. This argument has implications beyond the foundation world or even other institutions that have adopted diversity policy or are considering its adoption. In his *New Republic* article entitled "Philanthropical Correctness," David Samuels warns of the magnitude of foundation support for diversity policy: "The ideologically driven pursuit of 'diversity' and 'inclusiveness' is perhaps the one area in which today's foundations are influencing public policy with anything like the force of their powerful predecessors of the '50s and '60s" (Samuels 1995, 25, 35). However, I will demonstrate that how diversity actually works within foundations deviates from the policies they have encouraged nonprofits and the larger society to adopt. Race may be quite significant in the personal lives of foundation personnel, but it has a more limited influence on dividing their organizational and occupational world.

Theories of New Insider Standpoints

The major theories of how diversity shapes organizational culture generate divergent hypotheses for whether and how the new foundation insiders contribute unique and important perspectives to their respective organizations. I focus on two major sources for these hypotheses: the diversity management literature and sociological standpoint theory. In the former, conservatives critique liberal models of diversity management, whereas in the latter, feminists reconstruct Marxist theories of collective consciousness. At stake in both debates is the relative significance of group membership (race or gender), structural location (social class or other positional hierarchy), and region (local politics and demography) in shaping the perspectives of individuals. I focus specifically on the narratives, expressed affect, and other meanings that insiders associate with their direct involvement with an institution, that is, their institutional perspectives. These are only one segment of the more personally centered identities that sociologists of ethnicity theorize from research on the relative significance of group membership in everyday life and over the life course (Tuan 1998; Waters 1999). Therefore, I suggest that the significance of race in institutional life and thus also the relative validity of organizational diversity policy are relatively autonomous from the significance of race in personal lives.

The divergence between liberal and conservative models of diversity management concerns the question of whether a generic diversity policy would benefit organizations anywhere in the United States. Generally speaking, most diversity management theorists and consultants assume that membership in a phenotypic or visible group directly shapes an individual's exposure to relevant experiences (Cox 1993). Proponents of liberal diversity policy make social psychological assumptions about how individuals think, perceive themselves and others, interact, and shape their social worlds. For instance, they may assume that personnel enter organizations with different social expectations depending on their race because they have already learned that society differentially rewards their group for certain behaviors, they have adopted certain schemas for processing information about other groups, or their sense of self depends on the repertoire of role identities to which they have previously had access (Hollander and Howard 2000). Therefore, organizations might expect that *exposure* to interpersonal interactions, cultural representations, and role performances and the group-differentiated *structure* of those exposures will jointly shape how individual personnel perform for the organization.[1] Individuals bring into their institutional lives the culture of their group, both its traditions and its historical experiences in the wider society. With respect to the new foundation insiders, they might expect the division of foundation perspectives on institutional responsibility into group-specific standpoints.

In contrast, conservative diversity commentators are skeptical of the relevance of personal lives to the workplace and make the normative argument that organizations *should* incorporate only those diversity considerations relevant to their particular goals. Frederick Lynch's (1997) monograph on the growth and excesses of the diversity management field traces the new boundary of conservative discourse on race and diversity. Although he agrees that businesses and other institutions ignore shifting demographics at their peril, he believes that an organization is most effective when its personnel adopt a raceless institutional culture when they enter, leaving at the door most of their personal lives, including the cultures of White Americans. He argues that criticisms of monocultural institutions often confuse the cultures of capitalism and formal bureaucracy for White male culture and thus mistake as obstructionist that which is actually necessary for institutional success. An organization, therefore, benefits from diversity not when it acknowledges and includes the personal cultures of all its personnel but only when cultural competence provides the organization a competitive advantage in gaining access to nontraditional consumer markets in particularly diverse localities. Instead of efforts at making organizations "look like America," Lynch recommends ignoring federal categories and tailoring common policies such as cross-cultural education to specific regions. Conservatives like Lynch would expect foundation perspectives on diversity policy to vary primarily by area; the seemingly unique views of the new insiders *should* thus be quite similar to those of their local White colleagues.

I agree with conservatives that organizational policies responding to national population projections tend to gloss the significantly uneven impacts of post-1965 immigration on different parts of the United States. However, conservatives also make a total distinction between group cultures outside organizations and institutional cultures within organizations, which leads them to conceptualize organizations as unaffected by their environments except when they choose to pay attention. For instance, Lynch criticizes the diversity field for a preoccupation with its initial focus on African Americans and women without similarly considering the cultural legacy left by the longer predominance of White males in major U.S. workplaces and other institutions. I suggest that skepticism of the position that institutional perspectives reflect group memberships does not require us to ignore the potential effects of social structure on organizations. Instead of assuming that organizational necessity magically transmutes group members into institutional actors, sociologists directly theorize the relationship between structure and consciousness and question the validity of identity politics in ways that permit a better understanding of the complex relationships between social structure and organizations.

Although I deal with the sociological literature second, its discourse about identity politics actually predates the management literature and has long centered on the effects of hierarchy. Beyond how well individuals represent their group cultures and perspectives, identity politics involves the process of contesting and renegotiating the balance of cost and profit accruing to membership in a particular group in relation to other groups (Nagel 1996). In this light, management conceptions of identity politics overlook their intended target: the stratification of group statuses. For sociologists, the central question is not whether social classification effects different perspectives but rather when and how social hierarchy effects multiple standpoints on society.

Sociologists employ the concept of *standpoint* to highlight the ways social location limits or opens one's view of social relationships. The sociological concept is sometimes confused with the opinions of individuals or their allegiances to partisan ideologies. In actuality, standpoints are truth claims premised on the structural visibility of social relations to their claimants. Feminist theorists have borrowed the concept from the Marxist observation that the capitalist emphasis on buying and selling, that is, the *exchange* of commodities, tends to mask the more fundamental relations of *production* (Hartsock 1987). For example, Marxists compare the invisibility of work on the shop floor with the visibility of showroom sales and stock trades. Both Marxist and feminist standpoint theorists argue that superordinate status discourages its possessors or inhabitants from developing a consciousness critical of the social relations that advantage them. Feminist theorists have reconstructed the Marxist analysis of consciousness to account for not only locational hierarchy (e.g., social class inequalities) but also group-based hierarchy (e.g., race and gender inequalities). Thus, the main divergence between the two approaches concerns the question of how much the salience of group membership reduces to its coincidence with a location that could be shared by other groups.

The Marxist approach defines social structure as the hierarchy of locations within work organizations. In a reversal of liberal diversity-management theory, differences within organizations cause the differences in the larger society. The group cultures that individuals might bring into their institutional lives originate not from their personal lives but from the distribution of their group in the organization. Organizations, therefore, confront diversity issues only when their personnel, consumers, or suppliers include members of groups that are dissimilarly distributed throughout the organization. If certain groups are concentrated at the bottom of the organizational hierarchy, their members will possess a "true consciousness" of both institutional social relations and broader societal inequalities. This *transcendence* arguably gives the standpoint of subordinates a value beyond simply difference from the dominant organizational culture. Accordingly, Marxists might expect the new foundation insiders to voice institutional perspectives that reflect their locational status within organizations and to converge with the perspectives of White peers in the same positions. Furthermore, the views of subordinates should transcend those of superordinates, *providing a more complete account of social relations.* However, by reversing the liberal diversity model, the Marxist approach arguably commits the inverse error of reducing societal hierarchy to organizational hierarchy.

Instead of reducing social structure and organizations to each other or treating structure as entirely exogenous, the feminist approach begins to distinguish institutional hierarchies from societal ones. Significantly, the feminist reconstruction of standpoint theory has shifted from defining structure as a gendered binary (substituted in place of class) to a matrix of intersecting hierarchies. The early formulation associated a binary structure of male oppressors over female oppressed, with a reversed transcendence of female perspectives over falsely universalized male perspectives. In turn, criticisms of mainstream feminism as falsely universalizing White middle-class women have resulted in subsequent formulations that combined gender, race, and class in an additive hierarchy that still determines the relative visibility of social relations from each intersection of group membership and location. At the apex of power and the nadir of standpoint sit upper-class White heterosexual men insulated in an elite world from which they generalize their perspectives as universal truth. At the nadir of power and the apex of standpoint sit Black lesbians in poverty, to whom all relations of power are visible because society targets them for the worst forms of exploitation, exclusion, and dehumanization. All other persons thus occupy intermediate social locations whose additive oppressions provide standpoints with inter-mediate levels of clarity into the nature and structure of power. Later theo-rists have both narrowed the oppressor category and differentiated catego-ries among the oppressed.

Collins's *Black Feminist Thought* (1991) exemplifies the promise and chal-lenge of the later attempts to combine both group-based and locational hierarchies in standpoint theory. Her conception of structure as a *matrix of domination* recognizes the inadequacy of binary models but does not fully elaborate how to adjudicate between subordinate standpoints. Instead, it wavers between an additive structure, with the "most oppressed" group possessing a transcendent standpoint, and a new pseudo-structure lacking a singular nadir and wherein all perspectives are ultimately partial. Her matrix suggests an ambivalence about the hypothesized inverse correlation between social privilege and transcendence.

I suggest that this ambivalence is rooted in her recognition that experi-encing oppression does not by itself produce transcendent consciousness. In fact, Collins redefines transcendence by asserting its dependence on loca-tional considerations experienced only by a fraction of group members. In brief, transcendence requires both subordinate group membership and an unusual proximity to superordinates. While granting that most standpoints are partial rather than transcendent, she privileges the views of (Black fe-male) *outsider-insiders.* Collins defines the latter as the individuals who carry the strategies for surviving and navigating oppression for their racial com-munities, live a dual existence in both White and Black social worlds, and thus are dynamically positioned to continually renew their culture of re-sistance. Collins's exemplar for outsider-insiders is the domestic worker, whose intimate place within White families shows her both their dependence on her people and its inconsistencies with their alleged superiority. The validity of this intimate position, however, seems tenuous when Collins generalizes it to later insiders, such as the minority academic, that is, bureaucratic locations more prevalent for people of color in post–civil rights America (Glenn 1992). Whereas the non-White domestic worked intimately with a class-diverse range of Whites and returned home to a segregated community, it is doubtful that her present-day counterpart has similar inter-actions with a variety of Whites or lives in a segregated neighborhood with a variety of Blacks.

Nevertheless, Collins complicates the expectations of liberal diversity proponents and earlier feminists that group membership effects different standpoints. On the one hand, her formulation of standpoint theory anticipates conservative skepticism of claims that membership shapes what individuals contribute to institutions, much less overall organizational productivity. On the other hand, she premises her skepticism not on an organizational imperative for conformity but on the additional conditions for transcendence beyond simply membership. These conditions of proximity to both nongroup members and group members suggest the significant, albeit secondary, role of locational hierarchy in distinguishing institutional perspectives. Feminist theorists, therefore, expect new foundation insiders to contribute transcendent standpoints to their organizations *only if* their institutional locations place them close to White colleagues. In the absence of such proximity, their perspectives should reflect the nontranscendent or only partial "view from below" articulated by non-White outsiders.[2] Indeed, like conservatives, feminist theorists identify a distinction in the perspectives between institutional insiders and outsiders, but unlike conservatives, they expect the external hierarchy between groups to override institutional membership, in part because the latter is also stratified between groups (e.g., non-White domestics and White family members). Among my interview subjects in the Greater Cleveland and San Francisco Bay Areas, however, the stratification of racial and ethnic groups in the two foundations is far less than total, the result of the local historical changes detailed in chapters 3 and 4.

Within philanthropic relations at the Cleveland Foundation and the San Francisco Foundation, specific norms of recruitment and formal responsibilities distinguish their *major institutional locations*: the board of trustees, the professional program-related staff, and the directors of grant-seeking organizations. Local elite institutions appoint most of the trustees for community foundations. These appointing authorities often include the banks where the funds are invested, the Chamber of Commerce, the United Way, major universities, the mayor's office, and other locally important organizations (such as the League of Women Voters in San Francisco). At the Cleveland Foundation and the San Francisco Foundation, these trustees serve terms of five years, during which they may hire or fire the executive director (or chief executive officer), who in turn hires and fires the other foundation staff, both professional and support staff. Trustees seek candidates for directorship whose breadth of qualifications sets them apart from the other professional staff.[3] In turn, the director seeks candidates for her staff with qualifications for particular program areas, such as education, the environment, or urban affairs. Because grant-seeking organizations often operate within one of these program areas or policy domains, their own trustees and directors also seek similarly qualified candidates for directorship and staff.

Foundation trustees represent the apex of power within the philanthropic relationship, having the responsibility for managing the executive director and the discretion over the largest grants and most significant organizational priorities. A significant characteristic of trusteeship is its part-time status; although they command the most discretion, trustees are less involved in the organization's internal affairs than their staff. Among my interview subjects, they held the most racially differentiated institutional location. The White trustees were almost all businessmen[4] from executive corporate careers and upper-middle-class or upper-class family origins. By contrast, most trustees of color, male and female, came from educational, governmental, and non-profit careers, and those few others in corporate sectors identified themselves as lawyers or doctors, that is, by their educational credentials.

Foundation staff directly represented their organizations to the grant seekers and understood grantee projects and concerns more concretely than did trustees, who in fact trusted their staff to screen and summarize the major proposals for them. Among my interview subjects, the Asian, Black, and White foundation staff all came from occupational backgrounds quite similar to those of trustees of color. In short, many of them had been grant seekers at some point in their career. Also like the trustees of color, their self-identified family origins ranged widely from poverty to the upper middle class.

The directors of grant-seeking organizations, or grantees, were both the institutional outsiders and the most subordinate within the philanthropic relationship. Through solicited and unsolicited grant applications, they sought foundation support for a variety of projects to serve mainly disadvantaged communities or client populations. Like the foundation staff, the Asian, Black, Latino, and White grantees among my interviewees came from educational, governmental, and nonprofit occupational backgrounds and from family backgrounds less affluent than the White trustees'. However, the grantees' educational credentials tended to concentrate at the four-year-college level, whereas foundation personnel had usually completed additional years of higher education. Rarely did grantees possess only high school diplomas, indicating the relatively high social position of even the lowest location in philanthropic relations.

The relative desegregation of each institutional location suggests a problem with the feminist approach to organizational diversity. While feminist theory combines group and location hierarchies and permits distinction between social and institutional contexts, it also conceptually restricts the relationships between these elements. For one, it locates the source of group hierarchies outside of particular institutions and instead in "society," or alternatively, in "history," rather than consider the relative autonomy of distinct racial hierarchies in different institutions, much less the potential for interinstitutional collaboration or conflict. In addition, Collins assumes group-based hierarchy to be primary and leaves little theoretical place either for superordinate group members to occupy subordinate locations or to be outsiders, or for subordinate group members to occupy superordinate locations. Instead, the central social actors are insiders of color (outsider-insiders) subordinate to White insiders and outsiders of color. I suggest that foundation staff of color best approximate Collins's outsider-insiders, but only in relation to White trustees and non-White grantees. Still unclear are the roles of their White colleagues among the staff, the trustees of color located above them both, and the White grantees below them or outside their organizations.

I suggest that the appearance of these potentially contradictory standpoints marks the occurrence of incomplete social change, whereby the possibility of transcendence depends increasingly on the variable alignment of the new social actors rather than their theoretically assumed affinities for locational, regional, or group interests. In the pure model (or preceding era) of oppression, group membership correlates with social location, which in turn is characterized as natural for group members. In the wake of non-revolutionary social change, intergroup inequalities persist; however, particular locations no longer confine group membership. As a result, the perspectives of those who have gained mobility or entry may not match the perspectives of other group members. Instead, specific locations have come to moderate how and whether group membership affects institutional perspectives.

These complications parallel a long-standing debate in the study of social stratification concerning the nature of the middle class and the importance of those structural positions in between oppressor and oppressed. While Collins expects outsider-insiders to align with the oppressed and Marxists expect an increasing polarization between capital and labor, some stratification theorists have suggested a third outcome for the middle stratum: alignment with its own distinct interests.[5] The probable orientation of the middle stratum, therefore, goes beyond its alignment with those above or below to the pursuit of its own interests. Rather than being inevitable allies for the oppressed or necessary for liberation as leaders of future society, they may be enduring agents—sometimes bridges, at other times defenders of a status quo against changes by those above or below.[6] Ultimately, because few individuals or even groups can claim pure oppressor or oppressed status, we can characterize most standpoints as structurally middle strata.

These complexities shift the question behind the various conceptions of identity politics from *Whose standpoint counts?* (people of color, consumers, subordinates, outsider-insiders, or "objective" White males) to *Whose side are you on?* However, to identify the relevant "sides," we can no longer rely on analytic categories of interest, which may empirically fall on either side of a discourse (assuming only two sides are distinguished). These developments suggest the importance of, first, empirically identifying distinct standpoints apart from analytic categories related to competing systems of hierarchy, and only then examining the alignment of analytic categories within standpoint camps.

Incorporating the possibility of transcendence, these two steps become three analytic questions regarding the institutional perspectives of the new foundation insiders:

1. How do the perspectives of the Latino, Black, and Asian trustees and the Black and Asian staff cohere with and vary against each other, their White colleagues, and their White, Latino, Black, and Asian grantees?
2. When and where do the new insiders participate in coherent standpoints that actually transcend alternative standpoints?
3. What are the alignments of analytic categories (i.e., race, ethnicity, region, and institutional location) into standpoints? When do the patterns demonstrate convergence, bridging, or autonomy for middle

strata characterized by contradictory positions? Across which hierarchies do the alignments flow more readily, and which hierarchies
seem to channel them instead?

I have applied these questions to examining how the new insiders understand the intrinsic characteristics of diversity policy. And I argue that diversity policy provides only a very limited account of how philanthropic actors
comprehend the participation of foundations in race relations but that its
appeal is understandable because *sometimes* racial membership is salient in
distinguishing institutional perspectives depending on institutional location
and topic.

More broadly, I suggest that the above theories can be placed along a
continuum of social change stages. Feminist standpoint theory might have
provided a good account of institutional perspectives in an earlier era of race
relations. Marxist standpoint theory might yet provide a good account if
group membership continues to decrease in salience. The normative conservative approach expecting, or more precisely, prescribing, conformity
within organizations might become valid if locational hierarchy also disappears, that is, with the additional arrival of the ideal typical communist
society. And the liberal diversity approach expecting organizational conformity to society might become valid if communism arrives without a comparable decline in the significance of race. For the current period, however, I
argue that racial identity politics remains salient, albeit with secondary significance *within* locational hierarchies, organizations, and/or geographic
areas.

The evidence for my secondary significance argument comes from analyzing the institutional perspectives voiced by my interview subjects in the
San Francisco Bay Area and the Greater Cleveland Area. To assess the range
of perspectives about institutional responsibilities amid intergroup relations, I analyzed our discussions of the advice that they might give foundations and nonprofits. Following the above implications for analysis, I identified coherent standpoints *before* considering the role of analytic categories
and the alignment of contradictory-category positions. For each institutional location—trustee, staff, and grantee—I attended to regionally similar
themes, topics over which regions differed, and regionally unique concerns.
Among these patterns, I further identified themes either exclusively produced *by* individuals at certain institutional locations or of particular ethnoracial backgrounds, or constructed *about* certain ethnoracial groups. Then,
comparing the themes across grant-making roles, I considered the relative

overlap between locational statuses, looking for whether any racialized perspectives carried across institutional positions and whether any racial, institutional, or even regional standpoints transcended other standpoints. This method of analysis forms the basis of my following arguments about the relative coherence, transcendence, and alignment of foundation perspectives on institutional responsibility. In brief, the resulting patterns demonstrate the limited validity of existing understandings of how diversity shapes organizational culture and suggest my alternative theory of the secondary significance for group membership, associated with incomplete social change.

The Racial, Institutional, and Regional Definitions of Foundation Responsibility

The concern for intergroup symmetry is perhaps the most unique of diversity policy's distinct characteristics. Organizations can more easily adopt its other aspects in traditional terms, for example, by creating special priorities for hiring more non-Blacks, immigrants, and international specialists. However, the goal of symmetry, where Whites themselves are included, also requires a qualitative shift in policy. Indeed, antiracist public policy is *minority-oriented*, either regulating discrimination against non-Whites or improving their status in society. The former concern attempts to prevent Americans from treating non-Whites differently from "normal," implicitly meaning how Whites regularly treat other Whites. The latter concern seeks to reduce the barriers confronting non-Whites and their cumulative deficits in education, training, social networks, and assets, that is, their lesser accumulation of human, organizational, social, and financial capital.

Put another way, traditional policies attempt to "restore" normal citizenship, implicitly meaning the opportunities Whites experience as a group in U.S. society. Despite the important role of Whites as the policy benchmark for American normality, the traditional approach provoked a backlash against "reverse discrimination." In response, some diversity proponents proposed a shift in policy to include Whites explicitly, not only to spell out the group's social privileges but also to advocate a pluralist conception of normality as an alternative to a "raceless" Whiteness.

Central to this de-centering of Whiteness has been the practice of *reflexivity*, whereby participants in race relations view themselves as already racialized subjects rather than "objective" raceless observers of racial others. Rather than regarding foundations as raceless entities identifying minority talent, a reflexive perspective might characterize foundations as White organizations already implicated in race relations by virtue of their historical and contemporary activities, personnel, and culture. However, although some interview subjects viewed their respective foundations as de facto White organizations, none sought to characterize them as instruments of White responsibility for redressing race relations. Instead, my interviewees vested the foundations with organizational responsibility and varied in the degree to which they characterized foundations as fallible organizations. In other words, they advocated reflexivity in philanthropy of an organizational, not racial, nature.

In this section and the next, I explore how the new insiders construct these institutional responsibilities in their advice to foundations and grant-seeking nonprofits. The empirical predominance of institutional rather than racial standpoints among the interviewee perspectives suggests that the axis of foundation-grantee reciprocal responsibilities is central to the practice of foundation diversity policy. Regarding the institutional responsibilities of foundations, the new insiders gave advice that was divided by their institutional location. While the non-White trustees diverged from their White peers to contribute uniquely reflexive, regionally specific perspectives, the non-White program staff converged with their White colleagues in regionally distinct standpoints.

RACIAL DIFFERENCES IN TRUSTEE REFLEXIVITY ABOUT FOUNDATIONS

Trustees of all racial backgrounds provided advice that differed by their region but focused mainly on their respective foundations instead of their local environments. They were especially vocal about (1) the racial-ethnic composition of their respective foundation boards, (2) grant-making practices, and (3) external relations. In fact, they tended to be more externally oriented than their staffs in defining the responsibilities of foundations. However, trustees were also relatively inattentive to the ethnoracial composition of their staff and their relations with staff. Within both regions, trustees of color demonstrated greater reflexivity, describing both successes and failures, while White trustees focused on how other foundations might learn from their successes.

Regarding board composition and interactions, both White and non-White trustees emphasized the effectiveness of board diversification, but it was trustees of color who additionally noted its limitations and the need for further improvement. In Cleveland, a White trustee noted his work on promoting African American inclusion on corporate boards as a model for foundations to follow; he asserted that "almost every board I'm on now has at least one Black member." Trustees of color, all of whom in Cleveland were Black, recognized that their White colleagues respected their individuality, not simply their representation of non-White issues. For instance, they did not feel that other trustees expected them only to follow the agendas of previous Black trustees. In addition, they remarked that their individual concerns and agendas had become "anticipated" over time by their White colleagues.

However, Black trustees also critically observed that the cultural style of White board chairs significantly impacted the relative involvement of trustees of color in decision making. They also critically noted that the contrast in personal occupational backgrounds between White and Black trustees was telling of the continuing inequalities in race relations, in particular, the scarcity of African Americans in corporate boardrooms. No matter how well the trustees worked together or how much they had individually accomplished, their difference in origins was a reminder of how recent the civil rights movement had been.

In the Bay Area, Asian, Black, and Latino trustees also noted the difference between their backgrounds and those of their White colleagues. However, they framed the difference more pragmatically, as demonstrating the importance of minority presence beyond simple representation. As one trustee observed, "Trusteeship allows minorities to mix with the business community in a meaningful way," allowing him to perceive its inner workings rather than see a monolithic entity. Like their Cleveland counterparts, White trustees in the Bay Area held up their board's diversification process as an exemplar for other foundations. They proudly noted their decision to increase the size of the board from its historical number as a model policy for increasing board diversity rather than initiating struggles over limited seats. They also praised their colleagues of color as demonstrating that their foundation had been "right to wait for good trustees of color," noting that they had waited years for one board member to agree to join the board rather than ask second-choice candidates. Nevertheless, trustees of color remained critical of how foundations in general often diversified their boards in conventional ways. They observed that foundations tended to look for candidates who had already been professionally developed and vetted by others more willing to take risks. In addition, they warned of a "one of each" approach to diversification that tended to conflate intergroup issues with personality conflicts.

Cleveland and Bay Area trustees of color were uniquely vocal regarding grant-making practices, albeit for very distinct concerns. In Cleveland, Black trustees advised other foundations to look among applications for activities whose support "would lead to racial harmony" and also to prioritize "feasible involvement in racial and ethnic relations" over idealistic but less practical proposals. Meanwhile, in the Bay Area, trustees of color were especially concerned with the unintended consequences of funding priorities. They critically reminded other foundations that philanthropic decisions had to be weighed carefully because changes in priorities also changed grantee organizations even when grantees disagreed with the decisions.

Regarding external relations, trustees again raised regionally distinct concerns, and here again Bay Area trustees of color were especially balanced in discussing both successes and failures in their foundation's history. In the Bay Area, trustees defined their relevant environment as the philanthropic field in their region. The status of the San Francisco Foundation in local philanthropy came through clearly in one White trustee's pride in his board membership as "the crown jewel" in the work of local philanthropists like himself. Nevertheless, trustees also felt the Foundation needed to go beyond being recognized as "the best" and begin leading major initiatives. One trustee of color criticized the Foundation for not collaborating more with other funders and specifically recommended that it needed to "develop closer links with the local United Way." More substantively, Bay Area trustees divided along racial lines in a debate on Robert Fisher's interest in diversifying the Foundation's donor base. A White trustee confided that, although the goal was "noble and contemporary," he did not believe that there was "much to raise from ethnic groups," explaining his belief that if there were funds to be attracted, race relations would not be such an issue in the first place. However, others supported the push for philanthropic pluralism as an alternative to the extension of balkanization into philanthropy itself. One trustee of color even pointed to the emergence and growth of ethnic-specific funds independent of the San Francisco Foundation as evidence of their organization's failure at being recognized as inclusive of the entire community.

In Cleveland, both Black and White trustees emphasized their responsibility to act in broader contexts beyond local philanthropy. They praised their organization's strategy of regularly visiting other cities to learn about other policy and philanthropic infrastructures. Of particular note was a search for cities where Black-White alliances had persevered since the 1960s in order to locate models for new local institutions. They also asserted that "trustees must become advocates for foundation priorities," venturing beyond grant-making decisions and other internal responsibilities to persuade and influence other powerful actors to adopt foundation objectives. In brief, they were simultaneously more demanding than their counterparts in the Bay Area and less reflexive than the Bay Area's trustees of color.

REGIONAL CONTRASTS IN STAFF
REFLEXIVITY ABOUT FOUNDATIONS

Like their trustees, staff also offered regionally distinct advice regarding the responsibilities of foundations. Similarly, their regionally distinct perspectives focused on their organizations more directly than their local geographies. In fact, both sets of staff were quite narrow in their definitions of foundation responsibilities and limited their comments mainly to the internal composition and process of their organization. Unlike their trustees, the relative balance of discussion about success and failure fell along regional lines, with the Cleveland Foundation staff providing the least self-critical commentary either about their organization or foundations in general.

The San Francisco Foundation staff was especially vocal, providing direct recommendations and reflections on institutional experience, including successes for emulation, critical observations, and words of caution. They discussed (1) the racial and ethnic composition of the program staff, (2) board of trustees composition, (3) grant making, and (4) philanthropic philosophy—almost all in terms of both successes and failures. By contrast, the Cleveland Foundation staff was more reserved, and even the direct advice was comparatively more general. They did discuss staff composition, grant making, and philanthropic philosophy—almost all in terms of recognizing their successes—but were surprisingly silent about the composition of their board.

Regarding staff composition, Cleveland staff assumed the importance of taking an individual's race into account in hiring decisions and took pride in their foundation's accomplishments with this practice. They noted the organization's hiring Steve Minter as its first Black professional staff and his later promotion to executive directorship as the starting point for the contemporary priority given to diversity. Bay Area staff also favored the assumption that an individual's group membership mattered in hiring decisions but warned of the significant gap between achieving a diverse composition and arriving at a "truer" philanthropic pluralism. On the one hand, staff advised that even if anti–affirmative action sentiment prevailed politically, foundation "staff should reflect the diversity in the communities served by grants." Staff also emphasized the Foundation's early commitment to diversity as evident in its resolve to replace its first Black staff member with another African American. Regarding more recent years, they noted the San Francisco Foundation's success at having long maintained a "60:40 ratio of Anglos to people of color" on staff well before the regional population attained that composition.

On the other hand, Bay Area staff complained that diversity too often meant blindly staffing a department or organization with "one of everything," echoing a sentiment also voiced by their trustees of color. Furthermore, they also encouraged foundations to examine whether representational changes in staffing had actually altered institutional philosophies. In fact, one staff member warned that the increase in representational diversity on foundation boards sometimes led to a "decrease in attention to ethnics in poverty" because hiring criteria allowed racial membership to invalidly substitute for real community knowledge.

Regarding board composition, Cleveland staff were completely silent; Bay Area staff were more critical of their trustees and also more enthusiastic about the potential effects of trustee diversification than staff diversification. A simple reason for their less qualified support of trustee heterogeneity was simply that the foundation boards were generally less diverse than their staff. As one staff member observed succinctly, "Foundation diversity [is] easiest in grant disbursements, harder in staff hiring, and hardest in trustee appointments." Beyond ethnoracial memberships, they also complained that the trustees tended to be "over 50 percent Republican Party members."

Regarding grant making, Cleveland staff suggested that other foundations examine the Cleveland Foundation as a model. They advised others to follow their organization's historic lead in developing Black-White relations while increasing attention to Latinos and Asian Americans. The staff proudly recognized their organization's historical administration of the prestigious Anisfield-Wolf Book Awards since 1934, awards that now recognize books that "expose racism or explore the richness of human diversity." In addition, they noted the establishment of an African American Outreach Committee as an obvious policy and speculated erroneously that the San Francisco Foundation had a similar Asian American Outreach Committee.

By contrast, Bay Area staff offered more reflexive advice for foundations to raise the quality of their relationships with grantee organizations and also the latter's client communities. Emphasizing that "money doesn't change things by itself," one staff member suggested that foundations should "be less charitable" and more oriented toward "long-term development" and argued that foundations should relate to their grantees less through "telling and advising" and more through "teaching." Another staff member recommended that foundations partner with organizations that "already had trust in communities" rather than recognizing and imposing new leadership. In praise of themselves, the San Francisco Foundation staff voiced approval for how their organization had increased the diversity of its board before requiring grantees to submit organizational diversity reports, much less encouraging them to similarly diversify their own boards.

Regarding philanthropic philosophy, Cleveland staff simply suggested that foundations seriously consider assimilating diversity issues into their central philanthropic missions. They broadly asserted that foundations had "an obligation to include as much diversity in the process as possible." Furthermore, diversity was an important consideration because foundations were "in the business of finding talent and helping, supporting, and developing it."

By contrast, Bay Area staff philosophized about a more specific conception of diversity policy that emphasized its improvements over previous intergroup priorities but also expressed reservations about its actual promise. Suggesting how workforce diversity changed policy goals, they proudly pointed out the rephrasing of a diversity statement in their organization's mission statement, singling out how the old statement subtly bore the signature of those who associated diversity with "them" rather than "us." Bay Area staff reported on the emergence of an internal committee on diversity, whose first mission had been to engage conflicting staff perspectives on the outcome of the O. J. Simpson trial. Demonstrating a shift in attention from numbers to relationships, the committee reminded the foundation that diversity not only means how well foundation personnel reflect community demographics but also is an opportunity for the internal practice of the external relationships the foundation seeks to mediate, for example: "Why do we do what we do within the foundation and how does that relate to what we do outside?" As one staff member emphasized, "It's not just getting people to the table and that's enough. Instead, it's the recognition that the San Francisco Foundation is a microcosm of the San Francisco Bay area and that it takes hard work inside the organization not only to get along but also to better relate to our communities." Bay Area staff also critically observed that foundations often instituted diversity at the level of belief or values, such as in mission statements, rather than also in real action. In addition, they warned that the rising interest in diversity was "promising but should not be seen as a replacement for the continuing need for empowerment." In brief, they desired a diversity policy that transcended but did not abandon earlier policies such as affirmative action.

I found a complex pattern of greater reflexivity, albeit organizational rather than racial, among trustees of color than White trustees and among the San Francisco Foundation staff than the Cleveland Foundation staff. The coherent standpoints among the available perspectives divided first by region, second by institutional location, and third by race, though only among trustees, the superordinate location. New insider transcendence was limited to trustees of color and only in relation to their White colleagues in the same regional and institutional segment. Staff of color aligned in convergence with White staff, and trustees of color aligned autonomously from White trustees and also staff of color. With respect to the institutional responsibilities of foundations, the pattern of alignments suggests that locational hierarchy is more significant in institutional life than the group hierarchies to which diversity policy attends. And yet race remains salient, albeit within and not across institutional locations. In brief, foundation personnel are very divided on how to evaluate themselves, though none demonstrate racial reflexivity in their assessments.

The Regional Expectations for Nonprofit Grant Seekers

In contrast to their racial and institutional disagreements about foundation responsibilities, trustees and staff demonstrated regional agreement in their expectations of grant seekers. Regarding the responsibilities of nonprofits, we might expect reflexive perspectives to equate certain nonprofits with Asian, Black, or Latino communities instead of viewing them as raceless entities that happen to serve minority clients. In fact, many interview subjects employed both racially reflexive and traditional definitions of nonprofit responsibility. However, they also vested grant seekers with organizational responsibilities to represent minority clients and communities and to have different interactions with philanthropic organizations versus with government agencies and politicians. Regarding their expectations of nonprofits, the new insiders gave advice that converged with larger regional standpoints. The significant differences in reflexivity appeared along regional lines rather than group-based or locational hierarchy.

Trustees in the two regions shared some common concerns, but their perspectives on nonprofit responsibilities diverged along regionally different approaches to giving advice. Both San Francisco Foundation and Cleveland Foundation trustees admonished nonprofits to "focus" and "clarify their [organizational] mission" and develop their organization's technical capacities. However, the trustees differed by how they assumed grantees could arrive at some form of technical sophistication.

Bay Area trustees phrased their advice from what they imagined to be the standpoint of their grant applicants. "A good idea or cause isn't enough . . . you have to crawl before you can walk, walk before you can run," confided another trustee, defining organizational sophistication as beginning with ideals and maturing before attaining foundation support. The Bay Area suggestion that "[grantees] should have a valid need and a good implementation" contrasts with the more direct and less varied Cleveland versions of this advice for nonprofits to "get business training" for their staffs and "seek business volunteers" for their boards. Whether Bay Area trustees were more open to nonbusiness forms of technical sophistication or simply followed a less directive script for communicating their evaluative criteria cannot be determined. However, in both regions, trustees justified their superordinate status to grant seekers by constructing most of them as lacking technical capacities and in need of either more experience or more training.

Staff perspectives showed a similar pattern, with some common concerns but largely regionally different orientations to providing advice. Both San Francisco Foundation and Cleveland Foundation staff advised nonprofits not to rely solely on external grants and to "find something to be entrepreneurial about" (Cleveland) or create "self-generating streams of revenue" (Bay Area). In addition, staff also agreed with trustees that organizational survival would depend on having "sophistication," connecting their missions to a wider context than their particular issues. They advised nonprofits to "set their proposals in a larger infrastructure" of resources and programs originating outside their own organization. Beyond this point, however, staff perspectives diverged in a way similar to that of their respective trustees.

While Bay Area staff shared their criteria for proposal evaluation, Cleveland area staff largely shared observations on topics beyond the control of individual nonprofits. San Francisco Foundation staff uniquely discussed how nonprofits needed to "make [their] case for support," defined as more than documenting social needs. They also suggested that proposals go beyond "misery mongering" to promote how the proposed activities built on organizational assets. In addition, they advised organizations to "become savvy about long-term development rather than simply project development." Furthermore, if nonprofits asserted that they represented a community in need, staff confided that they looked more favorably on those grantees that demonstrated an "ongoing accountability" to that community.

By contrast, Cleveland staff offered naturalistic observations about the local nonprofit sector instead of specific tools for any given organization. The most empathetic commentary came from a staff member when she advised clarifying "vision and focus in both mission and implementation." However, she also more distantly observed that nonprofits "can't afford to make mistakes" because they are essentially "like small businesses, undercapitalized and understaffed, but expected to run like the biggest and best [corporations]." Other advice was likewise general, such as reminders to nonprofits that they are in a "high-risk business" and that they need "lots of resources to survive."

The one exception to the more pat advice of Cleveland personnel was their criticism of existing African American leadership, which they regarded as overly driven by individual personalities. One staff member claimed that "strong Black organizations are often just platforms for strong Black leaders" whose presence or absence could make or break their effectiveness. A trustee voiced a similar criticism of what amounted to an excessive African American reliance on charismatic authority. Responding to a general question about challenges for nonprofits, she employed examples from Black organizations as exemplars: "They need to be more careful about choosing leaders to follow, make sure they are for real, in for the long haul, and not just another self-serving individual." After citing a few examples, she concluded that it was unfortunate that "few leaders can tolerate competent advisors rather than surrounding themselves with idiots" who would not threaten their prestige. While interviewees tempered the intensity of such dissatisfaction with other examples of good leaders, they still noted the personalistic model of leadership as inadequate.

These regional orientations suggest deeper divergent assumptions about the capabilities of local nonprofit sectors and the relationship of foundations with their grantees. Cleveland Foundation actors tended to characterize the universe of grantee proposals as relatively predictable, or, as one staff member asserted, "The natural history of community organizations is similar everywhere." Another staff member explained that although the purpose of foundations was to "fund people and ideas[,] the ideas proposed were all old" and stressed the persistence of the "same social problems confronting each generation." Consequently, foundations usually had to "make decisions based on [evaluations of] energy, drive, and capacity" rather than innovation. Similarly, Cleveland area trustees advised nonprofits to consider the fit of grant proposals with existing institutions. They advised nonprofits to research the existing service infrastructure before asserting the need for a proposed initiative or project. Furthermore, Cleveland trustees asserted that a "dislike" of existing programs, however visceral, was just not sufficient "grounds for competition." By comparison, Bay Area trustees also observed a "vicious competition" for grants but explained it as the natural "problem of limited money" rather than an unnecessary consequence of grantee shortsightedness. In brief, Cleveland trustees assumed a "judge" role vis-à-vis nonprofits, demanding that they rise and conform to certain established expectations.

In contrast, San Francisco Foundation actors emphasized not nonprofit predictability but foundation peculiarity. Bay Area staff asserted that "foundations are all different" but emphasized that nonprofits need "to know what [foundations] were not" in order to pitch proposals successfully. Continuing the focus on foundations rather than nonprofits, staff advised nonprofits to pay attention to "generational" differences among foundations and relate differently to each: the newest "founder" philanthropies, the postfounder "family" institutions, and the postfamily "professional" foundations.

Like their staff, Bay Area trustees assumed a "coach" role, encouraging nonprofits to be strategic and become more competitive. Most advised grantees to maintain a level of independence from funder agendas. These perspectives ranged from advising simple autonomy to advising nonprofits to attempt to influence or even co-opt funders to their respective causes. Trustees noted that grantees "thought too hard" about what funders wanted and needed instead to rely more on "their own judgment" of priorities. One trustee advised nonprofits to be "careful about the stability of the organization rather than following funding fads"; another even suggested that presenting such "self-reliance" was actually more attractive to funders. On the more extreme side, a trustee complained that minority communities were not "doing their homework" on influencing the selection of community foundation leadership—in particular, the appointment of trustees—much less going beyond getting "one of their own" in the foundation to instead making a "system fix."

I did not find greater reflexivity among the new insiders than their White colleagues; instead, I found greater reflexivity among Bay Area trustees and staff than their Cleveland counterparts. The various perspectives cohered into two major standpoints divided by region, not race or institutional location. As a result, new insider transcendence was nonexistent. Indeed, the staff of color and trustees of color aligned in convergence with their White colleagues across group membership and institutional location and with each other. With respect to the institutional responsibilities of nonprofit grant seekers, the pattern of alignment suggests that regional considerations—whether local demographics, local culture, or immediate organizational culture—is more significant than social hierarchy of any kind. In brief, foundation personnel are quite united on how they evaluate grant seekers, and it is the West Coast personnel, not the new insiders across regions, who advance the most reflexivity—racial and organizational—in their assessments.

The Institutional Cohesion, Isolation, and External Orientation of Nonprofit Grant Seekers

So far, I have mainly compared the voices of the new insiders with the views of their White colleagues and found that, although the outsider-insiders sometimes contribute unique perspectives, these rarely cross the greater standpoint chasms between regions, if not also organizational roles. As shown above, the general argument finds further support in the comparison of foundation perspectives with the standpoint of grantee outsiders. In this section, I employ the grantees to represent a baseline against which to identify *the effects of insidership on foundation personnel of color*. To make this analysis, I have to bracket the extent to which foundation recruitment might include a systematic bias for certain subgroups of grantees and to which outsidership might affect grantee perspectives. In comparison to how foundations recruit their White trustees, however, they appear to recruit their staff and non-White trustees from a candidate pool more similar to that of their grantees. These procedures arguably reduce the effects of selection and outsider socialization and make plausible the interpretation that insider socialization produces the differences between the grantee and new insider perspectives.

Feminist theory suggests that insidership should transform "partial" outsider perspectives into transcendent standpoints. In other words, when outsiders become insider-outsiders, they should gain perspectives transcendent of both outsiders and traditional insiders. Unfortunately, the comparison of new insiders with grantees reveals multiple transformations involving both gains and losses. With regard to their definitions of institutional responsibility, the new insiders appear to gain the insider's view of regionally distinct grant-making decisions and culture, but at the cost of their uniquely cross-regional and critical analysis of the external relations surrounding foundation philanthropy. Ironically, it is the grantee standpoint that most differentiates philanthropic diversity discourse from the more internally oriented policies for workplace diversity. In sum, the new insiders do not always bring the grantee standpoint with them into philanthropy. Instead, insidership shifts their consciousness so that it becomes more like their White colleagues', even when interracial differences remain between structurally equivalent colleagues.

COST: AN AWARENESS OF
ORGANIZATION-POLITICAL LINKAGES

Whereas foundation personnel advised nonprofits to focus on general factors promoting organizational survival, grantees gave advice based on their specific organizational experiences and the issues particular to their ethnoracial constituencies. In other words, grantees narrowly characterized the institutional responsibilities of all nonprofits through their own challenges in meeting the social needs of their respective clients of color. Despite or perhaps because of this relatively inward focus, grantees also uniquely concerned themselves with the political history confronting and motivating their organization. Their perspectives on nonprofit responsibilities were very partial and isolated, sharing almost no common themes with foundation staff and trustees, whose perspectives converged with each other's into regional standpoints. When grantees become foundation personnel, their review of funding proposals gives them a broader view of local nonprofits but also removes them from the specific political goals they once sought to advance.

In both areas, rather than attempt to understand the complexity of the grant-making process, grantees advised nonprofits to cut through the chaos and establish personal relationships with foundation personnel. Cleveland and Bay Area grantees shared the belief that in securing foundation support, an important factor was "who you know" or even "getting the right person to ask," that is, preexisting social contacts with foundation staff and trustees. Relatedly, the grantees also agreed that foundation priorities were "fickle" and followed unpredictable trends, again making personal contacts more important than substantive fits between proposals and shifting funding priorities.

When grantees made regionally distinct observations about the relationship of nonprofits and local racial politics, these comments actually revealed national differences between group-specific political histories. In the

Bay Area, Asian American grantees saw nonprofit work and development as a potential stepping stone to broader political leadership; in the Cleveland area, African American grantees saw nonprofits, especially social service agencies, as the residue of failed political initiatives. As one Cleveland grantee advised, "Nonprofits need an early victory to survive, or else they turn into service providers." Rather than regional differences, these diverging perceptions of nonprofit-politics relations may simply echo the directions of Asian American and African American politics from the 1970s to the 1980s. While radical Black organizations were targeted for repression, other African Americans were incorporated into social service agencies, local political offices in increasingly Black central cities, or corporate human relations and affirmative action departments. By contrast, government repression largely ignored Asian American radicals (Omatsu 1994). Ironically, the latter and their more moderate peers focused instead on creating service and advocacy organizations focused on Asian Americans to fulfill needs neglected by Black-targeted government bureaucracies. In short, the same political incorporation that Cleveland Blacks saw in ambivalent terms as an insufficient resolution was regarded by Bay Area Asian Americans as their long-deferred next step.

A normative association between racial issues and the Black experience permeated both regions, regardless of their divergent demographics. When all interviewees, *not only grantees*, discussed Asian and Latino nonprofits or communities, they specifically noted their being Asian or Latino; in addition, they usually also distinguished Asian and Latino issues from Black issues. When Asians, Latinos, and Whites referred to African American issues, they would explicitly mark them as group-specific, whereas African Americans commonly generalized Black issues more broadly. No interviewees directly mentioned White-specific issues, leaving Whites instead as an omnipresent comparison group. Thus, Blacks were the implicit minority for policy attention, and Whites were the implicit majority handled through nonracial channels.

I suggest that these complementary norms originate from the history of nonprofit and political leadership. Because Black political participation started earlier than other minority movements and also pioneered identity-based politics for minorities, Blacks viewed the Black experience with politics and nonprofits as the definitive non-White experience and cast other experiences as derivative. By contrast, non-Blacks, *especially among grantees*, rejected the derivative characterization of their experiences; nevertheless, they tended to mention the Black experience as normative and constructed their goals not only as demanding "parity" with an implicitly White mainstream but also as "catching up" with Blacks. When a Latino grantee discussed the challenge of hiring college-educated staff, he specifically noted that Latino educational achievement actually lagged behind Black schooling. When an Asian American grantee worried whether having non-Asian clients gave greater status to his organization, he specifically noted their increasing activities in a predominantly Black neighborhood.

Unfortunately, grant making appears to involve a basic difference in how to define the responsibilities of nonprofits. On the one side are nonprofits captivated by their group-specific political mission, environment, and aspirations. On the other side are foundations making cultural evaluations of the local organizational ecology and its aggregate capabilities. When non-White grantees become foundation personnel, they, and their White grantee colleagues, appear to resolve this conflict by joining with their White trustees in common regional expectations of nonprofit development.

THE IRONIC PRICE:
A PRIORITIZATION OF EXTERNAL RELATIONS

Whereas foundation personnel advised other foundations to focus mainly on their internal composition and dynamics, grantees gave advice on the external context, impact, and image of foundation activities. More systematically than in their advice to other nonprofits, grantee interviewees emphasized the embeddedness of organizations, this time of foundations, in local politics and communities. When new insiders become staff and trustees, they retain the capability to develop autonomous definitions of foundation responsibility, but they also appear to lose touch with the national and regional critiques of how philanthropy interacts with its environment.

First, grantees in both regions identified links between foundation priorities and local political dynamics and perceived these connections as channeling foundation funding in ways that resonated with political clout or culture. Bay Area grantees perceived a San Francisco Foundation "aversion" to engaging Asian American issues and attributed it to the philanthropy's connections with the similarly averse Burton machine, a political network representing the left wing of local Democratic Party politics. Similarly, Cleveland grantees perceived the Cleveland Foundation's "neglect" of East Side communities and attributed it to the philanthropy's connections to a politically directed distribution of public dollars eastward to Black communities.

Grantees also shared a complaint that foundations missed the importance of the relationships that nonprofits forged with their communities beyond their association as service providers and clients. Bay Area grantees viewed the foundation perspective as oriented toward "counting grants" while missing how specific grants sustained particular relationships between agencies and certain ethnic groups: "Something they see as just one less grant is, for us, like losing our whole connection to, say, the Cambodian community." Cleveland grantees observed that foundations missed how developing a sense of community came from building personal relationships rather than simply "imposing strategies."

Third, grantees in both regions asserted that foundations focused too narrowly on low-income populations without considering the working poor or even middle-class coethnics. However, their arguments for including the less disadvantaged were different. Bay Area grantees felt that foundation priorities excluded the important bridges between the poor and their somewhat more advantaged peers, whom the poor aspired to join, whose family members were already supporting their poorer relations, and who were themselves not far above the poverty line. As one grantee stated succinctly, "The emphasis on the poor misses the whole community," limiting its capacity to help its less fortunate members. Quite distinctly, Cleveland grantees rebuked foundations for neglecting "the working guy" for the "welfare person" and for missing how the working poor were in as bad or worse a situation because the former was also supporting the latter through taxes.

Fourth, the grantees shared a perception that foundations conflated their work with for-profit activities but encountered distinct regional dilemmas. While grantees did not fault foundations for making comparisons between nonprofits and for-profits, they argued that foundations often did so without regard for "real-world" dynamics. As noted earlier, Asian American grantees in the Bay Area confronted assumptions that associated them with immigrant entrepreneurship and what they saw as a ploy to characterize Asian Americans as undeserving of public support. Meanwhile, in Cleveland, grantees observed that foundations wanted nonprofits to be "run like businesses," without noting inherent conflicts between "what funders want nonprofits to do and what businesses actually did." One grantee noted that although foundations were trying to encourage collaborations and wondered why nonprofits were so bad at cooperating, they failed to realize that corporations also usually competed with each other and collaborated only for unusual purposes such as competing against third parties or establishing monopolies.

If the grantee standpoint represents the pool from which foundations draw their staff and non-White trustees, then the new insiders may have begun their philanthropic careers with a broader and more critical perspective on how foundations conduct their external relations. When grantees become foundation staff, however, they appear to adopt a regionally specific staff perspective on the internal responsibilities of foundations. By contrast, when non-White grantees become trustees, they develop a racially autonomous standpoint that is transcendent over the White trustee perspective and retain a significant part of the grantee orientation to external relations. Indeed, trustees actually transcend their staff in attention to extraorganizational responsibilities. Whereas becoming staff appears to involve a commitment to formal organizational procedures, becoming a trustee permits new insiders to continue treating foundations as tools for larger political goals, albeit in a reduced fashion.

Conclusion: Toward Institutional and Regional Analyses

The empirical results demonstrate the institutional and regional structuring of philanthropic perspectives on diversity and therefore suggest the significant institutional and regional character of racial policies in recent U.S. history. Although the diversity movement purports to reshape national culture, its actual policy validity strongly suggests that we situate its aspirations in both institutional and regional contexts. Race becomes salient primarily within, and not across, specific institutional and regional contexts. This secondary significance for race as a social difference simultaneously confirms and challenges managerial and sociological perspectives on the legitimacy of identity politics in organizations. Identity politics provides the rationale for diversity policy, but regional, locational, and recruitment differences produce more significant effects on organizational culture than group membership (i.e., race).

To explore the actual effects of group membership, I assessed the distinctiveness of the perspectives on diversity voiced by foundation staff and trustees of color. Revisiting the four aspects of diversity policy from chapter 1, I found that foundation personnel rarely voiced the most qualitatively distinct aspect, modeling symmetric intergroup relations through racial reflexivity. No staff or trustee vested foundations with a White or otherwise racialized responsibility for improving race relations; however, they did evidence varying levels of *organizational* reflexivity, depending on region, institutional role, and race, with trustees of color and Bay Area personnel voicing the aspirations for more symmetric interorganizational relations. On the other hand, foundation personnel commonly expected from nonprofits a wider range of responsibilities for symbolizing their ethnoracial constituencies, developing technical sophistication irrespective of their specific mission, becoming accountable to their client base, and employing foundation grants differently from government contracts.[7] By comparison to the grantees, foundation personnel were more narrowly focused on their regions and less on cross-regional issues, or on their organizations and less on external relations.

Furthermore, the new insiders did not consistently produce distinct, much less transcendent, standpoints. These outsider-insiders largely became isolated behind organization boundaries and came to possess practically the same expectations of outsiders as other insiders. Indeed, they gained a familiarity with how foundations perceived the regional nonprofit sector, but at the cost of the political missions that motivated the grantees. Nevertheless, they established new, alternative definitions of institutional purpose, which ironically reproduced previously external group conflict within the higher levels of organizational hierarchy. These new missions, however, did not directly bridge their foundations with grantee perspectives. In brief, the pursuit of workplace diversity has transformed foundations, but not according to the theoretical expectations.

The conservative vision of diversity policy falls short of explaining the results because its assumptions about workplace culture ignore the existence of social hierarchy. On the one hand, the recurring appearance of regional standpoints in philanthropic perspectives on diversity confirms Lynch's (1997) assertion that the nationally oriented diversity movement has greater relevance in some places than in others. In addition, because the regional differences amount to differences between organizational cultures, they also confirm the conservative assertion that a singular "White male workplace" does not exist. Erroneously, however, conservatives assume that individuals check their group memberships at the door when they enter organizations and then adopt a particular organizationwide perspective that reflects the demographic heterogeneity specific to their region. In their account, workplace conflicts and the manifestation of White male backlash are primarily the result of intrusive federal regulations or overenthusiastic internal policies, which inhibit natural and more productive decisions about diversity. However, the results show that these regional differences are concentrated among grantors, whereas grantees tend to share cross-regional standpoints. Furthermore, among grantors, the results also show that institutional status and racial background do affect their perspectives on diversity, albeit within regional situations. In sum, while conservatives are correct to identify the importance of place, they fail to allow for the possibility that social hierarchies between, within, and outside organizations effect distinct perspectives on diversity.

By contrast, feminist theorists recognize the structuration of individual perspectives; however, they also fall short of explaining the results, mainly because their assumptions about social hierarchy ignore the relative significance of distinct statuses. This perspective presumes that group membership and institutional location blend *equally* to push superordinate intersections up and subordinate intersections down, challenging the middle strata with a menu of alignment decisions. Moreover, while not all Blacks are positioned to be outsider-insiders and not all women are positioned to produce feminist standpoints, theorists tend to assume that subordinate group membership is crucial. In brief, they treat being Black and/or female as a threshold for transcendence and expect group memberships to moderate how locational status effects individual perspectives. For instance, feminist standpoint theory expects gender to moderate the effect that scholarly work has on individuals so that academia pushes men to value intellectual abstraction but pushes women to recognize the contradictions between abstraction and socially valued "feminine" roles. In philanthropic and racial terms, foundation work might push Whites to value professional authority but push people of color to see the contradictions between professional authority and socially valued "minority" roles. In theory, the standpoints of non-White foundation officials would transcend those of both White foundation officials and non-White grantees. Tellingly, this approach has little to say about male nonscholars and White grantees.

In contrast, the results show that it is locational status, not group membership, that provides the threshold for transcendence, an effect more consistent with the original Marxist formulation of standpoint theory. However, the actual patterns of transcendence between perspectives veer from their expected depth and direction. Grantees are not transcendent over foundation insiders in their views on institutional responsibilities. Surprisingly, trustees are transcendent over staff with regard to foundation responsibilities for external relationships, partly inverting the expected direction of transcendence. Furthermore, group membership does influence institutional perspectives, effecting transcendence between trustees and affecting staff and grantees by augmenting their otherwise locational standpoints with additional concerns.

Similarly, the results show that the most variable middle strata were also not racially defined, or only partially so. As a middle stratum that is entirely locational in character, the foundation staff nevertheless aligns in multiple ways: converging upward with trustees in their views on nonprofit responsibilities and producing independent standpoints on foundation responsibilities. As the most significant racialized middle stratum, trustees of color were as variable in their alignments as the staff. Trustees of color similarly converged upward with their White colleagues on nonprofit responsibilities and staked out autonomous perspectives on foundation responsibilities. Other middle strata involving contradictory racial and locational statuses primarily converged with those in their same institutional status or organization. As suggested by the staffwide shifts in alignment, staff of color and White staff largely cohered together. Also, White grantees always converged downward with grantees of color in broader grantee standpoints.

The results do not clearly support any of the theoretical positions on diversity and organizational culture, but the feminist approach does correctly identify both the group-based and the location-based components in the social structure that effects standpoint variation. However, it fails to consider the possibility that locational structuration is stronger than the group-based contribution. In fact, the results confirm the inverse relationship: that it is locational position that moderates the effect of group membership on individual perspectives. Non-White membership pushes grantees to add concerns to a joint standpoint with White grantees. Similarly, it pushes staff mainly to add concerns to a joint standpoint with White staff. However, it has different effects on trustees of color, pushing them in multiple directions: to join White trustees on nonprofit responsibilities and to produce independent standpoints on foundation responsibilities. Thus, only among trustees of color does being non-White result in a substantially distinct standpoint possessing any level of transcendence.[8]

Furthermore, the middle strata do not align themselves to bridge institutional divides. Instead, in the case of trustees of color, they tend to establish autonomous standpoints distinct from and even transcendent over their White colleagues' but still different from the grantees'. These alignments suggest that wider intergroup conflict has mostly shifted into institutional settings, where it has then been segmented by institutional hierarchy.

As proponents of diversity have strategically developed politically insulated policies for improving race relations, their relative success has ironically undercut their arguments for policy adoption. They assert that organizational homogeneity makes it "harder to create trust relationships with [non-White] communities, to understand the fault lines, to listen to their radio programs, and to keep [one's] fingers on the pulse" (Arenson 2000). This argument invokes a past era of near total racial subordination, during which non-Whites were only grantees and excluded from foundation insidership. In the present, racial inequalities and segregation persist, but only partially structure the contributions of individuals to organizational cultures.

In addition, diversity proponents have successfully created not one but two regionally divergent policy models: eastern practices where diversity is primarily a strategic reconceptualization of elite-directed and Black-centered policy and western practices where diversity also pursues its distinct promise to shift toward symmetric relationships.[9] The result may be that different localities will selectively adopt aspects of diversity policy by their fit with their specific regional cultures, which in turn depend on or at least resonate with the nature of their urban political regimes. (At this point, the readers who have followed the alternative chapter sequence [field-level chapters 2, 5, and 6] should turn back to chapters 3 and 4 to find a fuller discussion of local organizational dependencies that moderate the structurally equivalent relationships among trustees, staff, and grantees.)

A significant complication for both the recruitment of nontraditional trustees and regional policy fragmentation is the earlier finding that a crucial factor for improving the scope and impact of foundation diversity policy has been the willingness of White male trustees to employ their ties with local and national elites. The future of institutional racial policies arguably depends less on the empirical contributions of the new insiders and more on the relative support of elite White males. The pursuit of workplace diversity has had two unexpected effects: a reduction in the salience of race for dividing institutional perspectives and an increase in the significance of regions, locational statuses, and the process of recruitment into those roles. And yet, it has also revealed the corporate character of the persistent, perhaps necessary, Whiteness in its trustee boards. I suggest that only when major corporations in the United States become significantly less White (and male) will diversity policy become wholly invalid and entirely lose its appeal. Indeed, the limited validity of diversity policy exists between two indicators of racial progress: the relative integration of institutional personnel and the continuing concentration of business leadership in the hands of Whites. In brief, the post–civil rights era is bounded not only between the 1965 Immigration Act and the possible mid-twenty-first-century arrival of a majorityless U.S. population but also between the 1964 Civil Rights Act and the (still incomplete) integration of major U.S. institutions, especially the leadership of major corporations. Until then, the shape and success of diversity policies depends rather ironically on the support of elite White males.

7

The Institutional Segmentation
of Post–Civil Rights America

Diversity policies have proven to be a revealing stage for race relations in the United States. In 1990, the magazine *Foundation News* signaled the foundation field's adoption of diversity in its special issue on "Pluralism in Philanthropy." The issue defined pluralism or diversity as the active inclusion of four non-White "cultures": American Indians, Asians, Blacks, and Hispanics. Five years later, the magazine revisited diversity policy in a regular department asking select funders to address a common question, this time regarding inclusiveness: What are inclusive practices and how do they—or don't they—strengthen a foundation's ability to achieve its mission (Zehr 1995)? In a statement titled "Foundations Aren't Inherently Good," the chair of the Association of Black Foundation Executives (also the head of a large community foundation) linked inclusiveness to both organizational performance and affirmative action. However, in a statement titled "More Than Just 'Diversity,'" the head of a corporate foundation distanced inclusiveness from racial, ethnic, and gender proportionality, redefining it as a diversity of viewpoints. In brief, while one funder reiterated the basic argument for diversity policy, another was asserting that foundations needed to go beyond race and ethnicity.[1] On the one hand, this call for a more inclusive policy scope recalls Frederick Lynch's (1997) condemnation of a race and gender "straitjacket" that diversity management inherited from affirmative action's protected categories. On the other hand, "going beyond" race is a rather ambiguous charge that can lead either to shifting policy attention off race entirely, as Lynch suggests, or expanding policies to include race plus other social differences.

This ambiguity in diversity policy parallels two important sequential shifts in the legality of race-based public policy. The first shift delegitimates race as the decisive criterion for decision making while legitimating its use when balanced by other criteria. The pioneering enactment of this shift was the *Regents of the University of California v. Bakke* court decision in 1976. In a highly politicized split decision, the U.S. Supreme Court "prohibited the university from using race as a criterion for setting aside spaces [in student enrollment] and allowed only that it be considered as part of a larger diversity standard such as region of the country" (Feinberg 1998, 11). The second shift goes further to delegitimate race as a uniquely undesirable criterion even within a broader range of criteria. An often mentioned example of this shift is the California state initiative Proposition 209, which passed in 1996, twenty years after *Bakke*; 209 prohibited preferential treatment based on race, color, ethnicity, or national origin, yet permitted "bona fide" qualifications based on sex. Drawing a starker contrast between race and other bases for diversity goals, the *Texas v. Hopwood* court decision, also in 1996, "clearly distinguished racial diversity from a broader conception of diversity when it held that diversity was not a sufficiently compelling rationale to justify race-conscious admissions at the University of Texas Law School" (Edelman, Fuller, and Mara-Drita 2001, 1627).

In the seemingly unrelated arena of transracial adoption, Congress has enacted the same sequence of shifts in legislation. To delegitimize preferences for same-race matching that allegedly locked non-White children in foster care, the Multiethnic Placement Act in 1994 forbade the use of race as a sole factor in adoptive child-parent matching but ruled that race could be one consideration among others. Only two years later, again in 1996, the Interethnic Adoption Provisions (lodged, curiously, within the Small Business Job Protection Act) ruled out race entirely as even a consideration. In adoption as in education, the status of race shifted from being a singularly protected category to "one of many" and, once again, to the singularly illegitimate basis for policy.

These legal shifts, however, are not universal, and the tension between the "one of many" and the "uniquely illegitimate" perspectives on racial diversity remains unresolved in many U.S. institutional settings. As Edelman et al. (2001) have observed, the law is "broad and ambiguous," rarely directly read and usually implemented through self-interested interpretations of statutes. Additionally, while *Bakke* is a national ruling, *Hopwood* applies only to the 5th Circuit of the Court of Appeals (Louisiana, Mississippi, and Texas), and Proposition 209 and similar initiatives have only single-state jurisdictions. Third, except for Proposition 209, these rulings and regulations confine their legal impacts to specific practices and fields, that is, student admissions to higher education and adoptive placements in families, and not even the state initiatives directly address the activities of private organizations and individuals.

The 2003 Supreme Court decisions in *Grutter v. Bollinger* and *Gratz v. Bollinger* on the permissibility of affirmative action in the University of Michigan's admissions policies for law school and undergraduate study illustrate all of these contingencies. Despite the popularity of the state-level initiatives against "racial preferences," big business and other major institutions submitted amicus briefs supporting Michigan prior to the national court's rulings. Even if the Court had found the use of race unconstitutional in the *Bollinger* cases, the decisions would have only indirectly affected its use in its original arena of employment or other sectors like contracting. Furthermore, the Court's distinct rulings in favor of the law school admissions policy and against the undergraduate admissions policy further fractured the institutional legitimacy of race policy while affirming its utility and even desirability. In sum, diversity policies are themselves heterogeneous and are so in ways that I argue reflect an increasingly visible and critical aspect of race in the post–civil rights era: its extensive *institutional segmentation.* In this chapter, I synthesize an institutional amendment to racial formation theory and discuss its implications for the revived multidisciplinary debates about the proliferation of multiculturalism and its potentials for Black exclusion and exceptionalism.

I argue that U.S. racial formation no longer exists as a coherent phenomenon because post–civil rights race relations have fragmented into institutional segments. As the preceding chapters have revealed, the historical emergence and contemporary practice of philanthropic diversity policy reflect more than the interplay of social movements with the state, that is, racial politics. Diversity policies also reflect the significant characteristics of their specific institutional setting or segment; these aspects are:

1. The relative autonomy of the institutional domain (e.g., the foundation world) from national politics.
2. The embeddedness of institutional members (e.g., individual foundations) in local politics.
3. The internal structure of the institutional domain (e.g., the relationships between the Ford Foundation, community foundations, and the Council on Foundations).
4. The hierarchy of roles (e.g., trustees, staff, and grantees) that structures the organizational culture of institutional members and how they relate to their external environments.

My findings suggest a rethinking of how racial formation theory under-stands race relations to be institutional.

Contemporary scholarship loosely characterizes racial phenomena as institutional through negative contrasts that limit its empirical utility to historical description. Against definitions of racism that focus solely on interpersonal abuse, racial formation theory views racism not merely as "a matter of attitudes and individual prejudices" but as associated with *racial projects* that "create or reproduce structures of domination based on essen-tialist categories of race" (Omi 2001, 273, 270). It also focuses on the for-mation of racial categories, the stereotypes or representations associated with each group, and the broader ideologies and cultural systems that justify the relative statuses of groups *or challenge them* as illegitimate. In-deed, this paradigm also identifies antiracist and other nonessentialist proj-ects not as racist but more simply as *racial*, thereby asserting the possibil-ity of human agency even within dominant social conventions. In further distinction from other structural accounts of race relations that amount to the secular predestination of utopic liberation or eternal oppression, ra-cial formation theory views race relations as involving complex political assymetries wherein racialized minorities wield differentiated levels and types of power rather than lack any significant power. Race is thus "ex-pressed differently at different levels and sites of social activity [with] shift-ing meaning[s] in different contexts" (270). Neither atomized attitudes nor total structure, this metaphorization of race as a highly situational "institu-tion" veers dangerously close to pure historicity and thus prompts the ques-tion of how "race" seems to maintain any coherence across different sites and contexts.

An alternative theoretical conception of institutions might serve to in-crease the explanatory potential of contemporary racial theory. Rather than viewing institutionalism as an intermediate perspective between agentic in-dividualism and predestined structuralism, I propose a pragmatic return to structural functionalism and its mapping of institutions, such as marriage, politics, education, the economy, and even philanthropy, as interconnected but distinctly organized spheres of collective activity. The current character-izations of racism as institutionalized and of race as an institution privilege a residually derived notion of constrained agency over the development of precise explanations of how race matters within and across distinct social contexts. I suggest that increasing attention to the specific institutional con-texts for racial phenomena would help ethnic studies balance the prevalent anti-essentialist critique that racial formation is situational with empirically based scholarship examining whether all of these situations are analytically equivalent, much less equal in social significance.

The indistinctness of the theoretical elements constituting racial formation theory reflects how ethnic studies has pushed the explanation of situationality into an exogenous black box. The term *racial formation* simultaneously describes a paradigmatic alternative to ethnic-, class-, and nation-based theories; the social process by which race is constructed; the outcomes of specific processes or projects; and even the broad constellation of projects that characterize a historical period. Somewhat facetiously, one might assert that during this (historical) racial formation, scholars who fail to adopt the (paradigm of the) racial formation perspective will miss the complex (process of) racial formation effected by the many initiatives promoting distinct racial formations (outcomes).

To be fair, Michael Omi and Howard Winant (1986) originally conceived of racial formation as anchored to a specific state and social movement dialectic that cast an unavoidable political shadow on expressions of race in all other institutions. As this book has shown, however, the diversity policies of foundations and possibly other organizations are more than just reflections of movement-state interactions.[2] Instead of abandoning the political anchor for a descriptive miasma of theoretically equivalent projects, I suggest that we view racial formation in the post–civil rights era as occurring in an *institutionally segmented* context: within and between semiautonomous institutional domains, including the important sphere of politics.

That said, the position taken here is necessarily suggestive because scholarly uses of the term "institutional" are nearly as variable as of "racial formation." In this book, I have similarly employed the term in multiple ways, including negative contrasts; however, I have advanced each institutional concept through separate and empirically based accounts. First, foundation racial discourse is institutional, meaning that the rhetorical inclusion of non-Black non-Whites reveals the existence of a relatively autonomous organizational field that is free to construct the content of its responses to political crises and federal regulation. Rather than reorient racial philanthropy toward protecting Whites from reverse discrimination, foundations maintained their mission of identifying talent and shifted their attention to non-White organizations that might survive the new conservative political climate. Second, the Cleveland Foundation is a preeminent local institution, meaning that it has become an organizational vehicle for coordination among corporate leaders and between corporations, politicians, and minority representatives for the purpose of governing the local economy, political insurgency, and economic inequalities. By comparison, the San Francisco Foundation is a "weak" local institution, meaning that it largely accommodates its local hyperpluralist regime, although it has also become an island of interracial cohesion and an organizational model for supporting projects distinct from federal policies. Fourth, the Ford Foundation is arguably the elite institution behind diversity policy in philanthropy and beyond, meaning that the organization is uniquely visible in the case histories of the Cleveland Foundation, the San Francisco Foundation, and *Foundation News*. Its regional interventions translate philanthropy's local political-economic dependencies into a field-level independence from national racial politics. On the other hand, its national political exile may have precipitated its definition of strategic philanthropy and inclusive expertise as fieldwide priorities. Finally, philanthropic culture is itself primarily institutional and only secondarily racial, meaning that group-based perspectives emerged only within and not across grant-making roles (and geographic locations) that segmented the discourse about diversity into trustee, staff, and grantee standpoints. In sum, philanthropic diversity policy is not only institutional in the usual sense of racial theory, as being more than reflections of individual attitudes and experiences and less than evidence for an inevitable structural fate, but also institutional in the sense of being organized differently by field-specific rhetorics, local urban regimes, elite national organizations, and organizational-role hierarchies.

This expanded conception of how the racial formation process is institutional has significant implications. Racial formation theory characterizes the state as the central agent and arena for maintaining unequal societal relationships either directly or by nonrandom neglect. While this perspective accurately highlights the importance of civil rights in U.S. race relations, it also neglects how the U.S. state is a relatively weak institution in comparison to states in other nations. Fragmented vertically and horizontally into overlapping and competing jurisdictions, U.S. law and politics are furthermore executed not only by elected officials and civil servants but also by a wide variety of largely private, unevenly regulated institutions: the sciences, professions, and organizational fields like foundation philanthropy. The case of diversity policy demonstrates how race, racism, and race relations are not only matters of individuals, groups, and the state but also a differentiated institutional terrain that moderates racial formation processes.

In the remainder of this chapter, I explore the implications of my findings for theorizing race and ethnicity. First, I suggest that an institutional approach to racial formation scholarship advances its development from a description of historical contingencies toward a potential explanation of how race remains coherent despite its extensive situational fragmentation. Second, I argue that the institutional segmentation of post–civil rights race relations accounts for the noted proliferation of both "good" and "bad" multiculturalisms. Third, I argue that an institutional analysis complicates certain monolithic predictions of African American exclusion from an emergent U.S. identity premised on valuing non-Black diversity. I close by calling for more comparative scholarship in ethnic studies and discussing how institutional segmentation theory improves existing comparative approaches to understanding race, racism, and racial inequality. In brief, I seek to provide an institutional specificity to contemporary theory and criticism about race/ethnicity.

Restoring Institutionalism to Racial Theory

While acknowledging my disciplinary bias, I suggest that the empirical analysis of institutions helpfully divorces racial and ethnic theory from the grips of an antipositivist criticism that offers only visions of theoretical utopia or innuendoes of doom, instead of also a concrete map of prospective social change. Less normatively, I argue that a theory about the *institutional segmentation of racial formation* specifies the more vague characterizations of race as political and explains the recurring association of racial formation processes with geography. The emergence of philanthropic diversity policy demonstrates how foundations constructed their own response to national (racial) politics by selectively identifying local policies and practices as exemplars or talent for fieldwide emulation. My findings suggest the importance of both racial politics and specific institutional factors beyond social movements, the state, and formal public policy.

Since the advent of racial formation theory (Omi and Winant 1986), scholars have so diluted its conception of institutional process that "racial formation" has become practically synonymous with the social construction of race. Instead of providing a specific account of race relations, racial formation theory functions as a metaphor for "constrained agency" and a paradigmatic alternative to accounts of group assimilation, comparative inequalities, and colonial oppression or resistance. Early racial formation theory included the limited but cohesive institutional element of a state and social movement dialectic that provided innovative explanations of the post–World War II civil rights movement years and the conservative reaction, cresting with the first presidential election of Ronald Reagan. The political dialectic organized the new theory's multilevel attention to the racial character of historical periods, the process by which racial meanings and arrangements changed, and the specific initiatives seeking to shift race relations from both the left and the right. With the growth of apolitical scholarship about "unconscious structures of privilege and representation" (Omi 2001, 270), these conceptual elements have lost substantive cohesion and appear to achieve integration only through an imaginary supersubjectivity, the invisible hand of race that imbues historical oppression and representations with a "continuing significance." I suggest that accepting the institutional segmentation of race does not ignore historical concerns but challenges social scientists to provide an explanation for the "obvious" continuation of racial history into the present and the practical coherence of race across varied contexts.

My theory of institutional segmentation thus does not replace racial formation theory but amends it by revisiting its first version. In their initial formulation, Omi and Winant (1986) argued that the Black-led civil rights movement heralded the rise of identity-based movements that challenged the U.S. state to shift the trope of race, and other social differences, from natural hierarchy to formal equality. They also asserted that these movements, to their detriment, quickly abandoned contesting the state for either "moderate" integration efforts or "radical" disengagement through socialism or cultural nationalism. Similarly, culturalist theories of race have ignored both normal and movement politics for a broader conception of "the political," including the micropolitics between individuals and the metapolitics between cultural representations. On the one hand, the growth of this scholarship suggests an overgeneralization of the notion of politics to include everything, thereby explaining nothing. On the other hand, it also suggests that the state is not the only significant institution affecting racial formation processes.

Rather than generalize politics as vaguely omnipresent because the state-movement dialectic fails to determine racial phenomena in every situation, I suggest reserving "politics" for state-related concerns and reconceptualizing racial formation processes along broader institutional lines. Instead of viewing racial politics as powerfully everywhere, we might recognize that the U.S. state is a weak state and thus view racial politics as stronger in its reach than its effects. That the state has a uniquely broad jurisdiction does not mean that politics influences every social context equally or that it is the primary force in every situation. The relative coherence of race across situations might depend on not only extralocal state rules and crises but also more proximate institutional rules and crises. It is insightful to interrogate the political character of varied racial phenomena like transracial adoption, affirmative action debates, media stereotypes, and diversity policies. However, it also matters that *families* adopt children, that *colleges* and *radio programs* debate affirmative action differently, that *Hollywood* and *Sundance* put distinct group representations into production, and that *philanthropy* and *police departments* implement different kinds of diversity policies.

Generalizing from my analysis of how philanthropic diversity policy emerged, I argue that the institutional placement of racial formation is itself a complex phenomenon deserving further study. Rather than simply providing stages for theatrical productions either originating from the Broadway of racial politics or emerging from a floating Hegelian Spirit of racial significance, the institutional contexts for racial phenomena have gained a relative autonomy from politics, and each other, since the 1960s civil rights era.

My analysis of the philanthropic rhetoric about diversity demonstrates that institutional discourse does not simply mimic political victories and defeats. Instead, the philanthropic domain *interprets* racial politics through a wider variety of institutional responses, including the shielding of unpopular policies and the development of new rhetorical justifications for them.[3] However, because domain members (i.e., individual foundations) are *embedded* in local politics, their available political allies and resources shape the implementation of their domain's autonomous responses to national politics. The Cleveland Foundation and the San Francisco Foundation played enduring roles in their urban regimes but varied significantly in the relative centrality of their respective contributions. The Cleveland philanthropy was stronger than the Bay Area philanthropy for the former's proven ability to convene and coordinate nonphilanthropic actors, especially corporate leadership. However, the Cleveland Foundation's strength reveals also both foundations' common weakness of needing other institutions and appropriate local political conditions to implement their organizational policies.

The Ford Foundation's visibility suggests that the foundation world possesses an internal structure with significant vertical differentiation. Institutions divide not only between domains such as philanthropy and higher education but also between the domain, its elite, and the other members. Although individual foundations are dependent on local corporations and political history, the elite development of those organizational members into national models provides the philanthropic domain with its cultural independence from federal racial politics. In turn, the centrality of the institutional elite depends on the availability of both locally successful partners and federal actors interested in foundation demonstrations of prospective public policy.

Like their individual members, institutional domains may also vary in strength, specifically their relative abilities (1) to enclose and "own" a specific set of activities, (2) to implement policies independently or at least through leading their allies, and (3) to control their respective members. With respect to the last capacity, organizational fields are particularly weak in comparison to other institutions, like the sciences and professions, which have greater control over the training, licensing, practice, and prestige of the individuals claiming membership and thus institutional authority. The Ford analysis suggests that organizational fields rely instead on elite members to regulate the behavior of members; or, less generously, domain cohesion is mainly the result of interorganizational patronage between elites and the other field members.

As the analysis of philanthropic standpoints about diversity demonstrates, location—both role hierarchy and region—segments how subordinate groups make cultural contributions to organizational culture. The institutional perspectives of the new insiders are a function of not only their distinct group memberships but also their locational similarities with White colleagues. Group-based perspectives arise primarily *within* the boundaries of grant-making roles and not across them. Institutional, organizational, and regional settings segment racial differences without reducing race to the status of epiphenomenon.

I suggest, therefore, that racial phenomena are neither endlessly situational nor vaguely disciplined by politics but are institutional in specific ways. Since the civil rights era, intergroup relations have been institutionally segmented. They occur largely within, instead of across, distinctly organized structures of authority and norms. Although politics is central among these institutions, intergroup relations within the other domains can include autonomous responses to the political realm. However, the relative strength of individual domain members depends on both their relationships with their local allies and their place in the internal structure of the domain. In the case of domains that are organizational fields, the place of member institutions depends heavily on the agendas of the elite members.

Racial formation is thus intimately connected with geography not only because the U.S. state is fragmented into local jurisdictions but also because location segments the group-based perspectives of individuals and institutional domains rely on organizational members embedded in local political economies. At the same time, geography is not determinative because elite institutions influence the selection and promotion of other members as models of the domain's autonomy from racial politics. To return to the theater metaphor, the national popularity of a play, for instance, a racial project such as diversity policy, depends not only on its reproduction in many and varied locales but also on how each theatrical company adapts the script to suit its artistic vision and target audience. The cohesion of race comes through both the mimetic proliferation of racial politics and their institutional translation for local audiences. Race, like Shakespeare's drama, persists because it is both extralocally recognizable and locally resonant.

Explaining Good and Bad Multiculturalisms

Viewing racial formation as institutionally segmented suggests an explanation for the proliferation of commentary about multiculturalism in recent years. In chapter 1, I defined multiculturalism restrictively as the intellectual trend promoting alternatives to the monocultural and assimilation-oriented conceptions of U.S. culture and society in university-based curricula and disciplinary knowledge. Commentators on higher education in the 1980s bemoaned the costs of postmodernism's challenge to a scholarly canon centered on elite White male history; more recent commentary has largely accepted its criticism of traditional scholarship and instead debates the appropriate path toward a *diverse* version of the "good society." In brief, the culture wars have moved off-campus and become relatively domesticated, and the concept of multiculturalism has become synonymous with diversity policy. In this section, therefore, I refer to multiculturalism and diversity policy interchangeably. I suggest that institutional segmentation explains these shifts in discourse about multiculturalism better than the discourses themselves, which are instead preoccupied with distinguishing "good" and "bad" formulations of multiculturalism. Furthermore, the results of my empirical research demonstrate that philanthropy has pursued institutional policy combining elements that other domains might see as good or bad. Rather than separating clearly into two opposing camps, multiculturalism divides into types characterized by both politics and institutional location.

On the political right, recent commentators seek to distinguish between policies according to their consequences for economic productivity. An immigration economist, Borjas (1999) raises alarm about "burdensome" immigrants admitted through family-unification preferences in U.S. immigration policy but calls not for closing immigration but for emphasizing occupational preferences to admit "contributing" immigrants instead. Such newcomers would also compete less with less-skilled and less-educated native workers, who are disproportionately domestic racial minorities. Similarly, Lynch (1997) argues for evaluating diversity management by its own promise to improve the performance of businesses. He predicts that such a reevaluation will discredit "moralist" multiculturalism inherited from race- and gender-focused government regulations while legitimizing "pragmatist" practices that engage genuine cultural differences that are either based on region, ethnicity, and work role or specific to customer base and international partnerships. On the one hand, Borjas and Lynch provide conservative perspectives by de-emphasizing concerns about historic inequalities and national cohesion. On the other hand, their views are also institutionally bound, generalizing the effects of multiculturalism on the *economy* to its value for the rest of society.

On the political left, recent commentators seek to distinguish policies by how they serve different political interests, specifically their willingness to address historical inequalities. Downey (1999) raises alarm about how "corporate" multiculturalism serves the cause of elite-directed municipal boosterism in Los Angeles, which makes only token attempts to improve race relations, such as promoting equity in the arts. By contrast, he praises "social justice" multiculturalism for challenging market inequalities and promoting cross-ethnic projects where "diversity serve[s] as a rallying point, but never an end in itself" (271). Relatedly, Gilroy (2001) criticizes another version of "corporate" multiculturalism that transforms once subversive Black art forms like hip hop into objects for White (and Black) leisure consumption. Additionally, he critiques "Black middle-class" multiculturalism for installing "blackness as the leading edge of the new doctrine of diversity" (Aronowitz 2001, 560), trading antiracism for upward mobility. Whereas Gilroy proposes the renunciation of identity-based politics, Omi (2001) suggests that antiracism cannot be pursued by abandoning racial identity. Examining antiracist organizations, he differentiates "good" and "better" practices by whether they employ the concept of race in a flexible manner; specifically, he examines whether the organizations are focused on changing only White attitudes or also interminority relationships, committed to cross-ethnic coalitions only rhetorically or actually involved in ongoing coalitions, and oriented solely toward interracial relations or additionally intraracial heterogeneity. On the one hand, Downey, Gilroy, and Omi make leftist contributions to the new debate about multiculturalism by de-emphasizing concerns about economic productivity and the prospects for national community. On the other hand, all three viewpoints have a common institutional character: they generalize from multiculturalism in the *political arena* to the rest of society.

In the political center, recent commentators have sought to distinguish multiculturalisms by the projected societal goals of their proponents. Appiah (1994) raises concerns about a "false" educational multiculturalism that teaches students about ethnoracial identities as if they were different cultures, an approach he regards as tangential to the intended goal of teaching respect for various identities. Instead, he suggests that a "real" multiculturalism would promote a new cohesive public history that did not confuse the right to respect with the fashion for cultural balkanization. From a different angle, Glazer (1997) also emphasizes the functionality of multiculturalism for national unity by distinguishing not different policies but their exaggerated claims from their deeper intellectual roots and rather traditional aspirations. While he remains dubious about the effectiveness of multicultural education for improving Black and Latino school achievement, he also views multiculturalism as the consequence of the persistent American refusal and failure to structurally assimilate African Americans. Nevertheless, he optimistically observes that beneath the "separatist" rhetoric beats a strong desire for integration. Hollinger (1995) divides contemporary multiculturalism into two previously allied intellectual movements with distinct prescriptions for national culture. Both trends seek to free Americans from the "ideal" of Anglo conformity and recognize the historical reality that colonized and immigrant peoples melted not into a single pot but into quintuple pots separated by race. Hollinger criticizes present-day *pluralists* for seeking to institutionalize the increasingly porous ethnoracial pentagon while praising *cosmopolitans* for seeking to increase affiliations between groups. In brief, "good" multiculturalism teaches Americans not to erase group cultures and identities but to transcend them by building a *civic* rather than an *ethnic* nation. On the one hand, these three perspectives are centrist to the extent that they de-emphasize concerns about economic productivity and historic inequalities alike. On the other hand, they also generalize multiculturalism in the domain of *education* to the rest of society.

The specific institutional locations of contemporary multiculturalisms (plural) characterize their design at least as much as do the political ideologies of their varied proponents. Particular conceptions of multiculturalism reflect not merely partisan positions but also institutional imperatives for benefiting from, selling, or exploiting multiculturalism; mobilizing multiculturalism; or teaching multiculturalism. Rather than assume that either economy, politics, or education is the central domain of society, I suggest that we examine how the rhetorics and actual practices of multiculturalism have impacts outside their domains and whether these segmented policies build up to or express any larger formations.

Indeed, my empirical research on philanthropy suggests that a given institution can pursue diversity policies that combine both so-called good and bad elements across the political spectrum. Were we to take the political dimension of the above camps as the primary characteristic of multiculturalism, we would be surprised if corporations evidenced concern with anything besides firm productivity, public relations, or marketing. Nevertheless, it is in the corporatist Cleveland area where the community foundation has focused more on addressing gross racial inequalities, mainly by convening corporate leadership repeatedly since the civil rights movement. And it is in the anticorporate San Francisco Bay Area where the community foundation has emphasized centrist community-building efforts instead. How multiculturalism is characterized and debated is therefore a function of not only racial politics (i.e., right, left, or center) but also the institutional segment (e.g., the economy, politics, education, or philanthropy) translating public policies into private diversity policy.

Reconsidering Black Exceptionalism in Institutional Terms

Given the central place of African Americans in contemporary multiculturalism and the history of philanthropic pluralism, it might be surprising that some scholars suspect the new American embrace of diversity to be a covertly anti-Black movement. In distinction from other, also critical perspectives on race relations, they argue that racial hierarchy in the U.S. is moving beyond its basic binary of Whites over non-Whites to uniquely exclude African Americans. I argue that these predictions and fears largely focus on race relations in institutional segments other than business management, corporate marketing, entertainment, higher education, political activism, sports, youth culture, and philanthropy. In brief, some claims of Black exceptionalism overgeneralize from racial exclusions in housing, intermarriage, and criminal justice to the rest of society. Certainly, U.S. racism has inflicted a disproportionate share of needless human suffering on African Americans; however, in important domains, Blackness has relatively high status. The post–civil rights period is not an exceptionally anti-Black era or even a "stalled revolution" in civil rights; instead, it consists of asymmetric and institutionally segmented intergroup relations.

The characterization of the post–civil rights era as uniquely anti-Black challenges the conventional ethnic studies account of the civil rights movement, the subsequent conservative backlash, and their effects on non-Whites, or, in the language of the scholarship, *people of color.* Facilitated by changes wrought by World War II, the Black-led civil rights movement eradicated de jure racial discrimination and inspired a cycle of protest, including the Asian American movement, the Chicano movement, the Red Power movement, second-wave feminism, White ethnic identity revivals, and, most significant, the Black Power movement. In response, a coalition of far right, new right, and neoconservative movements strove to contain further minority-related gains and succeeded with the presidential election of Ronald Reagan in 1980. According to racial formation theory, the political power of non-Whites significantly advanced but then stalled, leaving them all with heretofore unavailable civil rights but without full political equality, much less social citizenship, for example, equal participation in education, health care, economic security, and cultural self-determination.

Instead of asserting a shared fate for non-Whites, the new thesis of Black exceptionalism predicts a societal shift from the historic hierarchy of White over non-White to an emergent hierarchy of non-Black over Black. This thesis updates an older version that argued for a "caste versus class" distinction for the Black experience from the experience of European immigrants. Indeed, the "shared fate" analysis of racial formation theory and its predecessor, internal colonialism theory, arguably applied this older thesis to the historical experiences of Asian Americans, Latinos, and Native Americans.

Lately, however, the increasing evidence for group differences in assimilation strains the account of a common minority situation after the civil rights era. Studies of residential segregation, intermarriage, and criminal justice reveal that while Whites show resistance to closing their social distance with Asians and Latinos, their reactions to Blacks are qualitatively more negative. While Latinos and Asians still confront residential segregation moderately higher than that experienced by European immigrants in the early twentieth century, the segregation of Blacks remains significantly higher (Massey and Denton 1993), exposing them to unique levels of geographically related inequalities in job markets, schooling opportunities, and perhaps even environmental contamination. Similarly, whereas over 33 percent of married Asian Americans, Latinos, and Native Americans have White spouses, far fewer married African Americans have non-Black spouses of any race (Rubin 1994). Non-Blacks in specific regions have registered significant grievances with the criminal justice system; however, before the events of

September 11, 2001, national studies of police harassment noted its most prevalent target to be Blacks, in particular Black men.

Even before the prediction of a non-Black over Black hierarchy, the popular representation of Asian Americans as a model minority provoked critics of the stereotype to suggest that Whites were strategically positioning Asians as a buffer between Whites and Black demands for equality. Accordingly, the post–civil rights softening of White attitudes toward Asian Americans demonstrated a "racist love" (Cho 1992) that countered antiracist protest by selectively and conditionally accepting certain non-Whites. In a sense, recent critics of continuing Black exclusions perceive the increasing appreciation of diversity as an extension of racist love beyond solely Asians to all non-Black non-Whites.

These patterns of Black exclusion, nevertheless, are not by themselves an explanation of why a non-Black over Black hierarchy might have emerged. Change in the relative status of non-Whites is not new to U.S. history, and the historical record suggests the importance of factors beyond simple hierarchies of "taste" for one group over another. Almaguer (1994) has shown that prior to the Mexican Revolution of 1910, Mexicans were legally defined as White; indeed, Anglo Californians regarded them as "half civilized," feeling a closer affinity than with Asians who were racialized further "downward" for greater perceived differences in *language, religion,* and *culture.*[4] The reassignment of Mexicans to the bottom of the racial hierarchy came only later, in the aftermath of successful movements to exclude Asian labor from further immigration. In response, White business leaders chose to recruit replacements from Mexico to undercut White wages, placing Mexicans in more intense *competition* with White workers. The reassignment of Asians upward in the racial hierarchy has also been less than straightforward, punctuated with U.S. *wars and other international conflicts* with a shifting cast of Asian enemies and allies. In fact, the United States has swapped China and Japan between the enemy and ally statuses at least twice, with significant consequences for Chinese and Japanese Americans.

One causal explanation for contemporary Black exclusion asserts the operation of two transhistorical cultural principles linking White supremacy and anti-Black sentiment: it is best to be White, and it is worst to be Black (Lewis 1997). This version of Black exceptionalism argues that the real effect of the civil rights movement was to challenge and make unfashionable the first principle without altering the second, permitting other non-Whites to rise in status and thereby claim benefits that remained unavailable to Blacks (Sexton 2001). I contend, however, that this thesis of an unchanging and monolithic Black exclusion is an ahistorical proprosition that is rather casual in its engagement with not only the experiences of other non-Whites but also Black history itself.[5]

In particular, the thesis conflates two dimensions of the costs and profits accruing to group membership (Nagel 1996): the distinct material and cultural returns to racial status. Regarding material returns, research on contemporary social stratification demonstrates that income inequalities among White, Asian, Latino, and Black men do not result from distinct economic processes for non-Blacks and Blacks (Hirschman and Snipp 1999). Although it is no longer best to be White for wages, the only non-Blacks with rival wages are Japanese Americans. Blacks remain in the worst situation for wages, but they share that position with Native Americans and Latinos. Furthermore, Chinese American and Filipino American men would also be in the same position except for their investment in education, which is greater than that of Whites but produces smaller returns and lands them in an intermediate position between the two other wage patterns.[6]

Regarding cultural status, research on culture shows that high culture in the United States is no longer strictly European, much less characterized by the fine arts, but instead is composed of a "sophisticated" *omnivore*'s appetite for both formerly high culture and popular, especially ethnic, culture (Peterson 2002). While the shift suggests that it is no longer best to be exclusively White in one's cultural consumption, the implicit consumers for cosmopolitan tastes arguably remain Whites, especially those with the affluence and/or education to cultivate "worldly" tastes. The proposition that it has always been and remains worst to be Black in cultural terms seems selective given the long-standing and significant role of African American culture in American culture. From the minstrel shows to jazz to rock and roll to athletics to hip-hop today, Blacks and Black-inspired culture have been uniquely central to U.S. identity. Indeed, although U.S. national identity has historically been defined against a multitude of non-White others, American culture has uniquely exploited, benefited, and learned from African American–related cultural production.

In fact, the civil rights movements arguably magnified the significance of Black culture as Asians, Chicanos, Native Americans, feminists, and many others adopted aspects of African American political activism and culture. As Tom Wolfe noted in his classic, *Mau Mauing the Flack Catchers* (1970), non-Blacks learned to adopt Blackness in order to make demands on the state for attention to their own group-specific problems. One revealing anecdote involved attempts by East Asian activists to perm their hair to resemble Afros in order to be taken more seriously by White bureaucrats. In recent years, product marketers have focused far more attention on Black youth than is justified by the group's spending power in the hopes of launching broader market trends (Ford 2002–03). Indeed, for many non-Black immigrant youth living in cities, the process of Americanization is actually an acculturation to Black urban culture (Lee 1996). At the same time, the prominence of African Americans in U.S. professional athletics has been overstated, neglecting their comparative absence from team franchise ownership, management, and the majority of lower-profile sports. Nevertheless, in the ranks of high-profile athletic performance, their status is undeniably high. In important domains, being Black has had more political and institutional clout than being any other non-White.

The case of philanthropic diversity policy illustrates how the prediction of a non-Black over Black hierarchy is simultaneously a simplistic description of post–civil rights America and a distraction from the real significance of the African American experience in U.S. race relations. First, my examination of the fieldwide rhetoric about race and ethnicity does not reveal an exclusion of African American issues but rather a Black hegemonic presence throughout the 1960s, 1970s, and 1980s. Although the institutional discourse eventually presents philanthropic pluralism in terms of four equally important cultures, this construction may actually be a strategic presentation that masks the persistent identification of minority issues with Black issues. The publication of Black-specific articles does subside in the late 1980s, but the trade magazine does not exclude African Americans from its minority articles.

Second, the greater inclusion of Asian American and Latino issues in philanthropic policy occurs not in the stronger midwestern institution but in the weaker western institution. Ironically, the higher level of attention given Black issues in Cleveland is matched by the region's status as the second most segregated city in the nation, a social fact also indicated by the Foundation's failure in the 1960s to influence trends in public housing and education. Even in the Bay Area, however, foundation staff and trustees prioritize Black issues and populations, and Asian grantees complain about philanthropic attempts to "fit" Asian American issues into policy considerations premised on African American social needs.

Third, within the elite heart of the philanthropic domain, Black issues remain a major, arguably the primary, component of diversity concerns. Historically, the Ford Foundation has emphasized Black issues and supported projects addressing African Americans. As suggested in the field rhetoric, the elite institution has extended the meaning of minority policy to include Latinos, especially Chicanos, but without abandoning Blacks. I suggest that unless Ford reverses its historical tendencies and actively excludes African American issues from its policies, organized philanthropy will probably not shift its conception of race policy to focus only on non-Blacks. Although individual foundations may choose to follow the hypothesized exclusion of Blacks, most philanthropies addressing racial issues will arguably continue in the same path as the Ford Foundation.

Finally, individual perspectives on diversity do not fall into separate Black and non-Black camps. Philanthropic standpoints on diversity policy did not even cohere primarily around racial or ethnic group membership but around the institutional roles of trustee, staff, and grantee. When group-based perspectives did emerge within institutional standpoints, Black viewpoints were indeed distinctive but did not express a singular exclusion. Black-specific perspectives appeared not from the least powerful group of the grantees but from within the foundation trustees. Even among trustees, the institutional role that revealed the strongest racial divergence, the divide fell not between Blacks and non-Blacks but between White and non-White trustees, with Asian and Latino trustees in the San Francisco Bay Area expressing perspectives similar to those of their Black colleagues in both areas.

I suggest that the thesis of exceptional Black exclusion reflects the continuing capacity of certain rhetorics about African Americans to occlude the issues that are unique to other non-Whites—even over a decade since the advent of post-Black diversity policy. In brief, it is the scholarly version of the philanthropic tradition of defining minority issues through taste combinations with African Americans, as discussed in chapter 2. Like philanthropic rhetoric about race before 1990, the Black exceptionalism thesis projects how the African American experience differs from that of Whites, as a hegemonic filter for discourses about other non-Whites.

One example of this intellectual tendency is the proposition that race and ethnicity are identical concepts, distinguished solely by the social distance of a group relative to White Anglo-Saxon Protestants. It argues that American culture distinguishes "close" groups, such as Jews, as ethnics versus "distant" groups, namely Blacks, as races. This argument projects how Blacks (and Whites) experience race and ethnicity on non-Black non-Whites without examining their historical experiences and contemporary perspectives. Instead, it presumes that *either* race *or* ethnicity is salient for group membership. To be sure, many Whites and Blacks experience race and ethnicity in this manner. Most Whites rarely experience their race or ethnicity as salient forces in their daily lives. Because members of their race are so often in the majority, they generally have little conception of a "White culture" apart from a general national culture. And because interethnic marriages have occurred among White ethnics for generations, their sense of ethnicity may be strong but is largely optional and superficial (Waters 1990). On the other hand, Blacks often experience their race as salient, but like Whites, few Blacks have salient ethnic differences from other Blacks. Except for the minority of West Indian and African Blacks, most Black Americans long ago lost their distinct tribal traditions to the slavery experience. In brief, though Whites may *feel* ethnic, they and African Americans actually *live* race.

By contrast, the relationship between race and ethnicity is significantly more complicated for Asian Americans, Latinos, and Native Americans. For none of these groups was racialization as destructive of subracial groupings as it was for African Americans. Even before the arrival of post-1965 immigrants, Asian American communities were ethnically distinct from each other largely on the basis of national origins.[7] Consequently, many Asian Americans perceive race and ethnicity in a hierarchical relationship, wherein race is a container for many ethnicities, not as synonyms, as they are for Whites and Blacks. Similarly, the major Latino communities entered the U.S. polity at different points in time and even without a similar incorporation history. What complicates race and ethnicity for Latinos even more than for Asian Americans is the ambiguity over whether the supraethnic category "Latino" is actually understood as a race.[8] While a hierarchical relationship also exists in how Latinos experience race and ethnicity, whether it is race that contains ethnicity or vice versa also depends on the situation. Native Americans also share the hierarchical experience of race and ethnicity but with many internal contradictions. They may experience race as a container for distinct ethnicities, yet many Native Americans view those tribal cultures as structurally equivalent to the nation that "contains" the five major ethnoracial categories.[9]

That said, I am not arguing for the arbitrary analytic equality of the philanthropic food groups alternative. Instead, I suggest that we reevaluate the statuses of African Americans (and other groups) in institutional terms. African Americans are neither "just another" colonized people nor the "one truly" oppressed group; similarly, neither common colonization nor the Black experience alone is an accurate idiom for U.S. racial formation. Historically, Black people have arguably served as the "faces at the bottom of the well" (Bell 1992) by which other groups have learned to measure their relative social acceptance. But if any kind of Black exceptionalism characterizes contemporary race relations, it is not one of consistent Black exclusion over and across the institutional domains. Indeed, the post–civil rights emergence of institutionally segmented hierarchies fragments any one-dimensional claim of group exceptionalism.

What is *actually exceptional* about Blackness is not a static, maximum antipathy, but rather *a hegemonic visibility that has only rarely ever become an actual hegemony.*[10] Indeed, as popular writers have succinctly observed: "Black music is in, Black culture is in, but Black people will never be in" (Baker 1990, 74) and "Black youth [believe] themselves to be a powerful, autonomous force. In truth, they possess only the power to buy, and to influence others to buy. They have achieved a certain market status—not power" (Ford 2002–03, 6). This visibility does not challenge the racial status of Whites, but it is hardly insignificant to other non-Blacks who confront the more complex character of Black exceptionalism: its dual proximity to the White hegemony, albeit in distinct institutional domains.[11] In sum, *Blacks are simultaneously closer to and farther from Whites than any other non-White group.*

Toward a Comparative Institutionalism in Ethnic Studies

If racial and ethnic scholarship needs a yardstick by which to gauge social progress and to motivate antiracism, that measure of progress cannot be the experiences of African Americans or any other single group, especially when truncated down to the elements that simplistically characterize it as the "most oppressed." Furthermore, comparative ethnic scholarship can do more than artificially cast all groups as equally oppressed and arrayed around a White core. Indeed, simple versions of Black exceptionalism encourage a scholarly "return" to the traditional philanthropic frame of taste combinations, and theories of racial formation and colonialism flirt with the newer philanthropic frame of equally significant food groups. This book presents evidence of institutional segmentation that suggests an approach of identifying the institutional contexts between which groups may vary in their relative status and power and determining the precise relations between those institutional segments.

This approach of comparative institutionalism suggests a synthesis of other comparative approaches to ethnic social science that privilege foci on boundaries and hierarchies. In their debate over the question of whether sociologists should employ race as an analytic category, Loveman (1999) and

Bonilla-Silva (1999) identify different research programs as *the* important next stage in the study of racial and ethnic relations. Responding to Bonilla-Silva's (1997) call for studies of *racialized social systems*, Loveman proposes that scholars pay attention instead to the relative salience of race versus other social differences, arguing that Bonilla-Silva and other racial formation theorists crudely and unnecessarily manufacture race in their scholarship. She especially criticizes them for inappropriately projecting how race operates in the United States to their views of other nations. Instead, Loveman advances an alternative approach, the *comparative sociology of group making*, to identify what is actually distinct about race-based forms of social closure or socially consequential processes of boundary construction. In his reply, Bonilla-Silva suggests that Loveman rhetorically deflates the empirical significance of racism in her search for conceptual precision and renews his earlier call for scholars to conduct comparisons of racial structures between nations and across historical periods of the same nation. In truth, their respective research agendas are not mutually exclusive. Loveman's (2002) research on Brazilian nation building tracks how the government established racial *hierarchies* in order to construct a specific national identity. Similarly, Bonilla-Silva's (2001) research on U.S. and Latin American racisms charts the potential convergence of U.S. racial *categories* with Latin American conceptions.

I suggest that a *comparative institutionalism* articulates a connection between their respective concerns for boundary salience and the consequences of group hierarchies. Recalling the changing and contrasting composition of trustees at the two foundations, one might argue that the *salience of race versus other boundaries* such as gender depends on the institutional context and, in turn, its local political dependence. Whereas corporatist Cleveland facilitated a shift from an exclusively White male board to a majority White male and minority Black board, hyperpluralist San Francisco facilitated a shift from almost all White male board to a tripod of White males, White females, and people of color.

Recalling the interregional correlation between neighborhood segregation and philanthropic emphasis on minority concerns, one might argue that *racial hierarchies* vary not only between nations and historical periods but also by their proximate institutional domain. The real estate industry and philanthropy have responded differently to the public retrenchment against policies seeking to close majority-minority inequalities. In fact, worsening neighborhood conditions informed philanthropy's autonomous response to the rightward shift. What distinguishes the post–civil rights era may not be a new monolithic hierarchy but a crazy quilt of institutionally differentiated racial policies.

Recalling the role of the Ford Foundation in highlighting first Cleveland and only later San Francisco as model geographies for philanthropic rhetoric, one might argue that domain structure moderates the *relationship between boundary making and racial hierarchy*. As a relatively weak domain, the organization field of foundations relies on the activities of its elite members to provide a rhetorical cohesion and autonomy for the institution of philanthropy. The relative hegemonic presence of African Americans (vs. Native Americans) in philanthropic racial policy depends heavily on how the Ford Foundation selects from a geographic menu of specific boundary schema to construct hierarchical philanthropic priorities. In brief, the relations between domains and their members moderate the relationship between Loveman and Bonilla-Silva's respective foci on categories and hierarchies.

Returning to the questions that opened the book: How free and unique is diversity policy, then? How free and unique are institutions like philanthropy to promote racial formation alternatives to those broadcast by racial politics? The relative deviation of philanthropic pluralism from the four major aspects of diversity policy outlined in chapter 1 provides answers to the opening inquiries. Overall, the comparison suggests that proximate institutional strategies rather than political expedience (or even demographic imperative) have defined the post–civil rights proliferation of diversity policies across varied institutions. Foundations adopted diversity policy in a manner similar to the adoption of diversity management in corporations, rearticulating affirmative action–style practices and priorities to shield them from countervailing political trends.

Second, as in higher education, foundations de-emphasized the association of race policies with African Americans by rhetorically emphasizing an expanded policy scope beyond Blacks and sometimes even beyond race and ethnicity. However, the foundation with a more substantive post-Black constituency has less support from a broad base of White male corporate leadership of the kind that empowers the more traditional and arguably more conservative diversity policy of the Cleveland Foundation.

Third, while the new post-1965 immigration waves did strengthen the international dimension of primarily domestic racial diversity, local political history moderated the effects of demography. Hence, the Ford Foundation fashioned philanthropic pluralism as much out of its experience in regions like Cleveland if not more than its new attention to regions like the San Francisco Bay Area. In both regions, local political culture already established parameters for how each foundation made racial policies well before the demographic rise of the new immigrants either in its immediate environment or in the mass media.

Fourth, although the San Francisco Foundation made forays into the postlegal intergroup reconciliation aspect of diversity policy, most philanthropic diversity policy continues to intervene in race relations through the traditional asymmetric approach of altering non-White status without requiring Whites to take responsibility for the privileges of Whiteness. Indeed, the reflexive aspect of diversity policy may be its least transposable element across institutional domains. The prospects for a new model of "interracial justice" (Yamamoto 1999) may find its greatest challenge not in politically motivated opposition but in its perceived irrelevance or liability in certain institutional segments.

The implication of these results is not simply that diversity policy and philanthropy both possess a middle level of autonomy between being a shadow government and a servant to racial politics. If foundation diversity policy is representative of broader relationships between institutions and politics, then the segmentation of race relations has become the norm for post–civil rights America. We can no longer speak of race relations in singular terms; instead, we must turn to studying its relative coherence across institutional settings: between politics and the other institutional domains, between the domains, between domains and their geographically embedded members, and between elites and other domain members.

1 Diversity and Philanthropy

1 Since the start of the Gates scholarship program, the over-thirty-year-old Organization of Chinese Americans has replaced the Advisory Committee in its support role for the United Negro College Fund.

2 Against convention, I employ "her" and other feminine references as the universal gender and reserve masculine references for specific reference to males. If gender has become culturally arbitrary, the reader should become accustomed to the rule deviation by the book's end.

3 I conducted the forty-five interviews in the spring and summer of 1997, five years after the 1992 Los Angeles riots and four years before the September 11th destruction of the New York City World Trade Center. Each interview began with a structured segment, in which I asked interviewees to recall their organization's internal structure of authority, personnel composition, grant-making process, and racial/ethnic priorities. I recruited grantees in a less systematic fashion, inviting the directors of major local organizations with ethnoracial missions or clients. To grantees, I additionally asked about the quality of their relationship with the foundation. I asked all of my subjects to describe any changes they had experienced over the length of their association with the foundation. The interviews concluded with a more open-ended segment that covered the topics of their personal background; life history milestones; personal contributions to the foundation, organized philanthropy, and/or the nonprofit sector more generally; advice they would give nonprofits and foundations; and the state of local racial and ethnic relations since the start of their association or contact.

4 This expression was the unofficial motto of U.C. Berkeley during Chang-Lin Tien's tenure as its chancellor, 1991–1997 (Tien 1998).

5 Intermarriage, however, should not be confused with miscegenation or "race mixing," which has a longer history in North America than the legality of interracial marriages. Because a high proportion of the African American parents of biracial children have "White blood," both parents and children are quite conceivably already multiracial in their ancestry (Spencer 1999).

6   These aspects subdivide into at least fourteen empirical dimensions:

1. The general versus field-specific nature of the policy practices, for example, the philosophy of valuing difference versus a multicultural U.S. history requirement for graduation.

2. The philosophical and practical differences of a policy from affirmative action and the historical connections from the latter to the former.

3. The rationale for associating difference (intergroup heterogeneity) and increased organizational productivity.

4. The relative status of older equality and justice rationales within the diversity mission and their relationship with diversity rationales.

5. The balance of attention to non-Black groups and the classificatory schema for recognizing groups as contributing to diversity.

6. The assumptions about the past and future incorporation of newcomers and integration of people of color, that is, whether the U.S. culture is a melting pot or a quintupled pot (ethnoracial pentagon).

7. The relative incorporation of the new trends of intermarriage and mixed identity acceptance in assumptions about incorporation and integration.

8. The relative incorporation of or competition with social class–based rationales for social policy.

9. Judgments about better and worse demographic mixtures for diversity-related productivity.

10. The implicit collective memory of the civil rights movement and the 1980s backlash.

11. The implicit sense of national position in international relations and its impact on domestic race relations.

12. The balance of attention given to the issue domains of civil rights and new immigration and the association of groups with each issue.

13. The relative symmetry of change goals prescribed for Whites and non-Whites.

14. The relative emphasis given to the task of reconstructing intergroup relationships beyond legal compliance.

7   Mari Matsuda (1991) has found a parallel contrast between legal protections against racism and the phenomenon of accent discrimination. The dominant legal principle of *nondiscrimination* requires findings of prejudicial intent by individual perpetrators and a resultant denial of civil rights or other damage to individual victims. A secondary principle of *disproportionate impact* does not necessarily require prejudicial intent but does require a consistent impact on a protected class of persons. These criteria do not distinguish well between a speaker's linguistic competence and a listener's cultural incompetence. Rulings against accent discrimination cases have wrongly assumed the existence of "accentless American English." Given the relativity

of recognizing speech as accented, Matsuda argues that linguistic understanding does not reflect an inherent consistency among native speakers but is an effect of a cultural congruence between speaker and listener. However, because accent discrimination often does not have clear prejudicial intent, nor is it a universal property of any protected class of persons, courts have effectively ruled that the United States is a monoculture and that "incomplete" assimilation can be legal grounds for disparate treatment. The dominant logics that constitute race-specific public policies, then, provide an insufficient basis for the many diversity policies that go beyond affirmative action's disproportionate impact criteria. Matsuda proposes the solution of importing "reasonable accommodation" criteria from disability law into accent discrimination judgments. By seeking to shift law from prescribing a monoculture to accommodating cultural differences, her recommendation comes quite close to diversity policy. This proposal, though, falls closer to the legal goal of protecting victims than the diversity goal of altering relationships because even accommodation falls short of changing the core organizational cultures.

8   I would characterize the attribution of field institutionalization to congressional inquiries into philanthropic activities (Frumkin 1999) as an accurate but racially incomplete account of the social history that facilitated the eventual regulations.

2   Race Talk

1   While European immigrants faced prejudice and discrimination, the other four groups also confronted legally coded disenfranchisement in one guise or another, which constructed their group statuses as racial inferiors to Whites (Blauner 1972).

2   According to one source (History 1974), the Council had previously been the Council on Community Foundations, that is, the type represented by the San Francisco Foundation and the Cleveland Foundation.

3   For the issues during the newsletter years, I read through each issue and identified the articles with a central focus on race and ethnicity. For the issues during the magazine years, I examined the opening and annotated table of contents for articles with some focus on race and ethnicity. While the handling of the newsletters was more comprehensive, the magazine approach misses only those articles that mention racial and ethnic issues but not in a way that editors would consider significant enough to flag in the table of contents.

3   Business Philanthropy in Cleveland

1   Cuyahoga County approximates the boundaries of the city of Cleveland, the urban heart of the Greater Cleveland Area.

2   Neighborhood is operationalized here as a U.S. census tract, which covers a larger area than the block conceived in everyday use as a neighborhood.

3 The isolation index measures isolation from the larger society, usually assumed to mean the White population. However, one can also interpret a low isolation from Whites as a high isolation from coethnics, and vice versa.

4 Whether her first-name identification was associated with her race or marital status or due to her personal initiative is unknown.

5 In addition, as in other parts of the United States, Jewish Clevelanders occupy a possible fourth leg. Distinguished by religion from other White ethnics, they are nevertheless able to "pass" as White and ascend into corporate leadership. However, the traditional Jewish neighborhoods share space with the African American East Side, placing Jews and Blacks in both cooperation and competition with each other. Also, Jewish social service agencies constitute an alternative infrastructure to Cleveland's historic settlement houses and mainstream nonprofit organizations and civic associations.

6 In Cleveland, Catholic schools constitute the great majority of the local private schools.

4   Progressive Philanthropy

1 I am also indebted to Richard DeLeon's (1992) research on the distinct electoral currents that constitute San Francisco leftism despite its monolithic image to outsiders.

2 *Tales of the City* was originally serialized in a local newspaper, the *San Francisco Chronicle*.

3 Sickle cell anemia is a disease that occurs more often among African Americans and other descendents of certain regions where malaria was once prevalent: tropical Africa, the Arabian Peninsula, and southern India (Diamond 1994).

4 Alinsky is widely recognized as the "dean" of community organizers, who pioneered the methods of targeting and politically outmaneuvering power-brokers.

5 Interestingly, the Cleveland Foundation played a significant role in the Buck controversy. Homer Wadsworth and Steve Minter were called to testify as expert witnesses for the San Francisco Foundation, and Dolph Norton, ironically, was called to testify for Marin County. One interview subject recalled the additional participation of the "great Paul Ylvisaker" as an advisor to Paley.

6 While the public sector was embracing Black political entrists and neglecting Asian social needs, it was also, ironically, attacking Black political radicals while ignoring their Asian counterparts (Omatsu 1994).

5   Elite Visibility

1 See chapter 2 for definitions of the terms good causes, good works, and good strategies.

2   This definition of visibility is a rough approximation of the centrality developed and analyzed by social network scholars.

3   I am indebted to Neil Fligstein for making this distinction to me.

4   Arthur Gleason, 1906, "Mrs. Russell Sage and Her Interests," *World's Work* 13 (November): 8184, cited in Crocker 1999.

5   The one exception was the Oakland grant, for which the city was the recipient.

6   I am not arguing that McCloy and other members of the Eastern Establishment had a coherent agenda for Blacks or diversity, but instead that they gave substantial weight to Ford priorities in the wider society.

7   The Foundation encouraged the gradual indigenization of previously colonial institutions through supporting educational qualifications for political positions, promoted economically oriented central planning through the provision of foreign economists, and tried to improve government efficiency through the establishment of training institutes in public and private management.

8   Of the six organizations profiled, one operates in Egypt, but the remaining five operate in India and Bangladesh, demonstrating the Foundation's persisting connections with South Asia.

9   Judis (2000) describes the transition from Bundy to Thomas in 1979 differently. He claims that "with Thomas' appointment, business had won its decade-long struggle to emasculate the Ford Foundation" (164) and characterizes Thomas's interests in poverty programs, affirmative action, ghetto redevelopment, and women's rights as "an innocuous social liberalism" (163). By contrast, Judis regards the new president's treatment of consumer, environmental, and energy programs as abrupt abandonment and the desire for public interest law firms to become self-sustaining as a "laughable" cover-up for capitulating to corporate criticisms. My analysis in chapter 2 does not track foundation discourse on environmentalism; thus, I cannot test this assumption that consumer, environmental, and energy programs are fundamentally more "threatening" to business interests than policies addressing race relations, poverty, or sexism. However, chapter 2 does show that foundation rhetoric also strongly encouraged self-help to non-White communities after 1980, not just the above programs favored by Judis. Jenkins and Halcli (1999) also demonstrate that, during the 1970s, these environmental, consumer, and government accountability movements were the beneficiaries of a shift in priorities for social movement philanthropy, away from African American and other racial minority movements. Furthermore, they document that, during the 1980s, the race-oriented movements lost additional ground to the middle-class reformers. Therefore, I would characterize the discontinuity around 1980 in terms of the Foundation's strategic response to the changing political environment rather than its capitulation to capitalists by forgoing cutting-edge movements to support innocuous activism for race and gender equality.

10 I define field apparatus simply as the organization(s) with the authority and social closure over the representation of the field to itself and the state.

11 I am indebted to Richard York for this distinction between types of "global" phenomena borrowed from environmental sociology.

6 Validity of Diversity Policy

1 Furthermore, these factors, both prior and continuing, will have chaotic effects on organizational culture in the absence of an institutional policy promoting order.

2 Collins (1991) is silent on the perspectives of insiders who are proximate to White colleagues but isolated from non-White outsiders because she assumes that outsider-insiders return to their communities after work. Another theorist, Dorothy Smith (1987), sidesteps this possibility by characterizing transcendence as emerging from a community of insiders that collaboratively systematizes its members' individual perspectives into a collective standpoint. The crucial proximity to group members is thus not with noninsiders but other outsider-insiders. However, Smith does not address the effects of either proximity to outsiders or isolation from any coethnics, for instance, the classic situation of tokenism theorized by Kanter (1977).

3 Unlike in chapters 3 and 4, where I focused on the directors in greater detail, I aggregate them with the other professional staff in this chapter.

4 I discovered too late that White female trustees were largely missing from my ethno-racially diverse interview pool. While I did target them for invitation at the outset, only one agreed to participate, and she had time for only an abbreviated phone interview.

5 Although Wright (1985) characterized his many middle-class categories as "contra-dictory class locations" in their combination of capitalist and labor characteristics, he also avoided theorizing them simply as "at risk" for either proletarianization or co-optation.

6 Even in situations where the main conflict is between two ethnoracial groups, the balance of power in intergroup conflict often involves external actors. The limited success of the civil rights movement, for instance, rested on the ability of nonviolent demonstrators to provoke violent responses from White supremacists and, in turn, reluctant government intervention. Likewise, decades later, Chinese American parents sued the San Francisco school district to dismantle a policy limiting any ethnic group's domination of the elite magnet school. Various Asian American organizations split in their alignment for and against the consent decree initially brought forth by Black parents in the 1970s to increase educational access for all minorities. When the multiracial movement lobbied the federal government to change racial classifications to account for mixed-race individuals, it found an unexpected (and unwanted, for some) ally in Republican leader Newt Gingrich, who saw possibilities for weakening the data collection system supporting civil rights compliance measures. Characterizing the above debates as Black-White, Asian-White, Asian-Black, or mixed-monoracial misses how their outcomes depended on the appeal of competing standpoints to distinct intraracial fragments and third actors.

7   To be fair, it is arguable that social actors in asymmetric relationships often expect each other to easily perform functions that they themselves would describe as difficult tasks if their positions were reversed or if a structurally equivalent task were considered.

8   These findings, moreover, differ from the traditional reduction of group membership to locational statuses, for instance, the claim that social class mediates race effects so that one could predict life chances (or perspective) on the basis of knowing class background without needing to know racial membership. Instead, my argument is that both statuses structure philanthropic perspectives on diversity, but institutional considerations have primary significance, whereas race effects mainly emerge in the wake of that first cut.

9   Even though Bay Area personnel promote a primarily organizational reflexivity, the local willingness to seek a greater equality in organizational relations may also make local foundations more open to racial reflexivity.

7 Institutional Segmentation

1   The third funder questioned the importance of considering any social differences in their work. In the third statement, titled "Inclusiveness Is Not a Guarantee for Success," the head of a family foundation even characterized inclusiveness as a luxury and less necessary for small philanthropies that have yet to lose the "clarity" of donor intent.

2   My findings are paralleled in recent scholarship about racial and ethnic collective identities; these studies show that group solidarities are informed by the institution of politics but also precede state classification and develop new forms in the absence of state engagement.

3   My institutional segmentation amendment is similar to Edelman et al.'s (2001) concept of the managerialization of law, albeit writ larger than management. Edelman et al. employ their concept to explain the business adoption of diversity categories beyond federally protected classifications, arguing that over time, management transformed law by implementing civil rights law in ways more congruent with business goals. I argue that similar processes have occurred in fields beyond business management, for example, a philanthropization of law, an academicization of law, a police-ification of law. The proliferation of segmented translations of and responses to racial politics calls for a fuller understanding of intra- and interinstitutional race relations—one even deeper than what I provide in this book.

4   In an often-noted case, when the Japanese-Mexican Labor Alliance of Oxnard, California petitioned to join the American Federation of Labor as its first agricultural union, the national labor organization agreed on the condition that the union expel its Japanese members.

5   As Harlon Dalton (1995) observes, African Americans themselves often communicate the "standard story" of Black oppression in shorthand without directly engaging

many contemporary issues. The latter include questions about the impact of slavery on the present, the greater cohesion of the Black community under de jure segregation, the rise of a minority of successful Blacks, the impersonal nature of certain barriers to Black advancement, and the utility of other groups' strategies for getting ahead.

6   It is arguable that the apparent commonalty of Latinos and certain Asians with Blacks is a temporary outcome reflecting a high concentration of immigrants in each group. Their comparability may result from a foreign-born effect that will disappear as immigrant characteristics catch up with native-born Whites and Japanese. However, scholars of education have noted that immigrant student achievement often surpasses that of native-born coethnics who have become discouraged or even embittered by the domestic inequalities increasingly more salient than the benefits of immigration affecting immigrant aspirations. Furthermore, the nativity factor would not explain the comparability of Black and Native American wages.

7   While the earlier Chinese, Japanese, and Filipinos experienced a common cyclic history of invitation, labor exploitation, anti-Asian movement, and immigration exclusion, they did so in different decades and were somewhat able to evade racism directed at each other. This incomplete racialization has left Asian Americans with an often *situational* process of identification with either their ethnicity, racial category, nationality (i.e., American), or even specific panethnicity (e.g., South Asian), depending on the immediate or most powerful social context.

8   The U.S. Census lists race and Hispanic ethnicity separately in its questionnaires, but both the government and the general public frequently also collapse the cross-racial potentiality of Latino identity and construct instead a fifth race. In addition, some regions tend to treat Chicanos alone as a fifth race, while aggregating other Hispanics as a secondary "Others" category.

9   Although American Indians are a federally recognized race, Native Americans make up the non-White race that is the most intermarried with Whites. Also, their common historical experiences are quite similar to those of Native Hawaiians and even Pacific Islanders, who were once classified with Asians but now constitute a separate race from both Asian Americans and Native Americans. Although many Indians identify themselves as an ethnic group belonging to the United States, many others instead view their "ethnicity" in terms of national *sovereignty*. After all, no other non-White group has its own body of U.S. law.

10 Examining how White youth adopt Black culture, Perry (2002) has found that cultural adoption occurs primarily among suburban teens without regular association with African Americans and through the conversion of hip-hop from signifying Blackness to connoting "coolness" and status among other Whites. Whites look to Blacks, not Asians or Latinos, for cultural innovation and deracialize the cultural products in practice.

11 Personally speaking, I would prefer to be (and I am) a member of a group denied

cultural citizenship but granted economic trust (i.e., Asian Americans) than a group granted cultural renown but denied economic citizenship. That said, professional employment provides me the material resources to better accommodate cultural marginalization than an Asian American in a lesser economic position, who might opt instead for pursuing cultural recognition.

REFERENCES

Oral History Sources

I refer to archival collections, mostly in chapters 3 and 4, by the following notation:

History 1974: Bay Area Foundation History, Regional Oral History Office, Bancroft Library. The San Francisco Foundation funded an oral history of Bay Area foundations on the eve of its first director's (John May) resignation from the Foundation. The collection includes bound transcripts of interviews conducted by Gabrielle Morris, a staff member of the Regional Oral History Office, with individuals affiliated with foundations and other nonprofits in the San Francisco Bay Area.

Families 1982–1985: Cleveland Families Oral History Project, Western Reserve Historical Society. The collection includes transcripts of interviews conducted by Jeannette Tuve, a history professor at Cleveland State University, with individuals from long-established Cleveland families, including those with past affiliations with the Cleveland Foundation.

Also useful for fact checking, though not directly employed, was a third collection:

The Maurice Klain Research Papers (1956–1965): Cleveland Area Leadership Studies, Western Historical Society. During the 1950s and 1960s, Klain, a political science professor at Western Reserve University (now Case Western Reserve University) interviewed dozens of Cleveland leaders on the city's formal and informal power structure. The collection includes the transcripts, none of which may be linked to specific subjects while they remain alive.

Published Sources

Abarbanel, Karin. 1978. "For the Business World, vucg Has a Better Idea." *Foundation News.* 19(5): 17–25.

Abu-Lughod, Janet L. 1989. *Before European Hegemony: The World System A.D. 1250–1350.* New York: Oxford University Press.

Alchon, Guy. 1999. "Mary van Kleeck of the Russell Sage Foundation: Religion, Social

Science, and the Ironies of Parasitic Modernity." In *Philanthropic Foundations: New Scholarship, New Possibilities,* edited by E. C. Lagemann. Bloomington: Indiana University Press.

Allen, Robert L. 1969. *Black Awakening in Capitalist America: An Analytic History.* Garden City, N.Y.: Doubleday.

Almaguer, Tomas. 1994. *Racial Fault Lines: The Historical Origins of White Supremacy in California.* Berkeley: University of California Press.

Anyon, Jean. 1997. *Ghetto Schooling: A Political Economy of Urban Educational Reform.* New York: Teachers College Press.

Appiah, K. Anthony. 1994. "Identity against Culture: Understandings of Multiculturalism." In *Doreen B. Townsend Center Occasional Papers.* Berkeley.

Arenson, Karen. 2000. "Changing the White Male World at the Top of the Foundations." *New York Times,* November 20.

Aronowitz, Stanley. 2001. "Book Review: Against Race: Imagining Political Culture beyond the Color Line." *Contemporary Sociology* 30(6): 559–561.

Austin, James, and Andrea Strimling. 1996. *The Cleveland Turnaround: Responding to the Crisis (1978–1988).* Boston: Harvard Business School Publishing.

Baker, Kyle. 1990. *Why I Hate Saturn.* New York: Piranha Press.

Bartimole, Roldo. 1995. "Who Governs: The Corporate Hand." In *Cleveland: A Metropolitan Reader,* edited by W. D. Keating, N. Krumholz, and D. C. Perry. Kent, Ohio: Kent State University Press.

——. 1996. "Town without Pity." *Cleveland Free Times,* March 20.

Becker, Howard. 1995. "The Power of Inertia." *Qualitative Sociology* 18(3): 301–309.

Bell, Derrick A. 1992. *Faces at the Bottom of the Well: The Permanence of Racism.* New York: Basic Books.

Belluck, Pam. 2000. "Short of People, Iowa Seeks to Be Ellis Island of Midwest." *New York Times,* 28 August.

Berman, Edward H. 1980. "The Foundations' Role in American Foreign Policy: The Case of Africa, post 1945." In *Philanthropy and Cultural Imperialism: The Foundations at Home and Abroad,* edited by R. F. Arnove. Bloomington: Indiana University Press.

——. 1982. "The Extension of Ideology: Foundation Support for Intermediate Organizations and Forums." *Comparative Education Review* 26(1): 48–68.

Bernholz, Lucy. 1999. "The Future of Foundation History: Suggestions for Research and Practice." In *Philanthropic Foundations: New Scholarship, New Possibilities,* edited by E. C. Lagemann. Bloomington: Indiana University Press.

Bird, Kai. 1992. *The Chairman: John J. McCloy. The Making of the American Establishment.* New York: Simon and Schuster.

——. 1998. *The Color of Truth: McGeorge Bundy and William Bundy, Brothers in Arms.* New York: Simon and Schuster.

Blauner, Bob. 1972. *Racial Oppression in America.* New York: Harper and Row.

Blaut, James M. 1993. *The Colonizer's Model of the World: Geographical Diffusionism and Eurocentric History.* New York: Guilford Press.

Bloom, Jack M. 1987. *Class, Race, and the Civil Rights Movement: Blacks in the Diaspora.* Bloomington: Indiana University Press.

Blumer, Herbert, and Troy Duster. 1980. "Theories of Race and Social Action." In *Sociological Theories: Race and Colonialism,* edited by UNESCO. Poole, England: UNESCO.

Bonilla-Silva, Eduardo. 1997. "Rethinking Race: Toward a Structural Interpretation." *American Sociological Review* 62(3): 465–480.

———. 1999. "The Essential Social Fact of Race." *American Sociological Review* 64(6): 899–906.

———. 2001. "We Are All Americans: The Latinoamericanization of Race Relations in the USA." Paper presented at "The Changing Terrain of Race and Ethnicity: Theory, Methods, and Public Policy" conference. University of Chicago, October 27.

Borjas, George J. 1999. *Heaven's Door: Immigration Policy and the American Economy.* Princeton, N.J.: Princeton University Press.

Brooks, Clem. 2000. "Civil Rights Liberalism and the Suppression of a Republican Political Realignment in the United States, 1972 to 1996." *American Sociological Review* 65(4): 483–505.

Browning, Rufus P., Dale Rogers Marshall, and David H. Tabb. 1984. *Protest Is Not Enough: The Struggle of Blacks and Hispanics for Equality in Urban Politics.* Berkeley: University of California Press.

Chafkin, Sol. 1978. "Community-Based Social Service Organizations." *Social Development Issues* 2(2): 89–100.

Chatterjee, Pranab. 1975. *Local Leadership in Black Communities: Organizational and Electoral Developments in Cleveland in the Nineteen Sixties.* Cleveland, Ohio: School of Applied Social Sciences.

Chideya, Farai. 1999. *The Color of Our Future.* New York: William Morrow.

Cho, Sumi. 1992. "Racist Love, Racist Hate." In *Diversity and Excellence: Graduate Students of Color Handbook,* edited by J. Ferguson and M. Ponce. Berkeley: Graduate Minority Students Project, University of California at Berkeley.

Collins, Patricia Hill. 1991. *Black Feminist Thought: Knowledge, Consciousness, and the Politics of Empowerment.* New York: Routledge.

Coombs, Orde. 1976. "Will It See the 21st Century? Black-Controlled Foundation Determined to Succeed, but . . ." *Foundation News* 17(2): 44–49.

Cox, Taylor. 1993. *Cultural Diversity in Organizations: Theory, Research, and Practice.* San Francisco: Berrett-Koehler.

Crocker, Ruth. 1999. "The History of Philanthropy as Life-History: A Biographer's View of Mrs. Russell Sage." In *Philanthropic Foundations: New Scholarship, New Possibilities,* edited by E. C. Lagemann. Bloomington: Indiana University Press.

Curtis, Jody. 1988. "Into the Donor's Seat." *Foundation News* 29(6): 62–63.

Dalton, Harlon. 1995. *Racial Healing: Confronting the Fear between Blacks and Whites.* New York: Anchor Books.

Davis, Mike. 1990. *City of Quartz.* New York: Vintage Books.

DeLeon, Richard Edward. 1992. *Left Coast City: Progressive Politics in San Francisco, 1975–1991. Studies in Government and Public Policy.* Lawrence: University Press of Kansas.

Diamond, Jared. 1994. "Race without Color." *Discover,* November, 82–89.

DiMaggio, Paul, and Walter W. Powell. 1991. Introduction to *The New Institutionalism in Organizational Analysis,* edited by W. W. Powell and P. DiMaggio. Chicago: University of Chicago Press.

Doll, Bill. 1989. "Cleveland: Arts Renaissance." In *An Agile Servant: Community Leadership by Community Foundations,* edited by R. Magat. New York: The Foundation Center.

Downey, Dennis. 1999. "From Americanization to Multiculturalism: Political Symbols and Struggles for Cultural Diversity in Twentieth Century American Race Relations." *Sociological Perspectives* 42(2): 249–278.

Edelman, Lauren B., Sally Riggs Fuller, and Iona Mara-Drita. 2001. "Diversity Rhetoric and the Managerialization of Law." *American Journal of Sociology* 106(6): 1589–1641.

Espiritu, Yen Le. 1992. *Asian American Panethnicity: Bridging Institutions and Identities. Asian American History and Culture.* Philadelphia: Temple University Press.

Evans, Sara M. 1979. *Personal Politics: The Roots of Women's Liberation in the Civil Rights Movement and the New Left.* New York: Knopf.

Feinberg, Walter. 1998. *On Higher Ground: Education and the Case for Affirmative Action.* New York: Teachers College Press.

Fisher, Thomas, et al. 1996. "Institutional Development in Practice: A Case-Study from the Tibetan Refugee Community." *Development in Practice* 6(3): 217–227.

Fligstein, Neil. 1991. "The Structural Transformation of American Industry: An Institutional Account of the Causes of Diversification in the Largest Firms, 1919–1979." In *The New Institutionalism in Organizational Analysis,* edited by W. Powell and P. DiMaggio. Chicago: University of Chicago Press.

Folk-Williams, John. 1979. "On Being Non-Indian." *Foundation News* 20(2): 15–20.

Ford, Glen. 2002–3. "Powerful Illusions." *ColorLines* (winter): 4–7.

The Foundation Center. 2003, February 7. *Top 100 U.S. Foundations by Asset Size.* http://fdncenter.org/research/trendsþanalysis/top100assets.html.

Frankenberg, Ruth. 1993. *White Women, Race Matters: The Social Construction of Whiteness.* Minneapolis: University of Minnesota Press.

Frumkin, Peter. 1999. "Private Foundations as Public Institutions: Regulation, Professionalization, and the Redefinition of Organized Philanthropy." In *Philanthropic Foundations: New Scholarship, New Possibilities,* edited by E. C. Lagemann. Bloomington: Indiana University Press.

Garcia, Louis. 1980. "Hispanic Giving: Challenge of the 80s." *Foundation News* 22(4): 25–28.

Gilroy, Paul. 2001. *Against Race: Imagining Political Culture beyond the Color Line.* Cambridge, Mass.: Belknap Press of Harvard University Press.

Gitlin, Todd. 1995. *The Twilight of Common Dreams: Why America Is Wracked by Culture Wars.* New York: Metropolitan Books.

Glazer, Nathan. 1997. *We Are All Multiculturalists Now.* Cambridge, Mass.: Harvard University Press.

Glenn, Evelyn Nakano. 1992. "From Servitude to Service Work: Historical Continuities in the Racial Division of Paid Reproductive Labor." *Signs* 18(1): 1–43.

Goldstein, Joshua. 1999. "Kinship Networks That Cross Racial Lines: The Exception or the Rule?" *Demography* 36(3): 399–407.

Gordon, Leonard. 1997. "Wealth Equals Wisdom? The Rockefeller and Ford Foundations in India." *Annals of the American Academy* 554: 104–116.

Gordon, Milton Myron. 1964. *Assimilation in American Life: The Role of Race, Religion, and National Origins.* New York: Oxford University Press.

Grant, Julia. 1999. "Constructing the Normal Child: The Rockefeller Philanthropies and the Science of Child Development, 1918–1940." In *Philanthropic Foundations: New Scholarship, New Possibilities,* edited by E. C. Lagemann. Bloomington: Indiana University Press.

Gronbjerg, Kirsten A. 1993. *Understanding Nonprofit Funding: Managing Revenues in Social Services and Community Development Organizations.* Jossey-Bass Nonprofit Sector Series/Jossey-Bass Public Administration Series. San Francisco: Jossey-Bass.

Haines, Herbert. 1988. *Black Radicals and the Civil Rights Mainstream, 1954–1970.* Knoxville: University of Tennessee Press.

Hall, Peter Dobkin. 1987. "A Historical Overview of the Private Nonprofit Sector." In *The Nonprofit Sector: A Research Handbook,* edited by W. Powell. New Haven: Yale University Press.

———. 1999. "Resolving the Dilemmas of Democratic Governance: The Historical Development of Trusteeship in America, 1636–1996." In *Philanthropic Foundations: New Scholarship, New Possibilities,* edited by E. C. Lagemann. Bloomington: Indiana University Press.

Hammack, David. 1989. "Community Foundations: The Delicate Question of Purpose." In *An Agile Servant: Community Leadership by Community Foundations,* edited by R. Magat. New York: The Foundation Center.

———. 1999. "Foundations in the American Polity, 1900–1950." In *Philanthropic Foundations: New Scholarship, New Possibilities,* edited by E. C. Lagemann. Bloomington: Indiana University Press.

Hannan, Michael, and John Freeman. 1984. "Structural Inertia and Organizational Change." *American Sociological Review* 49(2): 149–164.

Hartsock, Nancy. 1987. "The Feminist Standpoint: Developing the Ground for a Specifically Feminist Historical Materialism." In *Feminism and Methodology: Social Science Issues,* edited by S. Harding. Bloomington: Indiana University Press.

Hero, Rodney E. 1992. *Latinos and the U.S. Political System: Two-tiered Pluralism.* Philadelphia: Temple University Press.

Hill, Edward W. 1995. "The Cleveland Economy: A Case Study of Economic Restructuring." In *Cleveland: A Metropolitan Reader,* edited by W. D. Keating, N. Krumholz, and D. C. Perry. Kent, Ohio: Kent State University Press.

Himmelstein, Jerome. 1997. *Looking Good and Doing Good: Corporate Philanthropy and Corporate Power.* Bloomington: Indiana University Press.

Hing, Bill Ong. 1993. *Making and Remaking Asian America through Immigration Policy, 1850–1990.* Asian America Series. Stanford: Stanford University Press.

Hirsch, E. D., Joseph F. Kett, and James S. Trefil. 1987. *Cultural Literacy: What Every American Needs to Know.* Boston: Houghton Mifflin.

Hirschman, Charles, and Matthew Snipp. 1999. "The State of the American Dream: Race and Ethnic Socioeconomic Inequality in the United States, 1970–1990." In *A Nation Divided: Diversity, Inequality, and Community in American Society,* edited by Phyllis Moen, Donna Dempster-McLean, and Henry Walker. Ithaca, N.Y.: Cornell University Press.

Hollander, Jocelyn, and Judith Howard. 2000. "Social Psychological Theories on Social Inequalities." *Social Psychology Quarterly* 63(4): 338–351.

Hollinger, David A. 1995. *Postethnic America: Beyond Multiculturalism.* New York: Basic Books.

Hudson, Ken, and Lawrence Carter. 2002. "Falling Down: White Males and Affirmative Action." Working Paper, Social Science Working Group, Sociology, University of Oregon, Eugene.

Jacobs, Meg. 1999. "Constructing A New Political Economy: Philanthropy, Institution-Building, and Consumer Capitalism in the Early Twentieth Century." In *Philanthropic Foundations: New Scholarship, New Possibilities,* edited by E. C. Lagemann. Bloomington: Indiana University Press.

Jenkins, J. Craig, and Craig M. Eckert. 1986. "Channeling Black Insurgency: Elite Patronage and Professional Social Movement Organizations in the Development of the Black Movement." *American Sociological Review* 51: 812–829.

Jenkins, J. Craig, and Abigail Halcli. 1999. "Grassrooting the System? The Development and Impact of Social Movement Philanthropy, 1953–1990." In *Philanthropic Foundations: New Scholarship, New Possibilities,* edited by E. C. Lagemann. Bloomington: Indiana University Press.

Joseph, James. 1972. "Black Perspective on Foundations: Blacks in Foundations. *Foundation News* 13(5): 31–33.

——. 1976. "Minorities and Foundations: Why the Distrust Lingers." *Foundation News* 17(4): 21–27.

Judis, John. 2000. *The Paradox of American Democracy: Elites, Special Interests, and the Betrayal of the Public Trust.* New York: Pantheon Books.

Kanter, Rosabeth. 1977. *Men and Women of the Corporation.* New York: Basic Books.

Kelly, Erin, and Frank Dobbin. 1998. "How Affirmative Action Became Diversity Management: Employer Response to Antidiscrimination Law, 1961 to 1996." *American Behavioral Scientist* 41(7): 960–984.

King, Rebecca Chiyoko, and Kimberly McClain DaCosta. 1996. "Changing Face, Changing Race: The Remaking of Race in the Japanese American and African American

Communities." In *The Multiracial Experience: Racial Borders as the New Frontier*, edited by M. Root. Thousand Oaks, Calif.: Sage.

Kravitz, Sanford. 1969. "The Community Action Program: Past, Present, and Its Future?" In *On Fighting Poverty: Perspectives from Experience*, edited by J. Sundquist. New York: Basic Books.

Kunen, James. 1969. "Foundations, Universities, and Social Change: Year of Decision." *Foundation News* 10(2): 51–57.

Kushnick, Louis. 1969. "Race, Class and Power: The New York Decentralization Controversy." *American Studies* 3(2): 201–219.

Lagemann, Ellen Condliffe. 1999. "Introduction: Foundations in History. New Possibilities for Scholarship and Practice." In *Philanthropic Foundations: New Scholarship, New Possibilities*, edited by E. C. Lagemann. Bloomington: Indiana University Press.

Lee, Stacey. 1996. *Unraveling the "Model Minority" Stereotype: Listening to Asian American Youth*. New York: Teachers College Press.

Lewis, Gordon. 1997. *Her Majesty's Other Children: Sketches of Racism from a Neocolonial Age*. New York: Rowman and Littlefield.

Lewis Mumford Center for Comparative Urban and Regional Research. 2002a. *Metropolitan Racial and Ethnic Change: Census 2000 (Cleveland-Lorain-Elyria, OH PMSA)*. http://mumford1.dyndns.org/cen2000/WholePop/WPSegdata/1680msa.htm.

———. 2002b. *Metropolitan Racial and Ethnic Change: Census 2000 (Oakland, CA PMSA)*. http://mumford1.dyndns.org/cen2000/WholePop/WPSegdata/5775msa.htm.

———. 2002c. *Metropolitan Racial and Ethnic Change: Census 2000 (San Francisco, CA PMSA)*. http://mumford1.dyndns.org/cen2000/WholePop/WPSegdata/ 7360 msa.htm.

Lopez, David, and Yen Espiritu. 1990. "Panethnicity in the United States: A Theoretical Framework." *Ethnic and Racial Studies* 13(2): 198–224.

Loveman, Mara. 1999. "Is 'Race' Essential?" *American Sociological Review* 64(6): 891–898.

———. 2002. "Nation-State Building, 'Race,' and the Production of Official Statistics: Brazil in Comparative Perspective." PhD diss., University of California at Los Angeles.

Lynch, Frederick R. 1997. *The Diversity Machine: The Drive to Change the "White Male Workplace."* New York: Free Press.

Macdonald, Dwight. 1955. *The Ford Foundation: The Men and the Millions*. New Brunswick, N.J.: Transaction Publishers.

Magat, Richard. 1979. *The Ford Foundation at Work: Philanthropic Choices, Methods, and Styles*. New York: Plenum Press.

———. 1999. "In Search of the Ford Foundation." In *Philanthropic Foundations: New Scholarship, New Possibilities*, edited by E. C. Lagemann. Bloomington: Indiana University Press.

Maharidge, Dale. 1996. *The Coming White Minority: California, Multiculturalism, and America's Future*. New York: Vintage Books.

Margolis, Richard. 1973. "White Philanthropy and the Red Man." *Foundation News* 14(2): 13–22.

——. 1984. "To Live on This Earth." *Foundation News* 25(2): 18–28.

——. 1988. "Native Profit." *Foundation News* 29(1): 18–23.

Martinez, Arabella and David Carlson. 1984. "Developing Leadership in Minority Communities." *Foundation News* 25(6): 40–45.

Massey, Douglas S., and Nancy A. Denton. 1993. *American Apartheid: Segregation and the Making of the Underclass.* Cambridge, Mass.: Harvard University Press.

Matsuda, Mari. 1991. "Voices of America: Accent, Antidiscrimination, Law, and a Jurisprudence for the Last Reconstruction." *Yale Law Journal* 100: 1329–1407.

McAdam, Doug. 1982. *Political Process and the Development of Black Insurgency, 1930–1970.* Chicago: University of Chicago Press.

McCarthy, Kathleen D. 1987. "From Cold War to Cultural Development: The International Cultural Activities of the Ford Foundation, 1950–1980." *Daedalus* 116(1): 93–117.

——. 1995. "From Government to Grass-Roots Reform: The Ford Foundation's Population Programmes in South Asia, 1959–1981." *Voluntas* 6(3): 292–316.

McKersie, William S. 1999. "Local Philanthropy Matters: Pressing Issues for Research and Practice." In *Philanthropic Foundations: New Scholarship, New Possibilities*, edited by E. C. Lagemann. Bloomington: Indiana University Press.

Miller, Carol Poh, and Robert Wheeler. 1995. "Cleveland: The Making and Remaking of an American City, 1796–1993." In *Cleveland: A Metropolitan Reader*, edited by W. D. Keating, N. Krumholz, and D. C. Perry. Kent, Ohio: Kent State University Press.

Minkoff, Debra C. 1995. *Organizing for Equality: The Evolution of Women's and Racial-Ethnic Organizations in America, 1955–1985.* The Arnold and Caroline Rose Book Series of the American Sociological Association. New Brunswick, N.J.: Rutgers University Press.

Minter, Steven. 1992. "Response." In *The Cleveland Foundation: Top-Down Solutions for the Hardest Problems*, edited by National Committee for Responsive Philanthropy. Washington, D.C.: National Committee for Responsive Philanthropy.

Mollenkopf, John H. 1983. *The Contested City.* Princeton, N.J.: Princeton University Press.

Nagel, Joane. 1996. *American Indian Ethnic Renewal: Red Power and the Resurgence of Identity and Culture.* New York: Oxford University Press.

National Committee for Responsive Philanthropy. 1989. *Community Foundations: At the Margin of Change. Unrealized Potential for the Disadvantaged.* Washington, D.C.: National Committee for Responsive Philanthropy.

Nicolau, Siobhan O., and Henry Santiestevan. 1991. "Looking Back: A Grantee-Grantor View of the Early Years of the Council of La Raza." In *Hispanics and the Nonprofit Sector*, edited by Herman Gallegos and Michael O'Neill. New York: Foundation Center.

Nielsen, Waldemar A. 1972. *The Big Foundations.* New York: Columbia University Press.

O'Connor, Alice. 1996. "Community Action, Urban Reform, and the Fight against Poverty: The Ford Foundation's Gray Areas Program." *Journal of Urban History* 22(5): 586–625.

——. 1999. "The Ford Foundation and Philanthropic Activism in the 1960s." In *Philanthropic Foundations: New Scholarship, New Possibilities*, edited by E. C. Lagemann. Bloomington: Indiana University Press.

Omatsu, Glenn. 1994. "The 'Four Prisons' and the Movements of Liberation." In *The State of Asian America: Activism and Resistance in the 1990s*, edited by K. Aguilar-San Juan. Boston: South End Press.

Omi, Michael. 2001. "(E)racism: Emerging Practices of Antiracist Organizations." In *The Making and Unmaking of Whiteness*, edited by B. B. Rasmussen, I. J. Nexica, E. Klinenberg, and M. Wray. Durham, N.C.: Duke University Press.

Omi, Michael, and Howard Winant. 1986. *Racial Formation in the United States: From the 1960s to the 1980s*. New York: Routledge and Kegan Paul.

——. 1994. *Racial Formations in the United States from the 1960s to the 1990s*. New York: Routledge Press.

Ostrander, Susan A. 1984. *Women of the Upper Class, Women in the Political Economy*. Philadelphia: Temple University Press.

——. 1995. *Money for Change: Social Movement Philanthropy at Haymarket People's Fund*. Philadelphia: Temple University Press.

——. 1999. "When Grantees Become Grantors: Accountability, Democracy, and Social Movement Philanthropy." In *Philanthropic Foundations: New Scholarship, New Possibilities*, edited by E. C. Lagemann. Bloomington: Indiana University Press.

Perrow, Charles. 1986. *Complex Organizations: A Critical Essay*. New York: McGraw-Hill.

Perry, David. 1995. "Cleveland: Journey to Maturity." In *Cleveland: A Metropolitan Reader*, edited by W. D. Keating, N. Krumholz, and D. C. Perry. Kent, Ohio: Kent State University Press.

Perry, Pamela. 2002. *Shades of White: White Kids and Racial Identities in High School*. Durham, N.C.: Duke University Press.

Peterson, Richard. 2002. "Roll Over Beethoven, There's a New Way to Be Cool." *Contexts* 1(2): 34–39.

Pifer, Alan. 1981. "Bilingual Education and The Hispanic Challenge." *Foundation News* 22(1): 20–24, 31–36.

Proietto, Rosa. 1999. "The Ford Foundation and Women's Studies in American Higher Education: Seeds of Change?" In *Philanthropic Foundations: New Scholarship, New Possibilities*, edited by E. C. Lagemann. Bloomington: Indiana University Press.

Raynor, Gregory K. 1999. "The Ford Foundation's War on Poverty: Private Philanthropy and Race Relations in New York City, 1948–1968." In *Philanthropic Foundations: New Scholarship, New Possibilities*, edited by E. C. Lagemann. Bloomington: Indiana University Press.

Richardson, James. 1996. *Willie Brown: A Biography*. Berkeley: University of California Press.

Rockquemore, Kerry Ann. 1999. "Race and Identity: Exploring the Biracial Experience." PhD diss., Department of Sociology, University of Notre Dame.

Rubin, Lillian B. 1994. *Families on the Fault Line: America's Working Class Speaks about the Family, the Economy, Race, and Ethnicity.* New York: HarperCollins.

Samuels, David. 1995. "Philanthropical Correctness." *New Republic,* September 18 and 25, 28–36.

Schlesinger, Arthur. 1992. *The Disuniting of America.* New York: Norton.

Sewell, William. 1992. "A Theory of Structure: Duality, Agency, and Transformation." *American Journal of Sociology* 98(1): 1–29.

Sexton, Jared. 2001. "Interracial Sexual Encounter and the Multiracial Movement." PhD diss., Comparative Ethnic Studies, University of California, Berkeley.

Shelley, Becky. 2000. "Political Globalisation and the Politics of International Non-Governmental Organizations: The Case of Village Democracy in China." *Australian Journal of Political Science* 35(2): 225–238.

Silberman, Charles. 1964. *Crisis in Black and White.* New York: Vintage Books.

Smith, Dorothy. 1987. *The Everyday World as Problematic: A Feminist Sociology.* Boston, Mass.: Northeastern University Press.

Smith, Steven Rathgeb, and Michael Lipsky. 1993. *Nonprofits for Hire: The Welfare State in the Age of Contracting.* Cambridge, Mass.: Harvard University Press.

Spencer, Rainer. 1999. *Spurious Issues: Race and Multiracial Identity Politics in the United States.* Boulder, Colo.: Westview Press.

Starr, Kevin. 2001. *California: The Dream and the Challenge in the Twenty-first Century.* http://www.ca.gov/state/portal/myca_htmldisplay.jsp?BV_SessionID=@@@@ 1903473256.1046652429@@@@&BV_EngineID=cadcgiihihgibemgcfkmchcog.0&sFile Path=%2fportal%2flinks%2fthe_dream.html&sCatTitle=California+-+The+ Dream,+The+Challenge.

Sundquist, James. 1969. "Origins of the War on Poverty." In *On Fighting Poverty: Perspectives from Experience,* edited by J. Sundquist. New York: Basic Books.

Sutton, Francis X. 1977. "The Foundations and Governments of Developing Countries." *Studies in Comparative International Development* 12(2): 94–119.

———. 1987. "The Ford Foundation: The Early Years." *Daedalus* 116(1): 41–91.

———. 1989. "Introduction to the Transaction Edition." In *The Ford Foundation: The Men and the Millions,* edited by D. Macdonald. New Brunswick, N.J.: Transaction Publishers. (Orig. pub. 1955.)

———. 2001. "The Ford Foundation's Transatlantic Role and Purposes, 1951–1981." *Review-Fernand Braudel Center* 24(1): 77–104.

Swanstrom, Todd. 1995. "Urban Populism, Fiscal Crisis, and the New Political Economy." In *Cleveland: A Metropolitan Reader,* edited by W. D. Keating, N. Krumholz, and D. C. Perry. Kent, Ohio: Kent State University Press.

Swidler, Ann. 1986. "Culture in Action: Symbols and Strategies." *American Sociological Review* 51(2): 273–286.

Takagi, Dana Y. 1992. *The Retreat from Race: Asian-American Admissions and Racial Politics.* New Brunswick, N.J.: Rutgers University Press.

Takaki, Ronald T. 1987. *From Different Shores: Perspectives on Race and Ethnicity in America.* New York: Oxford University Press.

——. 1993. *A Different Mirror: A History of Multicultural America.* Boston: Little, Brown.

Tendler, Judith. 1989. "What Ever Happened to Poverty Alleviation?" *World Development* 17(7): 1033–1044.

Tien, Chang-Lin. 1998. "Challenges and Opportunities for Leaders of Color." In *The MultiCultural Campus*, edited by L. A. Valverde and L. A. Castenell. Walnut Creek, Calif.: Altamira Press.

Tittle, Diana. 1992. *Rebuilding Cleveland: The Cleveland Foundation and Its Evolving Urban Strategy.* Historical Perspectives on Business Enterprise Series. Columbus: Ohio State University Press.

Toon, Elizabeth. 1999. "Selling the Public on Public Health: The Commonwealth and Milbank Health Demonstrations and the Meaning of Community Health Education." In *Philanthropic Foundations: New Scholarship, New Possibilities*, edited by E. C. Lagemann. Bloomington: Indiana University Press.

Tuan, Mia. 1998. *Forever Foreigners or Honorary Whites? The Asian Ethnic Experience Today.* New Brunswick, N.J.: Rutgers University Press.

U.S. Bureau of the Census. 1964a. "Part 1, U.S. Summary (Table 63)." In *U.S. Census of Population: 1960. Vol. 1, Characteristics of the Population.* Washington, D.C.: U.S. Government Printing Office.

——. 1964b. "Part 1, U.S. Summary (Table 141)." In *U.S. Census of Population: 1960. Vol. 1, Characteristics of the Population.* Washington, D.C.: U.S. Government Printing Office.

——. 1964c. "Part 1, U.S. Summary (Table 153)." In *U.S. Census of Population: 1960. Vol. 1, Characteristics of the Population.* Washington, D.C.: U.S. Government Printing Office.

——. 1964d. "Part 6, California (Table 21)." In *U.S. Census of Population: 1960. Vol. 1, Characteristics of the Population.* Washington, D.C.: U.S. Government Printing Office.

——. 1964e. "Part 37, Ohio (Table 21)." In *U.S. Census of Population: 1960. Vol. 1, Characteristics of the Population.* Washington, D.C.: U.S. Government Printing Office.

——. 1973a. "Part 1, U.S. Summary, Section 1 (Table 66)." In *U.S. Census of Population: 1970. Vol. 1, Characteristics of the Population.* Washington, D.C.: U.S. Government Printing Office.

——. 1973b. "Part 1, U.S. Summary, Section 1 (Table 67)." In *U.S. Census of Population: 1970. Vol. 1, Characteristics of the Population.* Washington, D.C.: U.S. Government Printing Office.

——. 1973c. "Part 1, U.S. Summary, Section 1 (Table 183)." In *U.S. Census of Population: 1970. Vol. 1, Characteristics of the Population.* Washington, D.C.: U.S. Government Printing Office.

——. 1973d. "Part 1, U.S. Summary, Section 1 (Table 187)." In *U.S. Census of Population: 1970. Vol. 1, Characteristics of the Population.* Washington, D.C.: U.S. Government Printing Office.

——. 1981a. "Chapter B, General Population Characteristics: Part 1, U.S. Summary (Table

68)." In *1980 Census of Population. Vol. 1, Characteristics of the Population*. Washington, D.C.: U.S. Government Printing Office.

——. 1981b. "Chapter B, General Population Characteristics: Part 1, U.S. Summary (Table 69)." In *1980 Census of Population. Vol. 1, Characteristics of the Population*. Washington, D.C.: U.S. Government Printing Office.

——. 1981c. "Chapter B, General Population Characteristics: Part 1, U.S. Summary (Table 70)." In *1980 Census of Population. Vol. 1, Characteristics of the Population*. Washington, D.C.: U.S. Government Printing Office.

——. 1981d. "Chapter C, Social and Economic Characteristics: Part 1, U.S. Summary (Table 246)." In *1980 Census of Population. Vol. 1, Characteristics of the Population*. Washington, D.C.: U.S. Government Printing Office.

——. 1993a. "Metropolitan Areas (Table 1)." In *1990 Census of Population. Social and Economic Characteristics*. Washington, D.C.: U.S. Government Printing Office.

——. 1993b. "Metropolitan Areas (Table 5)." In *1990 Census of Population. Social and Economic Characteristics*. Washington, D.C.: U.S. Government Printing Office.

——. 2000a. *P1. Total Population* (Census 2000 Summary File 3 - Sample Data) http://factfinder.census.gov.

——. 2000b. *P7. Hispanic or Latino by Race - Universe: Total Population* (Census 2000 Summary File 3 - Sample Data) http://factfinder.census.gov.

——. 2000c. *P21. Place of Birth By Citizenship Status - Universe: Total Population* (Census 2000 Summary File 3 - Sample Data) http://factfinder.census.gov.

Valverde, Leonard A. and Louis Anthony Castenell. 1998. *The Multicultural Campus: Strategies for Transforming Higher Education*. Walnut Creek, Calif.: Altamira Press.

Waters, Mary C. 1999. *Black Identities: West Indian Immigrant Dreams and American Realities*. Cambridge, Mass.: Harvard University Press.

Wetherell, Margaret, and Jonathan Potter. 1992. *Mapping the Language of Racism: Discourse and the Legitimation of Exploitation*. New York: Columbia University Press.

Wilson, William J. 1978. *The Declining Significance of Race: Blacks and Changing American Institutions*. Chicago: University of Chicago Press.

——. 1987. *The Truly Disadvantaged: The Inner City, the Underclass, and Public Policy*. Chicago: University of Chicago Press.

——. 1996. *When Work Disappears: The World of the New Urban Poor*. New York: Knopf.

Winant, Howard. 1994. *Racial Conditions: Politics, Theory, Comparisons*. Minneapolis: University of Minnesota Press.

Wolfe, Tom. 1970. *Radical Chic and Mau-Mauing the Flak Catchers*. New York: Farrar, Straus and Giroux.

Wright, Erik Olin. 1985. *Classes*. London: Verso.

Yamamoto, Eric K. 1999. *Interracial Justice: Conflict and Reconciliation in Post–Civil Rights America*. Critical America Series. New York: New York University Press.

Yarmolinsky, Adam. 1969. "The Beginnings of OEO." In *On Fighting Poverty: Perspectives from Experience*, edited by J. Sundquist. New York: Basic Books.

Ylvisaker, Paul. 1991. "The Future of Hispanic Nonprofits." In *Hispanics and the Nonprofit Sector*, edited by Herman Gallegos and Michael O'Neill. New York: Foundation Center.

Zehr, Mary Ann. 1995. "Three Funders: Inclusiveness. Do Inclusive Practices Strengthen a Foundation's Ability to Achieve Its Mission?" *Foundation News and Commentary* (Sept./Oct.): 32–34.

Zweigenhaft, Richard L. and G. William Domhoff. 1998. *Diversity in the Power Elite: Have Women and Minorities Reached the Top?* New Haven: Yale University Press.

Asian Pacific American Advisory Committee, 2, 259 n.1
Association of Black Foundation Executives, 58, 159
autonomy of diversity policies, 2–3, 34–38, 43–49, 239

Babcock Endowment, 124
Bad Cop, No Donut, 138
Bakke decision of 1976, 235
Bartimole, Roldo, 106, 109
Bay Area. *See* San Francisco Bay Area
Bean, Elmo, 79
Beaumont Foundation, 76
Behr, Peter H., 121
Belluck, Pam, 10
Berman, Edward H., 187–88
Bernholz, Lucy, 170
BICCA. *See* Businessmen's Interracial Committee on Civic Affairs
bilingualism, 51, 59
Bill and Melinda Gates Foundation, 1–2, 259 n.1
Black American Political Association of California (BAPAC), 129, 139
Black exceptionalism, 247–54, 265–66 nn.5–6
Black Feminist Thought (Collins), 207–8, 210–11, 264 n.2
Black issues. *See* African American issues
Black Panther Party (BPP), 129–30
Black Power movement, 12, 13, 60, 64, 248
Bonilla-Silva, Eduardo, 255–56
Borjas, George J., 247–48
Briggs, Paul, 83, 98
Brooks, Clem, 15
Brown, Bernice, 119–20
Brown, Willie, 130–31, 136, 139, 143, 144–45
Browning, Rufus P., 145
Bundy, McGeorge, 188, 190, 192–98, 263 n.9
Burke, Tom, 85

Burton, John, 130, 143
Burton, Philip, 130, 143, 144, 227
Bush (George W.) administration, 193
business management. *See* management theories of diversity
Businessmen's Interracial Committee on Civic Affairs (BICCA), 68–69, 81, 83, 88, 99, 157–58

California: Proposition 13: 135; Proposition 187: 14, 15; Proposition 209: 14, 15, 235; westward migration of the economy, 21
Carmichael, Don, 91
Carnegie, Andrew, 170
Carnegie Corporation of New York, 26, 170; international development programs, 183–84; organizational visibility, 159–68
Carnegie Foundation for the Advancement of Teaching, 161
Carter Center, 192
Case Western Reserve University, 73
Celebrezze, Tony, 92
Chafkin, Sol, 191
CIA connections with foundations, 185–86
Cisneros, Henry, 41
Civil Rights Act of 1964, 11, 15, 57, 196
civil rights movement, 6, 10–12, 31, 57; Black culture, 250–51, 266 n.10; conservative backlash, 29–30, 201–2, 240–41, 248, 256; equal opportunity legislation, 59–60; Ford Foundation funding, 195–98; identity-based politics, 107, 241; international contexts, 13–14; interracial justice theories, 16–17; post-WWII "Second Reconstruction," 11–12, 23–24; professionalism, 58–61, 64–65; radicalization, 57; San Francisco Bay Area, 129–31; uplift and higher education themes, 55–57. *See also* African American issues
Clark, Harold, 75–76, 158
Clement, Kenneth, 77, 78

Compton, Karl, 174–75
Congress of Racial Equality (CORE), 80, 197
conservative outlooks: corporate giving,
197; diversity management theories,
204–5, 230–31, 234, 245; emergence of
diversity discourse, 29–30, 201–2; foreign policy priorities, 193; immigration
policies, 13–14; multiculturalism, 8, 13,
16, 244–45; race-relations philanthropy,
106–7; reactions to civil rights policies,
29–30, 201–2, 240–41, 248, 256; traditional values, 16. *See also* Reagan
administration
corporate management. *See* management
theories of diversity
Council on Foundations (COF), 5, 34, 159,
261 n.2; emergence of foundation field,
167; Ford Foundation model, 198–99;
professional standards, 60, 167; racial
policies, 134; San Francisco Foundation,
125, 127; tax policies, 151–52
Cox, Eugene, 3, 176
Crocker, Ruth, 172
cultural competence, 29
Cuyahoga County. *See* Cleveland Area

Davis, Kinglsey, 189
DeLeon, Richard E., 143, 146, 262 n.1
Democratic Party, 107
demographic aspects of diversity, 8–10, 24,
108; beginnings of philanthropic pluralism, 26; cultural transitions, 9–10;
ethnoracial pentagon, 9; Midwestern
Black-White polarization, 108; mixed-
race individuals, 9, 259 n.5; post-WWII
population movements, 113; San Francisco Bay Area hyperpluralism, 110, 113–
17; shift away from Black-White perspective, 29, 31–34, 38–43, 234–35, 256.
See also immigration
Desai, Moraji, 184
disability laws, 17

diversity, definition, 3
diversity management theories, 7–8, 18,
204–5, 234, 245–46
diversity policies, 5–7; affirmative action
and multiculturalism, 6–7, 24, 242;
autonomy of foundations, 2–3, 34–38,
43–49; Black exceptionalism, 247–54;
domestic and international spheres, 6,
12–14, 24; elite field members, 152–54,
182–86, 195, 198–99, 233; equality, 39, 42;
institutional segmentation, 234–57;
intergroup symmetry, 6–7, 16–17, 24,
42–43, 213–14, 229–30, 233, 265 n.7;
leadership issues, 40–41, 46, 67, 191;
legal issues, 16–17, 260 n.7; local level
development, 153–59, 240–44, 256–57;
national models, 90–91, 147–48, 156,
198–99; neocolonial funding analysis,
195–97; new methodological approach,
27; origins, 29–33, 55–65, 197–99, 239,
263 n.9; reflexivity, 208–33, 257; regional
and institutional contexts, 229–33; shift
away from Black-White perspective,
234–35; structural challenges, 2–3, 34–
38, 43–49; tactics, 44, 45, 47; technical
attention, 39–40; validity considerations, 26–27, 200–203, 229. *See also*
Ford Foundation; institutionalization of
diversity; internal diversity policies of
foundations; philanthropic pluralism
Dobbin, Frank, 7, 16
Doll, Bill, 95–96
Downey, Dennis, 245–46
Doyle, Patricia, 77, 96

Eckert, Craig M., 195
Edelman, Lauren B., 235, 265 n.3
Edna McConnell Clark Foundation, 163,
165
educational segregation, 2
empowerment. *See* self-help philanthropy
Ensminger, Douglas, 185, 188

Indian issues. *See* Native American issues

India program of the Ford Foundation, 183–86, 188–89, 191

insiders. *See* internal diversity policies of foundations

institutionalization of diversity, 1–4, 17–27, 229–33, 260 n.8; cultural autonomy of foundations, 34–38, 43–49, 63–64; national and local interactions, 24–25; new methodological approach, 27; private philanthropy, 17–20, 260 n.6; racial formation theory, 27; shift away from Black-White perspective, 39–43, 256; validity considerations, 26–27, 200–203, 229. *See also* NGOS

institutional segmentation, 234–57, 265 nn.2–3; Black exceptionalism, 247–54, 265–66 nn.5–6; comparative institutionalism, 254–57; multiculturalism, 244–47; racial formation theory, 240–44; racism, 237–38; regional contexts, 243–44

integration. *See* African American issues

intergroup symmetry, 6–7, 16–17, 24; group inclusion rule, 42–43; internal diversity policies, 213–14, 229–30, 233, 265 n.7

internal diversity policies of foundations, 200–233; external perceptions, 227–29; grantee standpoints, 202, 224–30; grant-making responsibilities, 202, 220–24; identity politics, 201–2, 212; intergroup symmetry, 16, 213–14, 229–30, 233, 265 n.7; philanthropic efficacy, 201–2; race and institutional responsibilities, 203, 213–20; regional perspectives, 202, 214–24, 230–31; staff reflexivity, 217–20, 223–24, 229–33; theoretical expectations, 202–12, 230–31, 264 n.6; trustee reflexivity, 214–17, 232; validity considerations, 26–27, 200–203, 229

international contexts, 12–14; Ford Foundation programs, 174–75, 177, 182–92, 263 nn.7–8; market competition, 13; war on terrorism, 14, 193. *See also* immigration

International Republican Institute, 192

interracial justice theories, 16–17

interviews. *See* research methods

Iowa diversity project, 10

Japan, 13

Jenkins, J. Craig, 194, 195, 263 n.9

Jewish minority issues, 42–43, 262 n.5

John F. Slater Fund, 160–61, 162

Johnson, J. Kimball, 75–76, 153

Johnson, Lyndon B., 13

Johnson, Roland, 76

Jones, Adrienne, 79

Jordan, Frank, 144–45

Joseph, James, 40

Kelly, Erin, 7, 16

Kennedy, Robert F., 190

King, Frances, 78, 262 n.4

King, Martin Luther, Jr., 12, 57, 177

Kinglsey, Leonard, 121

Koshland, Daniel, 117–18, 121, 132, 133, 158

Kravitz, Sanford, 178–79

Kucinich, Dennis, 96, 101, 138

Kuhn, Mrs. Charles, 119–20

Kulas Foundation, 76

Lagemann, Ellen Condliffe, 170

Lane, Joan F., 120

language rights, 51, 59

Latino/Hispanic issues, 248, 266 n.8; bilingualism, 51, 59; characterizations of, in philanthropic discourse, 30, 49–54; charitable traditions, 28–29; Cleveland Area, 71, 72; emergence in national discourse, 29–30, 32, 38, 41–43, 57, 59; Ford Foundation support, 197; good-works philanthropy, 59–60; regional

Vanguard Foundation, 194

van Kleek, Mary, 172–73

victimhood theory, 31, 33, 39

Vietnamese immigrants, 50. *See also* Asian American issues

Voinovich, George, 96, 99–101

voter registration organizations, 154

Wadsworth, Homer, 68–69, 77–78, 95–101, 108, 142; Buck Trust controversy, 262 n.5; local and national collaboration, 99–101; management style, 95–97; racial priorities, 98–99

War on Poverty, 91–92, 107, 178, 191, 194, 197

We Are All Multiculturalists Now (Glazer), 8

White, Dan, 138

White, "Lou" Llewellyn, 119, 122

White, Michael, 105, 109

White issues, 14–16; adoption of Black culture, 250–51, 266 n.10; Black exceptionalism, 248–50; de-centering of Whiteness, 213–14; development of foundation field, 171–74, 179; elite philanthropy, 152–54, 182–86, 195, 233; ethnic identities, 42, 94, 248, 252–53, 262

n.5; historical advantages, 20–21; mainstream "American" culture, 50, 213–14; as minority, 110, 147; multiculturalism, 7–8, 10–13, 16, 244–47; reactions to civil rights movement, 60, 64, 196, 213, 248; self-segregation, 117; support of diversity policies, 233; as trustees, 233, 264 n.4

Widener, Mary Lee, 121

Wilhelm, Harry, 188

Will, George, 10

William H. Donner Foundation, 160–61, 162

Winant, Howard, 18–19, 238, 240–41

Wolfe, Tom, 250–51

World Bank, 186

Yamamoto, Eric, 16, 21

Yarmolinsky, Adam, 194

Ylvisaker, Paul N., 75, 80, 159; Buck Trust controversy, 262 n.5; Gray Areas Program, 177–81

York, Gwill, 77–78, 96

Young, Victor, 78–79

Zook, George, 75

Jiannbin Lee Shiao is Assistant Professor
of Sociology at the University of Oregon.

Library of Congress Cataloging-in-Publication Data
Shiao, Jiannbin Lee
Identifying talent, institutionalizing diversity : race and
philanthropy in post–civil rights America / Jiannbin Lee Shiao.
p. cm.   Includes bibliographical references and index.
ISBN 0-8223-3436-4 (cloth : alk. paper)
ISBN 0-8223-3447-X (pbk. : alk. paper)
1. Minorities—United States—Charities—Finance—History.
2. Multiculturalism—United States—History. 3. Charitable uses,
trusts, and foundations—United States—Case studies. I. Title.
HV3176.S32 2005   331.6'0973—dc22   2004011217